CALL ME TAI TAI

Passages from the Life of an Expat in China

JOAN KELLEHER

Copyright © 2023 Joan Kelleher

All rights reserved. No part of this publication in print or in electronic format may be reproduced, stored in a retrieval system, or transmitted in any form or by any means electronic, mechanical, photocopying, recording, or otherwise without the prior written permission of the publisher.

In some cases, the names of people have been changed to protect the privacy of others.

The scanning, uploading, and distribution of this book without permission is a theft of the author's intellectual property. Thank you for your support of the author's rights.

Design and distribution by Bublish, Inc.
Published by Battersea Origins Press

ISBN: 978-1-7369597-3-2 (eBook)
ISBN: 978-1-7369597-2-5 (paperback)

For my children:
Christopher, Lisa, Dennery, Kaleo and John.

CONTENTS

Chapter 1	The Beginning	1
Chapter 2	Silk Cushions and Altar Cloths	19
Chapter 3	Bok Choi and Banquets	33
Chapter 4	Settling in	41
Chapter 5	Silver Fish and Jiaozi	49
Chapter 6	Big Brother Is Watching	59
Chapter 7	Turn Right at the Cabbages	67
Chapter 8	The Golden Chair	77
Chapter 9	Boots Made for Walking	85
Chapter 10	Martial Arts Masters	91
Chapter 11	Night Noises	97
Chapter 12	Lost	103
Chapter 13	Shanghai	111
Chapter 14	The Nine Dragon Plate	125
Chapter 15	Potted Palms and Goldfish Bowls	133
Chapter 16	Hong Kong	143
Chapter 17	The Interpreter	151
Chapter 18	Chinese Opera	159
Chapter 19	Shan Shan and the Knot Lady	167
Chapter 20	The Brothers Hu	177
Chapter 21	The Forbidden City	183
Chapter 22	Harbin Ice and Snow Festival	189
Chapter 23	Mr. Huang	197
Chapter 24	The Hundred-Dollar Suits	205
Chapter 25	Tibet	211
Chapter 26	Manager Chang	231

Chapter 27	Entomophagy and Fried Ant Cookies	239
Chapter 28	Indigo-Blue Boxes	245
Chapter 29	Spring	251
Chapter 30	Blue Soft-Shell Crabs	257
Chapter 31	Superior Dragon's Well Tea	261
Chapter 32	The Sung Dynasty Pillow	269
Chapter 33	Summer Palace, Hebei Province	275
Chapter 34	Beauty Is Definitely in the Eye of the Beholder	281
Chapter 35	The Long Hot Summer	291
Chapter 36	Tiananmen Square	301
Chapter 37	Between Times	317
Chapter 38	Suzhou: Silk Screens and Classical Gardens	329
Chapter 39	Terracotta Warriors, Yurts, and Yak Butter Tea	337
Chapter 40	Return to Tibet	345
Chapter 41	Troubled Times	363
Chapter 42	A Narrow Escape	371
Chapter 43	They Are Back	379

Appendix	389
Acknowledgements	391
Author Bio	393

CHAPTER 1

THE BEGINNING

Away from home, further and further away,
No longer by comrades with ridicule treated.
Family ties or mutual love never break,
Though death may come at any time.

From: *"March Beyond the Frontier," Du Fu, c. 751

It was the first time I had been out of the apartment on my own, and I felt an uneasy relief as I set off to meet Ed at his office on Jianguomenwai Street. I walked unnoticed past two guards in rumpled uniforms and canvas shoes, rifle butts resting on the ground as they stood idly at the iron gates of our compound, then followed the arrows on the crude map I had drawn to the wide main road.

The air was thick and heavy. A dreary sky blended into the concrete buildings and became as one, and the cold dryness made my eyes weep. The factories had closed for the day, and muffled sounds surrounded me, with an occasional truck engine penetrating the hiss of thousands of bicycle wheels spinning, as handlebar to handlebar they came, a continuous stream of men and women in their gray unisex Mao uniforms. Time inched by as I waited at the crosswalk, the occasional ring of a bell a rude interruption to the earnest hum of wheels. I stamped frozen feet, sending sharp pains up my legs, held frozen fingers under my arms, convinced I was the only pedestrian in Beijing.

No sooner than one group passed through the traffic light, it changed color again, and the next group lined up, one foot on the road, one on the pedal poised for takeoff like competitors at the Tour de France. And, in that short interlude between red and green, I knew I couldn't cross the highway before it changed again.

Trapped on the gray granite pavement, facing an eight-lane road, I was a prisoner of the ghostly riders. My breath was captured in the air in front of me, like a stratus cloud in a winter sky; "dragon's breath," my children would say. I wrapped my long beige cashmere scarf right up to my nose as much to keep out the foul air as to keep warm. It soon became damp from my breath.

It was getting dark. I had to do something! In desperation, I made my move. Teeth clenched, body braced for impact, I stepped off the curb. Like a horse with blinders on, I looked neither right nor left—I saw no one—therefore, it was their responsibility to see me. Riders wove their way around me, slowing their pace but never stopping. I resisted the panic that urged me to run, which might throw them off balance, I thought, and, amazingly, I survived.

That experience became my first lesson in Chinese philosophy.

Eight months earlier, I was sitting on our patio, relaxing in the warm rosy glow of a Hawaiian winter's evening, watching Ed's cigarette smoke snake up and scatter toward the strawberry guava tree and the water beyond, my body tingling with fear and anticipation as I answered his question. "Yes, let's do it."

Our daughter Lisa would be going to college in New York that year, a long way away, I know, but it was what she wanted, and they had stables there, one of the reasons for her choosing that school; she almost lived at the stables here. She could hardly wait, and our new paycheck would certainly help with the fees. Seems we hadn't planned far enough ahead in the tuition department. And Chris had picked up his life with both hands; he was now a part-time student and working hard at his new one-man landscaping business he called "Nature's Helper." From the time he was nine, he enjoyed gardening—in fact, every tree in our garden, all ten of them, and every hibiscus bush Chris had planted for me. Digging holes in the hard-packed clay wasn't easy, but he took great pride in doing so, and, as he was working on a degree in environmental science, his choice of career was a great fit. So, it seemed the perfect opportunity for all of us to start afresh. The children were living their own lives, and Ed and I had long ago hit that time in marriage when endearing habits had become major irritations. The way he clicked his pen off and on incessantly became a time bomb waiting to explode in my head. His sneezing fits, without use of tissue or hand, drove me to distraction. His anger always simmered below the surface, and this seemed to increase with age, as he had fits about my long hair clogging the drains, my phone calls in the evenings. . . . We had tried marriage counselors, but, after each session, we eyed each other with open hostility, looking for signs of guilt, of betrayal, and the distance between us grew. A move to China seemed just the ticket for so many reasons. Besides, it would only be two years, not forever.

Two weeks later, Ed moved to Beijing, and I stayed on to wrap up my job and make sure Lisa was settled in New York. She was so excited about this school. It was a lovely campus, plonked in the middle of acres of unspoiled land, and the dorms were adequate, though I was a bit concerned about the coed status. Then, by mid-September, after twenty-five years of living in glorious Hawaii, I said goodbye to dear friends, who cheered my phony casualness, left Chris in charge of the house, and headed for the airport. It seemed so easy.

Twenty-two hours after leaving Honolulu, the Boeing 747 bumped to a shuddery landing at Beijing Capital International Airport. The bored stewardess's voice crackled over the intercom, announced our arrival, and invited all to "have a nice day." My heart beat a little faster. I squeezed my feet into shoes now a size too small, touched up my lipstick, and smoothed my hair with hands that shook.

Disembarking from the bright red, white, and blue interior, I was immersed in shadowy gray. Flickering florescent lights, skinny strips in the high ceiling, struggled to illuminate the cracked asphalt tile floor, the gray uniforms of airport security personnel. But they blended together in the same fuzzy gray dream. I followed my fellow passengers, men only it seemed, to the first checkpoint, where I left off my Chinese government health card, assuring anyone who read it that I was not totally insane, free from infectious diseases, including the bubonic plague, then moved to where an immigration officer sat in a kiosk so high I had to reach up to give him my passport.

He looked at me, then at my passport, back and forth. My passport was British; maybe there was a problem with my visa. I'd been to Taiwan two years ago, a family vacation. I held my breath. He squinted his beady black eyes over tiny, smudgy glasses, pulled his mouth into an upside-down smile, and finally thumped my passport and motioned me to leave. I felt the same mixture of relief and dread that immigrants must have felt when they passed through Ellis Island.

I walked into baggage claim, worried about the book I carried, though Stephen King should be okay, no sex, no politics. What about the canned food? Cheese and cigarettes? Scotch whisky? Even in 1986, China was still a closed society, suspicious of all things Western—except currency, "hard" currency, which could be traded on the international market. That's why Ed's job paid so much. Living in Beijing was considered a form of exile.

I looked for Ed, expecting to see him waiting for me, to see his smile, to feel his touch. People crowded around in untidy queues, making it difficult to see beyond their backs. I stood on tiptoes, searching, hoping.... He wasn't there. My stomach churned. I suddenly felt very alone. Unexpected tears welled up, and I busied myself with my handbag, embarrassed my disappointment might show.

A tall, skinny young man walked toward me and stood almost on my toes. His sudden arrival shook me out of my escalating panic.

"Tzu Chow," he told me with a broad smile. He thumped his chest. "Driver." I could have hugged him. Instead, I pointed to my two huge suitcases. He hoisted them up as if they were empty, and I followed as he pushed importantly through others in line to the customs agent. My cases were plunked onto a table, along with my hand carry. The customs agent stared at me, and I felt guilty of every form of smuggling. Tzu Chow leaned forward and made a joke. I think it was a joke; both men smiled. I saw a handful of cigarettes slip from Tzu Chow's pocket into the customs agent's hand. My customs form was stamped, and we were free to go.

The gray four-wheel drive was parked, illegally, outside. More cigarettes exchanged through a practiced sleight of hands.

Exhaust fumes and coal fires polluted the thick air and burned my eyes and irritated my throat. The few trees planted in the roundabout were bare of leaves. There was no grass that I could see, only dry, packed earth. I shivered, unaccustomed to the cold, dry wind of autumn, and climbed gratefully into the back of the jeep. The engine spluttered to life, and we started the hour-long ride to the city.

There were sheep and goats grazing in almost barren fields along the way. "*Yang*," I thought. I remembered the word from my language tapes, mainly because it was the same for both animals, but not the tone, and I was too timid to try it out on Tzu Chow. Wooden shacks leaned topsy-turvy dangerously near the bumpy road. I hadn't expected to see countryside. I unbuttoned my jacket, leaned back into the leather upholstery, and stared out the window. Skinny elms whizzed by, edging flat fields, and, in between all this monochrome, I saw the bright orange mass of a late autumn sun slowly sinking, blending into the earth. Like the warm fires of my childhood in a dark room on a winter's day, its glow offered the promise of comfort.

The metal door of the elevator banged open, and a short, steely looking woman pulled back the crisscrossed inner door. We jerked our way to the top floor without a word. On the concrete landing waited a small, thin woman, hands nervously clasped together.

"*Ni hau?*" she asked, and I returned her greeting. She then entered into a heated conversation with Tzu Chow, and, after he dumped the suitcases inside the apartment, he left. No cigarettes passed hands, and I knew who was boss.

This was my ai-yi, my housekeeper, and, over time, my language teacher and my friend, though she never crossed into the familiar. She was shy, a little awkward as she carried my suitcases into the master bedroom. I tried to tell her with sign language to leave them for Ed—they were heavy—but she smiled and blushed and took them, one at a time, both hands holding the handles, and bumped them into the bedroom. She made sure I followed, turning her head to look at me, a mother hen with her chick.

I looked around the large three-bedroom penthouse apartment, furnished by its first occupants. Good, solid furniture. Modern. Western. Probably very smart six years ago but shabby now as if the gray air outside had been sucked up by the upholstery and carpeting. And, with its bare walls, the space took on that empty, neglected appearance of a three-star hotel.

Ed arrived a short time later, and I supposed the heated discussion between Ai-yi and Tzu Chow was about picking him up from work. I could hear him in the hall; his voice was deep and rich, as distinct as his laugh. My heart beat a little faster; a smile formed on my face. The door opened, and in he came.

"So, you made it," he greeted. "This is Marvin Chang and his wife, Lily."

Ed seemed taller somehow, distinguished. I'd seldom seen him dressed in suit and tie. Hawaii businessmen dressed in flowery aloha shirts. His new look suited him. I wanted to tell him so, and I stared at him, trying to catch his eye. Engrossed in conversation with Marvin Chang, he walked into the den. We hadn't seen each other for seven months. Why did the Changs have to be here now? They were probably the reason he hadn't met me, and I disliked them unconditionally, standing there with their smug smiles.

Ed had told me about the Changs. Ed was Marvin Chang's replacement. They were Chinese Americans originally from Taiwan now on their way back to the US. Evidently, Mr. Chang's fluent Mandarin wasn't an advantage for him here; the local Chinese resent their own coming back and lording it over them, especially the Taiwanese.

"We're not staying," Mrs. Chang announced as if reading my mind. "Tzu Chow is driving us to our hotel." I watched Mrs. Chang talk to

Ai-yi and noticed her stern tone. She then turned her attention to me. "I've told her you are very important people," she said, "that your husband is president of the company."

I looked at Ai-yi, her hands thrust deep in her apron pockets, nervously picking at something unseen.

"Ed's not president," I said. "You know that. He's the general manager."

"Same thing," she answered. "And you are foreigners, don't forget. The phones are bugged," she added, and she continued on about the elevator operators, who make notes on visitors. "Ed can't slip any girlfriends in here, so don't worry." She smiled. My face flushed with anger as she continued with her list of terrors. "Of course, there are also the inconspicuous men who will follow you on the streets. Don't worry, they won't bother you. They just make notes on what you do, mostly who you see.

"Ai-yi is chosen by the Chinese authorities, you know. Can't get rid of her. Oh, and she has every Wednesday afternoon off. Goes to her leader for debriefing. All the ai-yis do.

"You can trust her though," added Mrs. Chang. I wondered how she had found that out—and what "trust" meant—but I silently scoffed at the hidden camera and other "spy" ideas. And, as for Ed slipping any girls in here, she was obviously thinking of her husband, not mine! Mrs. Chang was unhappy at their forced departure, I thought, and trying to put me off. Well, she wouldn't do it!

"I'll show you around tomorrow," she told me as they left. I wasn't given the chance to decline.

Ai-yi was next to leave. Through for the day, she left quietly, with a few words of greeting, which Ed responded to in English.

Alone at last, I needed Ed to talk to me, tell me about this exciting city, make a gesture of welcome.

"Get you anything?" he asked. I decided on hot tea and followed him into the kitchen. It looked pleasantly familiar. I had shipped linen and towels with Ed, along with all my copper saucepans and a small kitchen table with two chairs. The pots hung on a black iron butcher rack and shone warmly in the overhead light, making a cozy contrast to the darkness hanging thickly outside the window.

"How are the kids?" he asked.

"Seemed okay," I said. "We shall soon find out."

I watched Ed make the tea. The whiskery shadow made his once-tan face look whiter, his hair grayer. But, as he moved toward me, I could smell the familiar scent of stale cigarette smoke that always clung to his hair and clothes. He was still the same Ed.

He handed me a cup of tea. "You'd better get some rest. You can shower first if you like," he offered. My head buzzed with fatigue, and maybe jet lag made me overly sensitive, but his indifference made me angry. I'd expected him to at least talk more about the children or ask about the journey... hug me—though I couldn't remember the last time we hugged, so where did my expectations come from? I bit my lip to keep back tears. I rarely cried, and this wasn't the time to throw a tantrum. There'd be other days when we would talk, plenty of time to really get to know each other again.

I awoke in the early hours of the morning, that empty time between night and day. Panic gripped me. It turned my stomach into liquid, pricked my scalp with a thousand icy needles. It sat heavy on my chest, restricting my breath to shallow heaves. It dragged me back to half memories of cramped cupboards under the stairs and dark, damp holes in the ground. Memories that had been buried until now. I stared out through closed eyelids and willed them to go away. Ed lay snoring beside me, deep in sleep. Everything's all right, I said to myself. A strange bed, that's all. I took one of the pillows, wrapped my arms around it, and held tight.

Ed was up first that morning. He always got up early, around five, and I usually followed, but this morning I didn't awaken until he came into the room to get dressed.

"Ai-yi comes around eight," he told me. "She leaves at five or six. Whatever you need, just tell her."

"Just how do I do that without the language?" I didn't mean to snap; it just came out. How about a "hi" or "good morning;" that's what I had expected—on my first day, at least.

He said he would send an interpreter he sometimes used. She would come around ten. Ed left for the day, and, for the first time in my adult life, I didn't know what to do and had nowhere to go. I was four years old again and abandoned with strangers.

When Ai-yi arrived, I wanted to appear busy, so I picked up one of the books I'd never had time to read and thumbed through it. It didn't interest me. I arranged the pictures I'd brought of Chris and Lisa, favorite pictures in worn silver frames. I brushed Lisa's tumbling curls back from her chubby face with my fingers. She was four. Ed called her "Pumpkin." "Come here, Pumpkin," he'd say, and she'd squeal as he picked her up and twirled her around. "More, more," she'd say. "Higher, Daddy, higher." He'd been a great dad when the children were little, up until Chris was about nine. Then he withdrew.

It started with a typical Saturday morning. I was cleaning the plumeria blossoms off the glass patio table, an endless job. Ed and Chris were playing catch. Deciding to put the umbrella up to catch the flowers, I turned, and, out of the corner of my eye, I saw Ed reach back with the soccer ball and throw it as hard as he could. It sped through the air, hitting Chris in the stomach. He doubled over with the impact, a look of shock on his face. It happened so fast; it couldn't be deliberate, right? I must have seen it wrong. Not a word was said; Ed just walked back into the house, closing the door behind him. We continued to go to the beach, all four of us. And trips, of course, London every year, sometimes stopping off to see Ed's family, New Zealand to visit my cousin Jack, Disneyland, fun times. But something had changed that day; we all felt it. And, at home, Ed remained distant, leaving the parenting to me.

I walked around the apartment. The ceilings were high, and the windows let in a grudging light on the north and south sides. Sliding glass doors led to balconies off the living room and our bedroom. I went outside. Black grit swirled on the concrete floor. The polluted air hung low to the ground. I could see the wide expanse where I knew Tiananmen Square and the Forbidden City should be according to the crude map in the tiny Beijing guidebook (a present from the American Embassy).

Across the wide highway that encircled two sides of our compound, I saw a small patch of grass with several tall, skinny trees, under which moved a group of people, men or women; it was hard to tell in their padded gray uniforms. I watched them as they moved in unison, unbelievably slowly, graceful, effortlessly performing tai chi movements as endless trucks whizzed by spewing clouds of exhaust, honking at the bicyclists slowing them down. The heavy pollution clamped itself around my head, forcing me reluctantly back inside.

Ai-yi was busy in the kitchen. I wanted to talk to her, give her a grocery list, tell her about the Ivory liquid for washing my clothes. Ai-yi moved quietly, careful not to click dishes together or close cupboards noisily. The quieter she was, the more intense the atmosphere became, the longer the silence, the deeper my discomfort. Ten o'clock came not soon enough.

The interpreter's name was Kathy. Her dark hair was long and curly, and she wore makeup and a smart black suit. She had finished graduate school in the US a few years ago and spoke fluent English. Ai-yi made tea, and I asked Kathy to have Ai-yi join us. She did so, shyly, never making eye contact, and we sat at the large round glass-topped dining table, leaving wet rings where our cups rested.

"What's that word Ai-yi keeps saying?" I asked Kathy. It sounded like "foreign" to me.

"Ai-yi was told to call you *Furen*. It means madam."

What a loathsome sound. I wanted another name, a friendly name, something like *ni hao, xie xie, cha*. I particularly liked that one; *cha* was slang for tea in England. So, every word Kathy threw out I only paid attention to the sound. Then she asked, "What about '*Tai Tai*'?"

"Yes, perfect! Call me Tai Tai!"

More heated discussions. Ai-yi had real concerns with using it. It means "housewife," a common name, not good enough for a westerner, explained Kathy, but I held firm. "Tai Tai" was *me*. I wanted that name.

"Call me Tai Tai," I insisted. And so it was, unless Ai-yi and I were in the elevator together. Then, when she answered the nosey elevator operator, she used *furen,* giving me a guilty sideways look of apology.

"Kathy, tell Ai-yi she can have Saturday afternoons off."

Ai-yi resisted at first, then gave me a smile. "Tai Tai, *xie xie.*" She had a dimple in her right cheek.

Ai-yi arrived promptly at eight in the morning and worked until five or six, Monday through Friday, with a half day off on Wednesday for debriefing. Every day, the gritty pollution invaded our space, and, every day, Ai-yi conquered it. She took great pride in the apartment, and, when I asked her to arrange our canned vegetables by label, she took on the task with enthusiasm. We sorted out the laundry soaps, and Ai-yi stuck labels on each container. She seemed pleased that I used Ivory liquid for my clothes and shampoo for my sweaters, while regular powder was used on Ed's. Something she could share with the other ai-yis to give her additional status. Working in a penthouse already gave her an edge.

The only item we disagreed on was the use of the awful wash-and-wax floor cleaner Mrs. Chang had given her. This caused some debate and took a while to cure. Ai-yi was partial to the product's efficiency. I loathed the fact that it just moved the dirt around and stuck it in another place.

Mrs. Chang arrived around two, and Tzu Chow drove us to go shopping. The streets were wide, impersonal, the buildings plain, built of hand-mixed concrete and handmade brick. I saw nothing of the old city I had expected. We drove the two blocks to the Friendship Store, where foreign money buys luxury goods and a limited supply of Western food, which we didn't enter, then to a government-owned antique shop, which we did. I bought a small table, paid for it in foreign exchange certificates (FECs) purchased with dollars, and left it for repairs. I felt forced to buy a pair of tall *verte de chene* ceramic vases that I took with me and wondered what kind of arrangement Mrs. Chang had with the shopkeeper.

"You'd better get used to hearing '*maiyou,*'" she told me. I had no idea what she meant, and she seemed to enjoy telling me. "It means 'we don't have.' When I came here, every other word was *maiyou*. I had trouble finding a carrot. By the way, I left iodine crystals to wash your fruit and vegetables with. If you run out, you can always use bleach."

Rickety slat sided trucks sped by us, their waterproof tarps flapping around trying to get free. Dust covered every surface, stuck there by the elements. Maybe they had travelled the Silk Road, through deserts and mountains. . . . My daydream was interrupted by Mrs. Chang's persistent chatter. "How did your children take the move?" she asked. Her pushiness annoyed me.

"Just fine. Both are undergraduates now," I answered.

"Of course, the money's good here, probably helps with tuition. It did for my daughter."

I feigned interest in the grimy facades of flat-faced buildings and remembered that day seven months ago and my impetuous answer to Ed's question: "Yes, let's do it. It's a chance for all of us." The money was an incentive; it doubled our existing salaries combined—and then some. But that wasn't all. It was important for Chris to have this opportunity to live on his own, and we had both agreed it would be a chance for us to start again, work out our differences, find a way to make peace. These were powerful incentives for me, my son, my marriage.

"Yes, the timing was right," I answered.

We drove back through the north gate of our apartment compound. Small plots of trees and trimmed bushes sprouted up in islands between buildings. A brick wall with broken bottles embedded in the top surrounded the compound, and armed soldiers wearing canvas shoes stood at iron gates.

"Ten feet high," Mrs. Chang told me, indicating the walls. "Can't sneak anybody in here."

"How many buildings are there?" I asked.

"I heard sixteen, but you're in the end one, near the wall, so you only notice the buildings around here. That's why you have such a great view. They have a playground too, for youngsters."

The occupants were foreign diplomats, with a few expat business types, like us, she told me, then she continued with her warnings: our mail would be opened; some would go missing; cameras were hidden in every room, monitoring us night and day. "Even the bathrooms," she added. Her parting comments were for me not to worry if I heard screaming during the night; one of the tenants had taken up a form of vocal chi gong.

I rummaged the cupboards and fridge looking for something to cook Ed for dinner. The meat was frozen solid, and the fresh vegetables consisted of one onion, leaving omelets my only option. That decided, I grated cheese, beat the eggs, and looked at the stove. All four burners were built to accommodate woks, commercial size and fueled by gas. I plonked myself at the kitchen table, rested my head in my hand, and fought off sleep.

"What's up?" Ed asked. I hadn't heard him come in, and there he was, drink in hand.

"Hi there. Defeated by the stove."

"Hate the goddamned thing myself," he said. "I usually eat out. You sit, I'll cook." He took off his cuff links, the lapis ones I'd bought him, rolled up his sleeves, and whisked the eggs into a pan. Ed liked to cook; he cooked at home sometimes, but I didn't feel like a guest there.

"My new name's Tai Tai. Like it?" I asked.

"Fine."

"It means housewife, goes with my new career."

"Okay," he said with a smile, sliding eggs onto my plate.

We ate in silence. I started conversations in my mind and filled in his responses, trying to figure out a way to begin. There had been so much to do before I left Hawaii, and leaving the children had been much harder than I'd expected. I sighed. Everything that came to mind sounded like a complaint, or Ed would take it as one. There should be so much to talk about, but I settled for Mrs. Chang's paranoia.

"They don't bother with us, do they, Ed? You're in business, not government." I waited for his answer to reassure me.

"You never know," he said. "Finished?" He stood up and cleared the table.

"You'd better get some rest," he offered. "Catch up on yourself."

I wanted to shake him, hold him by his shirt collar, and yell, "Look at me! I'm here. Talk to me." But I swallowed the words and the lump in my throat, and, with a "goodnight," I walked to the bedroom and closed the door. I sat on the bed and looked around. I recognized the bed covers—I'd bought those at Liberty House—but nothing else. In a corner of my mind, I saw another room, small and dark, with sloping ceilings and a small bed against the wall surrounded with boxes and cases, each filled with witches and devils. Outside the tiny-eyed window, the sky was filled with fiery noise, which shook my body as it tried to come inside and devour me.

And I sat there, in that unfamiliar, dark place, longing to share the fears I had for Chris, wondering if leaving him was the right thing to do. Our family doctor said it was, and his psychiatrist had agreed that Chris "deserved the chance to make it on his own." I would never have left otherwise. The negative responses from members of the support group I belonged to who said he wouldn't make it were upsetting. But then they saw this illness as life destroying, while I saw the desire and motivation that drove Chris to achieve his goals in spite of what life threw at him. And there he was again, in his kindergarten school play. He was Peter Rabbit, with a long speaking part, and, to everyone's horror, right in the middle, he fell off the stage. He didn't miss a beat, just stood up and climbed back on the stage, speaking his lines without a stop. His summer excursions to the Big Island with Hawaii Bound, where he learned to rappel down the mountains, survive on his own in the vast forests, respect the land and everything on it, from the smallest pebble to the tallest tree, his Eagle Scout Court of Honor, and the pleasure these accomplishments gave him, while all the time he was fighting demons I knew nothing about. That was Chris at five, at twenty-two, and all the years in between.

Nobody knew, of course. Chris wanted it that way. Especially for Lisa, though I knew there would be a point in the future when I would have to tell her. So, apart from my closest friend, our emergency contact, nobody outside Ed's family knew. And they never, ever spoke about it, not his two brothers, his sister, his many aunts and uncles, his father. His stepmother might have, but she'd passed away by then. Nobody asked how Chris was doing, how we were coping; they just pretended the inherited gene that had missed them, that had missed Christopher too, had never happened. They were a family who found oblivion in their delusions.

Then I remembered a strange conversation I'd had with Ed's stepmother years before. She was a gentle, kind woman, a schoolteacher by profession. We were sitting in their kitchen drinking coffee, and she suddenly started talking about her son, Ed's half-brother. "I was so worried," she began. "He excels at math, so I had him take an IQ test, asked his teacher what he thought. He said that his grades were due to really hard work. I was so relieved. I'd been concerned he might be a genius, like his father, and all that entails." At the time, I wondered why she'd shared this with me. We hardly knew each other, but I now saw it as a warning, alerting me to the possibility of mental illness and implying that she thought I already knew. I had no idea, and her comment just hung there, waiting years for the penny to drop.

These thoughts haunted me, especially when I wasn't busy, and I had a habit of spiraling down where I didn't want to go, so I reminded myself how well Chris was doing, that China was only a two-year assignment, that I planned on going back home every five or six weeks and for Lisa's school vacations. Of course, I would stay longer if necessary; Ed and I had already agreed. And, with that in mind, I finally slept.

CHAPTER 2

SILK CUSHIONS AND ALTAR CLOTHS

There's an embroidered curtain hanging outside the blue railings.
And a scarlet screen that's painted in blossom-and-branches style.
And a patterned cushion of dragon's-beard rushes eight feet square.

From: **"It's Cold," Han Wo, c. 750

I once read the dispute that language was created by men to communicate while hunting and by women to exchange gossip. I haven't formed an opinion either way, but I do know that words alone aren't the only means to share information. During the next week, I learned about Ai-yi's family. I started our exchange by greeting her every morning. I'd wait until she had taken a quick, sly shower and changed her clothes in the back bedroom, then greeted her with a broad smile. "Ai-yi, *ni hau*?" I'd ask. The first day, I received a head-lowered, mumbled response, the day after a smile. Encouraged, I showed her Lisa and Christopher's photos. We made eye contact, and the communication began.

Through a complicated mixture of charades, facial expressions, and words in our own languages, I learned that Ai-yi was married, and her parents lived in the country. Her father was a classical painter of flowers. Her married daughter lived with her mother-in-law and had a baby girl of her own. The only item we struggled over, or rather I did, was that Ai-yi was the mother of twin sons. I finally got that when she puffed up her thin cheeks and pushed out her stomach, then straightened out to her tall, slim self, and held up two fingers. "Twins," I said, pointing to my son's picture twice, and I felt very smart when she laughed and clapped her hands in delight.

Sometimes I referred to my English/Chinese dictionary, and Ai-yi would help me repeat the word, correcting the tone. It gave me courage to try sentences. I'd have them arranged, rehearsed in my mind, and, during the day, I'd pop them out. Most of my early attempts came with corrections. Ai-yi wanted perfection.

Ed had what he called "the meet-and-greet banquets" every night that first week and arrived home late. After Ai-yi left for the day, my imagination took off, and with it came a sense of unease that became physical and crawled over me. It was so quiet. The stereo wasn't working, nor the TV, so I couldn't play any of the videos we had on hand, and I found myself listening to the walls breathe. I thought of the hidden cameras and saw eyes of strangers watching me. I pulled at the gap in the sheer curtains to cover the encroaching darkness outside and gasped at my own reflection. And, as soon as night came, I went to bed, buried myself under the covers, and gave in to my rambling thoughts.

What the heck am I doing here? I asked myself. Moving to a country where buying a carrot is a major undertaking—and with my marriage in the shambles it was. What magic dust or witchcraft did I have up my sleeve to resolve the unspoken issues between Ed and me? And Chris, what if he had a relapse? I had emergency plans in place. I could be back in twenty-four hours. Would that be enough? But, in my anxious nest between the sheets, I gave up worrying about the questions—and even less about the answers. What did it matter? I was here! I'd already chucked everything in, including my career, on the whim of fate. That was another huge adjustment I had to make, leaving my job. I had worked at the same company for twenty-two years, part time only when the children were small. By the time I'd left for China, I was manager of four departments, which amounted to some fifty employees. I knew each of them, and I missed every one of them. Happy, busy days.

By Thursday, I could stand it no more and waited up for Ed.

"I need to get out of this apartment," I announced as soon as the key turned in the lock.

"No one's stopping you," he said, hanging up his coat.

But this isn't Hawaii or London, and I don't know where to go, I wanted to tell him. I need a map. I'm scared. Look at me. None of the words could be uttered; my brain and emotions were mush.

"Why don't you meet me at the office tomorrow?" he offered. I got out the little map and drew arrows pointing to the main road. It looked easy enough, and so began my first adventure.

I finally made it through the obstacle course of a thousand bicycles, like some sort of initiation rite, and climbed up onto the pavement with a feeling of relief. I walked into the office building and to the receptionist, who returned my smile with a cold stare. I was interrupted, midbreath, by a hawk-faced Chinese man in his midthirties.

"You must be Ed's wife," he said with an American accent and extended his hand. "Michael. Follow me."

Ed's office was along a corridor and behind a closed door.

"He's expecting you. Go right in," he invited, tapping on the door and turning the handle.

Ed reclined in a large black leather armchair behind a neat leather-topped desk. His executive toolset was in one handy container, a dozen sharpened number-two pencils in another, his calendar and phone on the credenza behind him, his pen in hand. Behind his desk, stunning calligraphy in a black frame dominated the room. He looked every bit the big shot, the *laoban*.

"You found it," he said, announcing the obvious. I felt irritated.

"Yes, past every bicycle in Beijing. You need a car to cross the road here."

"Crowded this time of day, factories closing. Ready?" he asked, taking his top coat off the hanger and opening the door. "We'll go out the back way."

"Where did you get the calligraphy?" I asked.

"Oh, that. Someone gave it to me."

"It's beautiful. What does it mean?"

"Eternity."

"And?"

"The Chinese return favors, even if it takes a thousand years, so they say."

I found out later that the "someone" was a very beautiful Chinese woman, a reporter for the *China Daily*. I felt a pang of jealousy when I saw her in Ed's office one day. She left as soon as I arrived.

Tzu Chow drove us to the old Yuanlong Gu Embroidery Silk Store near the north gate of Tiantan. The ground floor was ablaze with colorful bolts of silk and stacks of cushion covers. Silk dresses hung on racks alongside embroidered silk pajamas and padded silk jackets, some lined in rabbit fur. The second floor sold double-sided embroidered pictures from Suzhou of goldfish swimming in place, their glorious tails spread out behind them, canaries sitting on branches of fruit trees in blossom—and antique silks. I bought three of these exquisite pieces in bright pink: an altar cloth with embroidered deer, probably Taoist, and two matching chair covers.

"What are you going to do with those?" asked Ed. "I thought we were here for cushions." It was his turn to be annoyed.

"They're lovely," I told him. "And so inexpensive," I added, then went to work choosing cushions. At three dollars each, I bought over a dozen and piled stacks in Ed's arms to carry to the counter.

"Think you've got enough?" he asked after his third trip.

"Six for each settee and a few spares. Should be."

Back in the apartment, I played with the cushions, arranging them by color and pattern, mixing the birds with the flowers, the hundred children with the cherry blossoms, the yellow silk with the brown velvet. Admiring the results of my handiwork, I thought of other things to brighten the place and make it homey.

"Ed, let's go shopping tomorrow," I said as I scrubbed potatoes to bake for our dinner. I didn't know why I suggested it; we had never gone shopping together before. Not one of his things, he had said. But situations change things, don't they?

"Work half day Saturday," he answered, pouring himself a drink.

"What about later?"

He took off his dark-rimmed glasses, rubbed his eyes with his index fingers, and responded with a heavy sigh. He wanted me to know it was a chore for him and a favor to me. "Okay, be ready around one."

Ed was always early—it was his company's motto—and, by five minutes to one, we were walking out of the building. Michael was waiting. I was surprised to see him. Ed hadn't mentioned anything. After a brief greeting, I was left tagging along behind while they strode ahead like lifetime pals. Walking as if joined together, they turned off the main street and entered what turned out to be the busiest street in the city, Wangfujing.

Shops lined both sides, and the pavements were crowded with pushy pedestrians and vendors selling sweet potatoes and roasted chestnuts from metal barrels. It was as busy as Oxford Street on a Saturday or Times Square any day. I wove in and out of shoppers, all traveling in the opposite direction. Huge potholes waited for the uninitiated pedestrian, and I could only take quick glances ahead for fear of falling in and being trampled flat. When I could no longer see the top of Ed's head, I felt my heartbeat speed up in panic. I had no idea where I was. There were so many people I couldn't stand in one place long enough to turn around. Then I saw them, standing outside a noodle house, chatting away as if they hadn't a care in the world. I wanted to yell at them both for leaving me, but instead I settled on a hostile look. With my heart pounding now in anger, without comment, we went inside.

"Ed," said Michael, "you'll really like the sweet-and-sour soup here."

Chinese customers filled the small room, noisily slurping soup, spitting chewed bones on the stained tablecloths, pouring hot tea over unwashed chopsticks. We stood behind a table, waiting for the occupants to finish. They seemed unaware of our presence.

Michael did the ordering, Ed the paying.

They talked together of work and the drama of the week: the two-hundred-pound passenger who was found dead on arrival and the difficulty getting him off the plane. Seats had to be removed to get him out, but none of the Chinese employees wanted to go near—let alone touch—the dead foreigner, and the Chinese authorities didn't want him.

He'd died on the plane; therefore, he had no right to disembark, they argued. Michael turned the Chinese superstitions surrounding the dead into a humorous story.

Why hadn't Ed mentioned this to me? Why didn't he talk about his work? His work had been the mainstay of our conversations at home. My face stung with embarrassment; my stomach clenched into knots. I wanted to run out of the seedy restaurant, but pride and fear of being lost held me back. I planned on not eating—that is, until the food arrived: noodles in golden broth and a selection of dumplings. My glasses steamed up, and my stomach rumbled.

I held my anger until we got back to the apartment. "What am I doing here, Ed?" I asked. "Who is this Michael person?" I demanded. "Who are you? I don't know you anymore!"

Ed went into his usual mode for confrontation—silence, a stony glare. He pushed out his full bottom lip and poured a drink. I took a deep breath and clenched my mouth shut. Okay, I thought, I'll give you your ten minutes.

That's what the marriage counselor had told me: "Give him ten minutes. Let him settle down after he gets home before you say a word." Settle down? I had wanted to ask. I worked too. When did I get to settle down? But, of course, I didn't. I wanted to have the counselor on my side, to tell my husband how neglectful he had become to his family, how cruel his indifference was, his fits of anger, his absences. We had both vied for the counselor's approval. So, I applied the ten-minute rule whenever Ed went into his frigid state of non-communication and said not another word, and, usually, by the time the ten minutes had passed, Ed was into his second double and I into banging pots, quietly, on the stove, forcing myself to forget what it was I had wanted to say.

That's how we had operated the past ten years—what made me think it would change? But this time my humiliation in front of strangers made me reckless.

"What do you want from me?" I screamed. We'd never had a real fight, and I'd never screamed like that before. Snide remarks thrown back and forth trying to outdo each other inflicting pain was as far as we went. Ed always had the last word. He was a master at deflecting. And, if that didn't work, he would use his ultimate weapon, anger, and explode, and I would have to resist the urge to take the bait that would feed his anger.

He remained silent, lighting a cigarette to go with his third drink. I stormed off into the bedroom before the tears came, slammed the door, and slumped on the bed, my body shaking.

It had been so easy for Ed and me to disconnect. More so after Christopher's diagnosis. He into his world of work, vodka martinis, the evening paper, while I rushed around doing . . . what? Avoiding confrontation mainly, pretending everything was just fine, no problems. Here we were. I smiled at the world. Your average 1980s American family: two careers, two children, one dog, and two cars. Keep the peace at any cost—my mother's motto, though I didn't understand it when I was young.

The room was getting dark and cold. The central heating wouldn't be turned on for another week or two. I went into the bathroom, stood in the tub, and let hot water run over my body until the cold inside me washed away. Have a good look, I said out loud to the hidden eyes. I wrapped my wet hair in a towel, threw on a terry robe, and went to the kitchen for a hot drink. Ed was already there, opening a can of tomato soup.

"Like some?" he asked. I sliced a loaf of French bread, and we sat at the kitchen table in impotent silence.

And the silence ate at me. It always did. And, before the anger I felt could give voice, I took myself off to bed.

I was at work when the call came in just after lunch. "Paranoid schizophrenia," the doctor said. "Do any relatives have it? If so, find out their meds."

Schizophrenia? What did that mean? My body turned to ice; my head buzzed. Scenes of Hitchcock's *Psycho*, the shower scene, the screaming music, filled my thoughts. I hung up the phone, tried to get back to work, but the world as I knew it had changed. I left the office without a word.

I looked at the people waiting for the bus, tired people, each with their own sorrows, and I knew, without a doubt, that we are all, rich and poor alike, connected on this journey through life. Hand in hand, shoulder to shoulder, we go silently from beginning to end.

The bus took us over the Pali through the Ko'olau cliffs with waterfalls and thick forests climbing up to the sky, and I wanted to get off, to run as far and fast as I could up into those mountains and stay there forever.

Chris was there when I got home. I had to be strong. "We'll get through this," I said, and we hugged as he wept. He must have been terrified. It was all about his future now. "Don't tell Lisa" were his first words. I promised.

Chris was four when Lisa was born, and he took his role as big brother very seriously. When Lisa was three, we moved from Kaneohe to Kailua, not far but still a change. During that time, Lisa developed a fear of Count von Count from the children's program *Sesame Street*. Every night I would search under her bed, in the closet, behind the curtains, all to make sure he wasn't there. I worried that Count Dracula, as she called him, would mess up her math skills. Years later, I found out that some nights, when it seemed extra dark or she was overly tired, Lisa would creep into Chris's room and cuddle up. She knew her big brother would keep her safe.

As soon as Ed came in, I told him, quietly, in our bedroom, asked him what he knew about this dreadful illness. He denied any knowledge but called his brother. And another part of Ed's secret life was exposed. His father, a brilliant, brutal man, had a double diagnosis, schizophrenia and bipolar disorder, and, even though I heard them talk about the hospitalizations, Ed said, "I didn't know." I didn't believe him. He was the eldest. And a feeling of betrayal cut through me. "Why didn't anyone tell me?" I wanted to scream the words as loud as I could, but the children. . . . That question still haunts me.

Three years previously, when Chris was fifteen, he went to the same doctor for behavior I found disturbing. Ed had tried to cover it up, dismissed it, dismissed my concerns. He said I was being a worry wort. "Nothing to worry about," the psychiatrist assured me. My thoughts ran away with me, the what ifs. What if I'd known about Ed's father? What if the doctor had picked up on it three years ago? I shared these thoughts with Ed. He didn't respond.

For the next four years, Chris and I worked together to reclaim his life. I read all I could about this devastating illness. There wasn't enough to answer my questions, to satisfy my need to know that there was a cure. Surely there was a cure. This wasn't a new disease. But, apart from medication to help control some symptoms and counseling to offer support, the battle was yours and yours alone to fight.

The first year was the hardest while his doctor tried various medications looking for the right balance, and Chris struggled to finish his school semester . . . fighting to keep the voices away. Terrified he might be sent to Hawaii State Hospital, a facility with a bad reputation, housing mostly the criminally insane. The medication resulted in tardive dyskinesia, causing his fingers to stiffen, so I typed his school papers. He spent most days in his room, so much so that Lisa asked me if he was depressed. It was a tremendous relief for me to tell her he was. This would give her a reason she could understand. Society said it would be much better to think he suffered from depression rather than schizophrenia, a word that wrongly conjured up Norman Bates, I now knew. And I remembered my twenty-two-year-old sister being sent away to be "treated" for tuberculosis. This was 1951, after all, better to believe she had a life-threatening contagious illness than an out-of-wedlock pregnancy.

While most of his friends had left for the mainland, for work or school, the ones who remained he avoided. He was convinced the voices he heard in his head could be heard by others. I suggested we put that to the test, and we sat in the kitchen with a tape recorder running, a thirty-minute one. We replayed it . . . silence. Chris wasn't fully convinced and didn't want to take a chance. He was ashamed, afraid of what his friends would think. He didn't give them a chance to understand.

We talked about things he could do, activities to get out of the house. Scuba diving interested him. Hawaii is a great place for water sports, and he took diving lessons, passed tests, worked with a team. Then, one day, Chris started running, just like that, early mornings when it was cool. From running, he started hiking again, something he had always loved to do since his Scouting days. Sometimes solo, sometimes with the Sierra Club. My heart lifted when I saw him come home from his hikes, his face relaxed, all the deep worry lines softened, his eyes shining. And

I knew he would make it. There were challenging times ahead, some terrifying, but Chris was back. That was four years ago now, and I still found tremendous comfort remembering.

Saturday night's silence carried over into Sunday morning. Anger nipped at me. I wanted to scream out years of frustration, smash dishes, throw books, anything to transform the silent antagonism into something healthy. We could do it now, tell each other how we felt—the children weren't around. Instead, I sat on the settee connected to the umbilical cord of a tape recorder and listened to my fifth set of Mandarin language tapes, hoping this one would do it for me.

"I usually go out for coffee Sunday. I think you'd like the place."

I promptly received Ed's offer as a gesture of good will and packaged my anger away for another time. I realized I was being manipulated, the reward after Ed knew he'd upset me. He could never apologize; that would mean admitting something was wrong. This was our usual pattern, had been for years. The only difference was that I now recognized it.

Tzu Chow had weekends off. The jeep was parked outside our building.

"Brave you, driving here," I told Ed, and I meant it.

"I only drive the main roads, and only weekends. Bicyclists aim at Western drivers. Looking for easy money, I guess."

Another awkward truce.

Traffic was surprisingly light, a couple of slat-sided rickety trucks, a few taxis, some pedicabs, and we drove in a straight line to one of the first Western hotels built in Beijing, the Jianguo Hotel. Its small, cramped lobby bragged a drycleaner and a bakery selling imported German sausages. I inhaled the warm, comforting smell of fresh-baked bread.

After buying bread and liverwurst, Ed led me to the central lobby. In this small Western hotel, the expat community gathered. Squashed around tables, peeking through palms, sipping coffee and eating cream pastries, they gossiped while the elderly Chinese string quartet made music. The room was alive with potted palms and Strauss waltzes.

We sat at one of the round marble-topped ice-cream tables and ordered coffee and French pastries.

"It's really lovely, Ed."

"Glad you like it," he said, handing me the sugar. He still wore the gold ring I'd had made for him in Hong Kong. It had his initials embossed on its square face. He had beautiful hands, large yet graceful, and, even though he always used too much force to tighten washers, he had held our babies so gently, so competently.

"Thanks," I said. Our hands touched ever so lightly in the exchange, and that touch sent a tingle up my arm, like static electricity. I looked at his face; his hair was receding from his temples, and I could see the thin scar on his forehead from a childhood accident. I thought of the time we went skiing together and how his ski had broken in half and flapped behind him as he crashed down the hill yelling, "Tally ho."

We weren't a couple then, just good friends. I was engaged at the time, and Ed was Jim's roommate at college. We met at a party Jim had at his mother's house, a welcome party for me. Ed came up to me. "I wanted to meet the woman Jim's so crazy about." He smiled. His teeth gleamed white. Over the next few months, we went to school functions, on a few double dates with my friend from work. Ed laughed a lot, made me feel comfortable. I told Jim I really liked Ed, that he reminded me of my brother. Jim looked at me, his expression serious. "Stay away from him," he said. "He's all mixed up." It was such a strange comment, so I put it down to jealousy, but I never forgot it.

It would be three years before we saw each other again, and, in that time, I had broken up with Jim, arranged a transfer from work, and moved from Connecticut to beautiful San Francisco. Ed and I kept in touch with the occasional letter, then, during a very cold November, I was sent to Boston to work, with a month's vacation promised after the job was done. I thought of going to London to see my mother, but I had just received a letter from Ed, who was now living in Hawaii. "Why don't you come here?" he wrote. I was freezing, and I thought of sunshine, warmth, beaches! I made flight and hotel reservations, and off I went. We'd been a couple for one month before we married. Just one month, yet I had been so sure. It wasn't many months later that I saw signs of trouble—his drinking, his hot temper, his dark moods—but I knew I could make it right. He would soon settle down and be the happy, loving person I'd first met.

The orchestra played slightly off tune, which I found delightful. We smiled together, and Ed offered me his pasty, which I didn't hesitate to accept. We stayed until the end of the program, and, as I climbed in the jeep, I saw the musicians leave. Dressed in their bow ties and black canvas rubber-soled shoes, they were the picture of dignity as they balanced violins and cellos alongside their bicycles and pedaled off. Ghosts from another time.

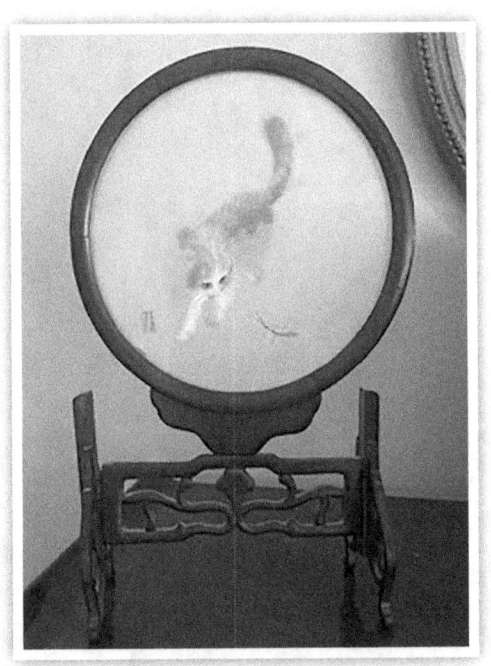

CHAPTER 3

BOK CHOI AND BANQUETS

Fish and meat are temporarily forbidden,
Come, taste our vegetables and fruits.
Lower your head and drink a cup of wine;
Raise it and listen to some golden verses.
When you are in high spirits your body becomes light
And you want to soar up high, riding on the wind.

From: "Holding a Dinner Party," Wei Yingwu, c. 780

Ai-yi shopped for vegetables on Mondays, and I put on my coat, ready to go with her. Her eyes opened wide in surprise. She tried to put me off. The market was dirty, she said. I wouldn't like it. But I wanted to see it for myself. The markets of my childhood were abundant with life and color. Vendors selling polished apples with names—Cox's Pippins, Mrs. Smith's, Macintoshes—and juicy black cherries and flame-colored carrots with their green frilly tops. Friendly places smelling of the earth.

The frozen-faced elevator operator asked Ai-yi where we were going. Did I speak Chinese? I could understand more than I could speak, and I sensed Ai-yi's discomfort at having me tagging along and saw it on her face when she referred to me as *furen* and told her that, no, I didn't speak Chinese. Ai-yi gave me a look of apology, but I sensed that, in some way, she was protecting me.

Our destination was an open "free" market a few blocks behind the compound where the new breed of entrepreneurs had set up shop. Beyond their long wooden tables lived my neighbors. I could see the beginning of the narrow unpaved street; there were no streetlights, and the single-story stone buildings looked as if they were part of a long wall, ready to fall into a heap. I looked around at the shoppers, women and old men bartering over prices, dressed in their dull gray uniforms. Their greasy dyed-black hair cut blunt and short, all signs of individuality hidden. I was the only westerner, and, in my long butter-yellow down-filled coat and my red hair fluffing about in the wind, I knew I'd been too rash, too insensitive to Ai-yi's feelings by coming with her. I felt embarrassed, out of place. A nosey trespasser.

Tables stood on both sides of the road, and, up close, I realized buildings must have stood there until quite recently; some of the rubble still littered the ground. Samples of goods lay on flat boards; stock was kept in sacks and wooden crates. Ai-yi walked up to me and whispered that she would show me the vendors to trust. This egg seller was not one of them. "Never know how old," Ai-yi told me, "until you open up. The vendors on the other side of the street all cheats, scales not working properly, sell old produce, cheap price." Ai-yi bought from two vendors only who shared a table: huge mud-encrusted carrots, fat onions, tiny emerald-green bok choi, huge arthritic ginger roots, and potatoes. The chosen produce was weighed on handheld scales, and Ai-yi argued that the mud weighed more than the vegetables, and an extra carrot or potato was grudgingly added. Tables where fruit should be lay bare. I was hoping for apples or pears. Ai-yi said perhaps another day. *Maiyou*.

I wanted to help Ai-yi carry the heavy bags back to the apartment, but she didn't look my way, and I knew it would cause her more embarrassment if I were to ask.

As soon as we entered the kitchen, Ai-yi opened the money drawer, scribbled numbers on a piece of paper, and put in the tiny torn remnants of *renminbi* ready for the next purchases. We had spent the equivalent of eighty cents.

"Banquet tomorrow at the Beijing Hotel," Ed announced when he came in from work. "Up for it?"

I was cooking a pot of onion soup for dinner. I struggled to find the Chinese word for broth and finally settled on using bouillon cubes and water.

"All right," I answered, biting back the desire to ask why this particular event was open to me. I knew my words would pop out as sarcasm. And Chinese food sounded particularly appealing, going out more so. Would I be expected to entertain?

"Don't worry," Ed told me. "Most of them go for the food. They only get to eat these meals with foreigners."

Except for birthdays and special treats, we hadn't eaten out in Hawaii. The main reason was the expense, and we seemed able to relax more at home, sitting around the table, sharing the events of our days. In the last few years, though, we had started to eat our meals in shifts. The last time I remember sitting in the kitchen around the table was a Wednesday, hump day. Ed seemed tense, so I tried making light conversation, said the wrong thing, something really stupid. "Ed, I think we put the wallpaper up the wrong way." I pointed to a panel that was obviously out of kilter. He stood up, went to the offending paper, and tore it off the wall. I froze, felt ice-cold panic spread throughout my body. I watched as he stormed away. I looked at the children; Chris was staring at his plate, Lisa staring at the wall, eyes wide. They were scared! They had seen Ed lose his temper: the time our dog tore up his audio tapes, spreading the floor with spools of gray, when the lawn mower stopped. Irritating things would set him off, but he'd never been violent. I had no idea what to do. I wanted to hug them both, tell them not to worry, that everything was fine. I looked at the wall. Only the loose piece was missing. Would I be making too big a deal of this? Worrying them even more? I settled on distraction.

"Look at the time," I said. "Lisa, time to get changed." Wednesday was Lisa's riding day. She was at the stable three days a week, overnighting Fridays. Saturday she would muck out the stalls, swim in the pool, and ride as much as she could. "Time to go," I said, picking up the car keys, and off we went. Chris went to his room.

At home that evening, I sat on the settee next to Ed and asked, "What was that all about?"

"Tired, I guess," he said.

"You really scared the children. Why are you always so angry?"

"I'm not angry. It's you."

I knew I was sensitive, took things seriously, and I was always walking on eggs around Ed, careful not to upset him, trying to make him feel happy, loved. His favorite aunt had told me how emotionally abused he had been as a child. His father resented his oldest son, blamed him for all that went wrong. Found fault in everything he did. Used him as a target for his anger, his deep rage.

I sighed. There was no point in pursuing this argument; it would accomplish nothing positive, just entrench us further into our current moods.

Ed never lost control in front of the children after that. I think he scared himself, too.

Strange I should think of that now, though being away from home had evoked a lot of memories, some happy, some worrying. Natural, I supposed. Without the usual distractions, there was a lot of free time to think.

We entered doors to the middle wing of the sprawling three-wing hotel, one wing built by the Chinese, one the French, one the Russians, all of whom obviously had their own ideas on "grand" and didn't talk to one another. We crossed the dingy lobby and up a short flight of wide stairs. Wooden doors almost as high as the ceiling stood open, leading into the immense banqueting hall. Dark red walls met matching carpeting. A stage with red velvet drapes stood at the far side. Massive, grubby chandeliers drooped from the high ceilings, tried to brighten the interior. Stale cigarette smoke, dust, and stained carpets scented the air, accumulated since its construction in 1915.

Our hosts were lined up to greet us, about twenty Chinese men in dark suits standing to attention.

"This is my wife," Ed told the interpreter at his side, who translated to a small thin man in the center of the line. He had that look of quiet power worn into his lined face, which reminded me of my tai chi master. I extended my hand. "*Ni hau?*" I greeted with my best smile, hiding my nervousness. He turned toward me. His blank expression was replaced with surprise; he took my hand and met my gaze, eyes open, unguarded.

We found our table and joined six other guests, Chinese and male, already seated. The linen was starched and bright white. Bottles of Chinese beer and ashtrays were at every setting. A haze of smoke already hung low in the room.

"There are always speeches," Ed told me. "The Chinese like to hear themselves talk." Translations weren't made, but I tried to look interested, though, with the echoing sound system and my lack of language, I understood little, if anything.

The sound of applause was replaced by the clinking of plates. Thick, steaming shark's fin soup was poured from tureens into our bowls, boneless chicken with black mushrooms, sautéed scallops with bok choi. The dishes came, one after the other, and, with each dish, a clean plate. The chopsticks were the tricky kind, long slippery ones made from bone or plastic. I knew better than to attempt my skill with rice, so I left my bowl untouched.

Fresh pots of steaming tea and a cold sweet almond soup ended the meal. I looked for noodles, which never came.

Except for light conversation about food, nothing else was said. Any discomfort I might have felt was buried in the attentive service and the gusto with which our fellow guests devoured their food. Meal over, there was no sitting around. Our host stood, chairs were pushed back, and everyone left as they had entered, quietly and on their own.

"That's the best part about these functions," Ed said. "Eat, drink, and no bull sessions afterwards."

"Great idea," I said, thinking of the times I'd had to stand around in four-inch heels, smiling, looking interested, bored to death, waiting for the "buddy" groups to break up so we could leave.

"Was I the only woman there?" I asked, looking at all the men walking past us.

"There were a few women, Chinese Party types. The Chinese don't bring their wives to these events. Not a bad system." I pinched his arm lightly, and he grinned. I had noticed a few women, tall and skinny, wearing dark "power suits." They had stood back, like shadows.

We were five blocks from our apartment and one from Tiananmen Square. The drive back was on streets that were empty except for the odd taxi or pedicab. The wide road was well lit, and no tall buildings marred the sky. High streetlights glowed without shadow, accentuating the stark trees.

"You made quite an impression on Dzao," Ed told me when we were in the apartment. He was talking about our host.

"How do you know that?"

"Because he rarely shakes hands."

"I liked him," I answered. "He seemed sincere."

"You don't know him" was Ed's parting comment as he walked into the bedroom. But I still felt a sense of confidence. The Chinese are like everyone else, I thought. They respond in kind, a smile for a smile.

I can fit in here.

CHAPTER 4

SETTLING IN

An old friend of mine has prepared chicken and millet
And invited me to come home to his farmhouse.
Green trees come together beside the village;
Blue hills slope away beyond the city walls.

From: "Visiting an old Friend," Meng Haoran, c. 760

I saw very little of Ed, perhaps an hour in the morning and a few hours in the evenings, and then he kept busy with papers from work or newspapers and magazines smuggled off inbound flights, and his vodka, while I puttered around looking for things to do. We had both silently agreed to avoid confrontation and maintained our old habits of coexistence, careful in the words we used, the things we said. I put my concerns aside, wouldn't give them any room in my mind. And, when they bubbled up, demanding out, I told myself, "Keep busy." Luckily, our shipment arrived that week.

Six scruffy men stood in the hall, leaning on wooden crates. Ai-yi gave them a quick survey and decided they needed to be bullied into working. "Take off your shoes," she ordered. "Open the crates in the hall and carry the items into the apartment. *Furen* will show you where things go. Clean up your mess." And I had to decide right then where to place the stuff I thought I couldn't live without: my two sewing machines, the huge, complicated knitting machine I had used just once before, silk-resist dyes I'd taken classes to learn how to use, and that stupid stationary bicycle. That monster went in the back bedroom, the rest either in cupboards or on the desk in the same back room. Job over, the men knelt on the floor, picking up every trace of packing material, and I saw the holes in the socks sagging around their ankles and inhaled the rotting stink of unwashed feet.

By the time they were ready to leave, this surly bunch was as meek as lambs. Ai-yi was obviously a woman to be reckoned with and took her job as housekeeper to the "president of the important foreign company" seriously.

I looked down at shoes waiting for feet, rubber-soled, canvas-topped, holes where toes poked through, and the one leather pair that had split seams down the back. Their owner waited until last to slip his feet into his shoes. He stood tall by the door with a proud look on his face, a slight smile at the corners of his mouth. My mind flashed to my childhood and my own broken-back shoes. I knew how awkward it was to walk in shoes that slipped off your feet and tripped you up and what it felt like when there was no choice.

I called Ai-yi aside. I wanted to give them a tip but knew that would get everyone in trouble, so I thought perhaps a cup of tea or a bottle of beer. Ai-yi looked indignant at the idea of serving these men, and so they left with empty crates full of empty wrappings. Why didn't I think of cigarettes?

Our stationary bicycle proved to be a bad idea. I used it twice, Ed not at all, and I noticed the strange way Ai-yi looked at it. At first, I thought she saw it as another frivolous Western contraption for lazy people, something innocuous enough to report to her leader. But Ai-yi didn't own a bike, and those who did used them as their primary means of transportation, like we used cars.

Two years later, I found out that Ai-yi transferred from two crowded busses to get to our apartment because she couldn't afford a bicycle, though Ai-yi never mentioned it; she was too proud.

I was bored! Isolated in an apartment, I was inspired to do absolutely nothing, and I felt guilty. I should be doing *something*, I felt. With so much empty time, my thoughts turned to Ed and spun me in a circle of frustration and confusion, urging me to provoke him into a fight, force him into acknowledging my presence. Up until a few weeks prior, I was a working mother with very little time just to dwell on issues I didn't want to face. I thought of the clothes I wanted to design, all the stuff I'd brought to make that happen, but, with this mysterious city spread out around me, I was too restless to concentrate. I was a child again, shut up alone in a gloomy bedroom while the sun still shone and the birds sang and I lay there, a prisoner, suffocating and yearning to escape.

Walking in a strange city requires a mission, or at least the façade of one—one mustn't look lost or confused, especially here. So, though intimidated by the memory of my first excursion to Ed's office, I was ready to try again, my destination the market Ai-yi had taken me to. Ai-yi now shopped before she came to work, and I gathered she thought shopping totally inappropriate for someone in my position, whatever that meant. I waited for Wednesday afternoon, her "debriefing day," and, as soon as she left, I rang the elevator bell. It took ages to respond, and the operator slammed open the metal concertina doors and took in my entire persona with one swift, bold look—I felt she was waiting for me to apologize for disturbing her. I gave her a small, friendly smile that she ignored.

With my shopping list in pinyin and some crumpled *renminbi*, I walked along the side street to the unpaved road. Yellow dust, stirred up by the wind, spun in circles at my feet. I tried to blend in. I was short. Maybe if my coat were black, I wouldn't have stood out so. People ignored me, or they stared at me with that blank, closed look I couldn't read. I pushed my hands deep in my pockets, head lowered to hide my unease, feeling stupid and totally out of place. I forgot everything Ai-yi had told me and went to the first table. Shopping was no longer a good idea; I wanted to get it over with.

Women in dark, noncolored clothes and with expressionless faces stared at me and stepped back from the table, a signal for me to go to the front of the queue. Smiling, I shook my head "no" while repeating my thanks, "*Xie xie*," feeling even more embarrassed about buying food

I was supposed to purchase at the government-run Friendship Store, for using *renminbi*, for having a thick coat, especially one in such a light, decadent color that spoke of "capitalistic pig."

It was my turn, and, with my primitive language skills, I asked for potatoes and leeks to make *potage parmentier* for dinner. The woman serving me wore several sweaters, one over the other, in various shades of black. Even with that, it was clear to see she was painfully thin. Her lined, weathered face spoke of years working outdoors, and her short, greasy black hair was pushed behind her ears. She wore woolen gloves with the fingers cut off, and her broken fingernails were caked in mud. I felt her gaze and, before she could turn her head, saw the sly smile on her face and was surprised when she started jabbering away in a friendly tone. Her potatoes were good, the leeks fresh from the farm that day, she told me. The other customers crowded around and watched in silence. Suddenly, they started to yell, all at once. I jumped. My skin crawled; my ears rang as the blood rushed to my head. Panicked, my instinct was to run. I turned to look at them. "What had I done?" I wanted to ask. My embarrassed vendor tapped my arm and pushed some *renminbi* into my hand, some extra potatoes in my bag. She then forced an enormous turnip into my arms and gave a smile of good will. I don't like turnips, but I had to take it. I looked around at my fellow shoppers, and, for the first time, I smiled openly. Some looked surprised, some made a weak attempt at a smile, but they all met my eyes. *"Xie xie,"* I thanked them, and I was warmed by their mumbled responses.

More confident now, I decided to walk toward the neighboring houses. This required passing the meat and fish stalls. Black hunks of flesh and chopped-up fish stank even in the cold, and live ducks and chickens left the market in sacks or draped over bicycle handles by their skinny legs, squawking at this indignity. Plenty left without their head, butchered with the same dirty cleaver on an unwashed wooden board. I heard their cries. My skin crawled. I kept on walking.

Potholes dented the earthen street; stone-slab sidewalks were raised up to house level. They were so narrow that the opening of a door would knock a pedestrian into the road. Centuries of smoke blackened the stone walls of the houses. There were no windows, and wooden doors hung crooked off their hinges. There was not a trace of rubbish, not even a cigarette butt or a leaf off a tree. The only evidence of habitation was the odd bicycle leaning against a wall and an occasional whiff of raw sewage.

The shadows were getting longer, the air cooler, the massive turnip heavier. I sensed eyes peering at me through brick walls, watching my every step. My skin crawled. I knew I would be completely lost if I didn't turn around right then.

I rushed back through the market and to the apartment. I left the turnip on the outside steps, waiting for a turnip lover to snatch it up.

The uneasy feeling stayed with me for a long time, as if I'd entered a secret world closed to me. Flashes of my childhood came: I was standing in that dark hallway holding my gas mask tight. I knew this foster family didn't want me. I could tell. They didn't smile or say hello.

Over the next five days, I walked so much my calves convulsed into one huge cramp of solid wood. I could barely move. Concerned at my limping, Ai-yi called Kathy, which led to the magic of Chinese massage at the Holiday Inn.

The Holiday Inn Lido is a modern hotel built alongside open fields near the airport. They bake great bread and make fabulous sausages, all created by their German kitchen staff; they sell imported canned food at exorbitant prices and have a massage studio. I'd had massages before for the usual reasons—stiff neck, sore back—Swedish and pressure point, but never Chinese, and the masseuse recommended by the hotel manager was male. Ed came with me and went grocery shopping while I waited nervously for the masseuse. I asked him to pick up some canned Italian tomatoes; it had been ages since I'd fixed a pasta sauce.

There were charts on the walls, and I stood in front of one labeled "twenty-four-hour organ body clock," trying to decipher its mysteries. A gentle knock on the door came, and in walked a tall, thin middle-aged man, dressed in a knee-length starched-white coat, his pale face etched in worry lines. Trying to smile, I pointed to my legs. He felt my calf, nodded, and signaled me to lie face down on the massage table. Covering my entire clothed body with a huge white sheet, he rolled those muscles until my eyes teared. He rubbed his hands together and held them over my legs. I felt the heat vibrating from them penetrating my wool slacks, and my frozen calves began to melt. I could have hugged him in gratitude, but he seemed removed, dignified, so I thanked him, paid him, and he bowed slightly but didn't smile.

I discovered that my excellent masseuse was a doctor trained in Western medicine, and he received more money moonlighting as a masseuse than his fifty-dollar monthly salary as a surgeon.

The next evening, with my legs now performing their job without complaint, I stood in the kitchen inhaling the rich aroma of a red sauce, added a little more red wine, and threw in some dried basil. The kitchen soon smelled like home, and I thought how much I missed Hawaii. It is certainly a beautiful place, with perfect weather and warm, friendly people, great for raising children. But I had longed to live nearer family; we were five thousand miles from our closest relatives, and I believed being around aunts and uncles, cousins and grandparents was really important to a child. WWII had put a stop to that for me. Ed had a really big family, and I'd often brought this up, but the longer we stayed, the more entrenched we became, the muter the request.

Ed poked his head into the kitchen. "Smells great in here," he said.

"Just thinking about you."

"Good stuff I hope."

"Well," I said, "we've finally moved from Hawaii, not east as I wanted, but we've moved."

"Can't have everything," he said, putting a spoon in the bubbling sauce. "This is great." That was the end of it.

Moving had been a sore point throughout our marriage. "Where do you want to go?" he'd ask. "Somewhere near family" would be my usual response. And Ed would make promises he knew he wouldn't keep. "Next opening on the East Coast," he'd say. And life took over—work, school, Scouts, horseback riding, friends—and soon it became just too complicated to even think about leaving.

"Why did you never want to move?" I asked.

"I didn't want to go back to all that fighting," he said.

"What fighting? I thought everyone got along."

"You get a bunch of hot-headed Italians in business together and it's going to be hell. I didn't want the kids around that."

I was astounded. "Why didn't you tell me years ago?"

"Ancient history," he said.

"But it's not," I said. "That history has controlled our lives."

He shrugged and walked into the den.

My head buzzed with frustration. Why couldn't we talk about our feelings? Why did secrets and lies hold us prisoner?

Part of me knew, and I had to admit to myself that it was a relief not to be forced to face the past. There were memories I wanted to stay buried too, though I now knew a little bit more about Ed.

We sat at the small kitchen table, and I watched as Ed used the bread from Lido's German bakery to wipe up every trace of pasta sauce from his plate.

"Did they always fight?" I asked. "When we were there, everyone seemed happy enough."

"You saw them separately, not together," he said. "Get more than two of the brothers in one room and there'd be a fight."

"What about your aunts?" I asked. He had two.

"They stayed out of it, got their husbands to do the fighting."

"How awful for you," I said. "You were the eldest child, weren't you?"

"Yep."

This was the most Ed had ever shared with me about his family. I wanted to know more but knew I'd have to tread very carefully. So many questions stored in my head for years now screamed for attention. I had no idea what to ask. What I really wanted to know was what made Ed so distant, so difficult to understand, why he had problems with intimacy, friendships. Why he couldn't hold my hand for more than a few seconds.

"What about at home?" I asked.

"What? The times my mother had to lock herself in the car all night long . . . ?" He got up from the table. "Have a report to finish." And, with that, he left the room while I sat there in shock. Words left me. I didn't even know what to think. Then I realized I now had more questions than before.

CHAPTER 5

SILVER FISH AND JIAOZI

Snow-white fish on crystal tray,
Delicacies abundant await the satiate
Who merely toy with the chopsticks of rhinoceros horn.

From: "Ballad of Beautiful Ladies," Du Fu, c.753

Ed had arrived five months before me, made friends in the expat community, and was fairly established with his Chinese business partners. We saw each other early mornings, Saturday afternoons, and Sundays. He was still totally engrossed in his work, and the earlier promise of sharing family history wasn't sustained, and I had no idea how to reactivate the dialogue. For years, I was held captive by the thought that, if I knew more about his childhood, I would be able to understand Ed's remoteness, his reason for shutting down, and help him through it. But what did I know? I'd only just started remembering some of my childhood, and, while it was nowhere near as traumatic, I found I couldn't speak of that either. And I began to wonder if we'd ever be able to share, to connect, and that maybe it was just me. That I should not be here. Though leaving Ed wasn't an option at this point, as I was terrified that any insinuation that our marriage was in serious trouble might send Chris into another crisis.

Besides, here I was in this intriguing country. I should concentrate on the opportunities surrounding me. Not make any hasty decisions. After all, the twenty-odd years of silence wouldn't be resolved in mere months.

Then Ed announced another banquet, our third that week. He had found my presence useful. I was an icebreaker, a neutralizer, handy when meeting stiff government officials. The truth was I enjoyed meeting these men. Though our limited conversations were through translators, I found them gracious in an old-world way. Then I thought of the food, and my stomach cringed at some of the dishes we'd been treated to lately: duck's feet—nails intact—and nightmarish fat gray sea slugs cut in quarters. For all the people there, except us, these dishes were on par with Beluga caviar and wild Scotch salmon, and food couldn't be refused; to do so would make us appear ignorant—or, worse, arrogant foreigners. I got to be an expert at moving food around, and I was grateful that, after every dish, my messy plate was replaced with a clean one.

"This restaurant is supposed to be good," Ed told me.

"Am I dressed okay?" I walked toward him, straightened my skirt, and twirled around. I'd bought a new wardrobe for China. All my clothes had been summer weight. I spent more than I should, but I reasoned I needed to look well dressed—not over the top, just quietly elegant, a departure for me, as I usually gravitated toward bright colors and floaty fabrics.

Ed responded with his usual "You look fine." I always wondered how he came to that conclusion without really looking. The only time he said anything was if I showed too much cleavage. Then he didn't wait to be asked. "A bit low there, Joan," he'd say, raising both eyebrows for emphasis.

Tzu Chow drove us to Beihai Park, where we walked across a bridge to a small island in the middle of a lake. And there it stood, Fangshan Restaurant. Forty guests in all sat at five round tables in the clean, elegant dining room, art-deco style, reminders of a decadent age long gone. Two other westerners were there, both men. I was now used to being the token Western female.

"This place must cost a fortune," I whispered to Ed.

"Yep. Don't worry, they've made enough money off me. They can afford it." Ed's theory was that westerners in general were looked on as cash cows, waiting to be milked. I didn't want to believe that was entirely true.

Instead of beer, bottles of Scotch and the Chinese equivalent, *Mao Tai*, sat in the middle of each table. There was a short speech, then we were served golden bird's nest soup, followed by huge pink shrimp with sugary walnuts, chicken baked in its own clay mold smashed at the table to release the tender meat—then out it came, the house specialty, a whole fish, silver and shining on an oval blue-and-white platter.

I declined the eye and took a tiny piece from the side with my slippery chopsticks and realized that I'd never really tasted fresh fish before, light and delicate in my mouth, moist and luscious. I could imagine the crystal-clear waters where it had lived. Fine spices blended together in a steamy fragrance, and the taste of the white flesh of the silver fish was enhanced by the perfume of the seasoning.

"Ed, this is delicious."

"Good," he responded, lifting a large section from the tail. As he reached toward my plate, the wool sleeve of his jacket gently brushed the back of my hand.

"Whole fish test the chef's skill. If it breaks, it can't be served," he told me.

There was one silver fish for each table, and the bones were picked clean.

I wanted to learn how to cook this amazing dish.

"Ed, can Tzu Chow take me shopping?" I asked on the way home. "I'd like to buy a fish."

"What are you going to do with a fish?" he asked. "Who's going to clean it?"

"Ai-yi will help me," I told him.

"Up to you. Tomorrow's okay."

The next day, I spoke with Ai-yi. I told her of my desire and asked for her help, first in finding the fish. Ai-yi seemed pleased at this request.

Tzu Chow drove, and Ai-yi poked his shoulder from time to time as she gave directions. We arrived at our first market. Filmy tanks like abandoned aquariums stood on tables, and fish looked out at me with bulging eyes. Their gills moved frantically in the grimy water. I'd no idea they would be alive. I wanted to change my mind, but it was too late to turn back and lose face, so I followed Ai-yi as she inspected each booth. She put on the authoritative air she did so well, bossing the vendors, complaining about each fish: too small—dull eyes—bad color.

We went to three markets, and, at the last one, I sighed with relief—we hadn't yet found the Best Fish. Turning to leave, I told her, "Another day, no problem," and then she saw it— a magnificent silver fish swimming alone in a huge tank. I told her it was too big, but Ai-yi was determined to fulfill her mission, and out came the fish from his tank, and into a plastic bag he went. Haggling over the price dragged on, and I thought, "Good, he'll suffocate before we get home."

It took a good fifteen minutes to get back to the apartment, then Ai-yi filled a galvanized bucket and placed him head down into the water.

He was so long his tail stuck out—and I saw it move, slowly at first, then vigorously flopping about, upside down in that bucket. I couldn't stand it, coward that I am, and walked aimlessly around the compound while Ai-yi prepared the fish.

It was five in the afternoon when I returned, and Ai-yi was scraping the scales off the fish. Thank goodness, the poor old fish was dead. And then he jumped, trying desperately to escape the hand that held him. *He was alive!*

My heart pounded. I couldn't bear to look and told Ai-yi to hit him on the head or put him in the freezer, anything to end his misery. She laughed. "Tai Tai, if he is dead before I scale him, the flesh will not be tender." I tried to tell her I didn't care, but she smiled as one does at a silly child and continued to tell me what a strong fish he was; he would be very good to eat. I could say nothing and, turning coward again, rushed out of the apartment for another aimless walk.

Ai-yi had left when I came back, and there was the fish, ready for cooking, diagonal slices cut in his silver skin and fine slices of ginger and chives inserted in the folds of his pale pink flesh.

Guilt overwhelmed me at the thought of my greed and the misery it had caused this beautiful animal. Should I give him a ceremonial burial befitting his courage and beauty? What would that prove? I pondered and looked at him again in a new light. This wonderful fish had gone through the trauma of capture, imprisonment at the market, and torture in my kitchen. Surely the best way to honor him would be to eat him. Besides, Ed liked fish.

Decision made, I cooked him in the huge wok, using all my skill when I turned him over to keep him whole. Just as Ed walked in the door, I laid his silver body on my biggest platter.

"Wow, I'm impressed," he said. "Where'd you get it?" He sat down at the table and took a piece with his fingers. "It's delicious."

"Enjoy," I said, and I told him the fish's story.

Ed had no compunctions about eating this noble creature, and we sat at the table with the beautiful fish and a bowl of rice. A meal to remember—and not one to be repeated in my kitchen.

When we weren't at banquets, we usually went out for dinner at Ritan, one of my favorite local restaurants. Cooking at home proved to be a problem. Ed wasn't about to become a vegetarian, and meat was difficult to get. Buying from the street vendors was out of the question. It could be dog or horse or cat or yak or squirrel. In any case, flies had feasted on it long before it was sold. Scrawny yellow skinned chickens, heads on, claws extended, lay in the cooler at the Friendship Store, hens that had exhausted their supply of eggs. Without diplomatic stores at our disposal, our only option was the Western grocery store at the Holiday Inn Lido. As well as their delicious German sausages, they sold imported canned food at exorbitant prices and occasionally Australian beef or lamb frozen solid into gray-pink blocks. In spite of its unappetizing appearance, it sold out quickly to westerners living in the hotel's apartments.

Ritan Restaurant was around the corner from our apartment, at the gates of Ritan Park. Ed drove all the same. The streets weren't well lit, and very few people were out at night. The extraordinary silence was eerie.

A well dominated the courtyard, and the eaves on the single-story building turned up to the sky at the corners. Ornate paintings of birds and peonies faded and chipped by age and weather decorated the doorways. Luscious smells escaped through the opening.

"It's lovely, Ed. Is it very old?"

"Don't know. I come here for the food." I looked it up later in the small Beijing Guidebook, which said it was built in 1531 as part of the altar for the Temple of the Sun. Buddhist or Taoist, it didn't say, but, in any case, it became one of my favorites, partly for its history and the beautiful park but mostly for the house specialty, *jiaozi*, dumplings.

In the summer, stone tables placed under shady trees presented a setting for customers to sample teas and have cups refilled by experts pouring hot water from kettles ten feet away without spilling a drop. And, on summer Sundays, it became a meeting place for old men with their prized songbirds housed in elaborately carved cages. The old men walked from the *hutongs* at the back of the park, hung their bird cages under the branches of *Hua Shu* trees, and sat admiring one another's pets while smoking thin black pipes.

Steam and cigarette smoke filled the crowded underlit dining room, and surly waitresses rushed around carrying overfull trays dangerously close to customers' heads. We were assigned a booth near the middle. The cracked mosaic-tiled floor was slippery from spills. I looked around at our fellow diners. Except for a few Chinese businessmen, they were Western—specifically, judging from the heavy rolled Rs and slurred Ss in conversations so loud they sounded argumentative, Russian. It was then that I noticed their noses: huge beak-like protrusions from thick, dark faces. And I knew why the Chinese slang for westerners was "big nose," and I smiled like someone in on the joke.

Our waitress came to the table, impatiently tapping the stub of a pencil on a greasy pad. Wasting her time, that's what we were doing.

"You order, Ed," I said. Ed liked to order.

He pointed to the pictures on the stained menu: red pork with spring onions, steamed shrimp with ginger, chopped cabbage with water chestnuts and crushed hot peppers, pork and dried shrimp with sesame seeds, steamed buns with sweet red bean filling for dessert, and beer, *pijou*, one of the few Chinese words he knew; the other was *Mao Tai*.

Then we waited, and, in that noisy place, I reached out and touched Ed's hand. "What's it like working here, Ed?" He shrugged. I persisted. "It must be at least challenging, difficult even."

He sighed. "Not really. Give me a desk and a chair, throw in a phone, and you could be anywhere."

"Wow," I said. "That's an impressive attitude." And I meant it. Then I thought maybe his constant dark moods, his distance even, must be because of me. Perhaps he just didn't want me here.

Ed looked around the restaurant, "Service is always slow," he said. He had finished two large bottles of beer, and the ashtray was full of stubs. I poured more tea, watched green leaves sink to the bottom of the tiny cup, and jumped when steaming platters were thrown on our table, waking me from my semi-trance. Fat, white, translucent dumplings glistened like satin cushions floating on a thin, rich brown layer of vinegar and soy sauce. The attitude of the waitresses no longer mattered. I got used to it after a while, even sympathized with them. They slogged away for a piddly wage without the lure of tips, not even a Western cigarette.

"I have to pierce some of these," I told Ed as I struggled with a fat shrimp dumpling. "They're so slippery."

"Nobody cares here. Do you want to taste the beer?" He knew I never drank beer.

I touched the back of his hand and smiled. "Thanks, Ed, but I'll stick to tea."

Maybe it would be all right; maybe I was just overreacting, having trouble adjusting. We talked to each other when we were out. Nothing important, but it held a promise for more intimate moments.

Time to see Chris again, stock up on food and, of course, cigarettes. We usually had a weekly phone chat, and, while he seemed to be doing well, I felt it necessary to see for myself. It was always with trepidation that I left, worried what I would find, how to handle any difficulties, and a mixture of relief and guilt when I came back. Chris always met me at the airport, and my first sight of him would tell me what to expect. He was thinner, which worried me until I realized he was watching his weight. His antipsychotic medication messed up his metabolism, and weight gain was inevitable, so he devised a plan.

"One big meal a day, dinner," he told me. "No sodas." His work was physically demanding, and I was concerned about that.

"Does that include Dr Pepper?"

"Yep." He smiled.

"Okay," I said. "Next time I go to Costco, I'll get you some muscle milk. It's a good protein drink."

He was smoking now too, but, if that helped him, I wasn't going to say anything. His day started at seven in the morning, and work kept him very busy. I saw him evenings only. On his weekend off, he went to volunteer, working at Lyon Arboretum; the Nature Conservancy, cleaning their grounds; at the Kaneohe Marine Corps Air Station building nests for booby birds; hiking, which I was very happy about. He needed to be busy. And, every time I left, my heart filled with pride and admiration for his courage, and I felt more confident with the decision we'd made. Chris was thriving. He still kept pretty much to himself, but he had his clients and a few hiking friends, which was more than he had just a few years ago.

CHAPTER 6

BIG BROTHER IS WATCHING

The Mighty wind blows, scattering the flying clouds,
After meriting the unification of the world, I returned home.
Will fierce warriors guard the four corners?

From: "Song of the Mighty Wind," Liu Bang. c. 202 BC

I woke up Monday to a gloomy day. The sun and sky were hidden in clouds of brown like a dirty snowstorm, obliterating everything in its path.

"Sand blowing in from the Gobi Desert," Ed said in answer to my question. "Might last for days. I suggest you stay in."

The strong tone of his voice made me want to go out. The tone that said, "Why do you need to learn to drive?"

Sand crept into our apartment through closed windows like some insidious slithery monster, covering everything in a layer of grime. The tallest building in Beijing was the new CITIC building a block behind us, and, at twenty-nine stories high, it was barely visible. Ai-yi polished and swept, but the grime prevailed.

"*Aiya,*" she moaned, tackling the windowsills in the den for the second time that morning.

With sign language and a few feeble words, I suggested Ai-yi go home. She reluctantly agreed to leave after lunch. I made a pot of tea, and, with sliced Swiss cheese and French bread, I plucked up the courage to make a sentence: "*Ai-yi, ni xihuan cha ma?*" I asked, holding the teapot over an extra cup, miming the request. Ai-yi's expression was one of absolute surprise, as a mother's might be at her two-year-old constructing a sentence. I sat at the kitchen table and placed a plate opposite for Ai-yi. Except for my "christening" day, we had yet to share tea or food. Ai-yi hesitated; she found something interesting in her apron pocket and picked away, looking around the room, anywhere but at me. I felt the blood rush to my face and stared at the table as I pulled out the chair. I'd done it again, embarrassed her. I was just trying to show my gratitude for making the hour-long journey to work that day. She could easily have stayed home; half of Ed's employees had. I handed her a paper towel to use as a napkin. She tore it in half and handed a piece to me. We smiled at my extravagance.

Ai-yi declined the bread I offered and, from her woven plastic bag, produced her lunch, then sat gingerly at the table.

"*Mianbao*," she smiled, "bread," and pointed to my plate. That was her first and, in my presence anyway, only English word. She rolled the "r." We sat facing each other, and I practiced my growing language skills hesitantly, as Ai-yi was quick to correct my grammar. We commented on the flat wheat bread of China and the white fluffy bread on my plate. Ai-yi opened a small plastic container and shyly picked out tiny strips of pickled vegetables with her chopsticks. That was her meal. Bread and a few pickled vegetables. I squirmed. The discomfort I felt was the same as sitting in my dentist's chair. I fell back on my old standby: talking.

I asked her if she would write Chinese characters for the furniture. Ai-yi smiled, pleased with the request. She was really pretty, I noticed, with her small oval face and short wavy hair, just beginning to gray, though her worn body and sad eyes told a story of hard times.

After she left, I went to the den and put a stack of index cards and a thick black marker on the kitchen counter. Every day, Ai-yi filled a card or two, and, by the end of the week, everything, including the refrigerator, had a sign stuck to it with scotch tape with Chinese characters, under which I wrote the pinyin.

"What's all this for?" Ed asked one evening.

"Trying to learn the language," I answered as I copied the characters on index cards and wrote the pinyin on the back to use as flash cards.

"Okay." He laughed. "If it makes you happy."

"Might be fun if you learned it too. That way we could practice together."

"I leave that to the professionals," he said. And I wondered why he never learned to say even the simplest things: hello, thank you—just two little words: *ni hao*? *Xie xie*. I suspected the Chinese nationals we met all spoke some degree of English, even though they never displayed it, and I thought it a very clever strategy. Like a cloak of invisibility.

The sandstorm continued for days, and I felt trapped in the apartment. Ed stopped by at the "DVD Library" one of the apartment dwellers had set up. Admission was four DVDs, and then you could borrow. But even the *Pink Panther* could entertain for only so long. So, it was a relief when the phone rang. The caller introduced herself as Rebecca Young. Her voice was soft and lilting, a southern accent.

"Hello, Joan. The girls are over, and I wanted to know if you were coming for coffee." I said I'd be delighted, but did she have the right person?

"Oh yes," Rebecca answered. "The embassy gives me the names of all new expats. Didn't you get my invitation?"

"No," I answered. I heard her sigh, and she gave me her address.

Ai-yi helped wrap a scarf around my hair and over my mouth. Even so, the fine sand stung my face and seeped into my hair and ears on the thirty-odd steps to Rebecca's.

Rebecca lived with her diplomat husband in the building next to ours, on the sixth floor. The apartment was one of three on that floor, and, with the sandstorm and small windows, it was quite dark, though cozy with its elegant southern-style furnishings and vases of elaborate silk flowers. Older than I, Rebecca was refined and gracious, a true diplomat's wife and at ease with it. Four other women sat sipping coffee and nibbling cookies, all Americans. Except for one woman who had two young children, we were mothers of adults.

"Welcome to our little get-together," Rebecca smiled.

I liked my hostess right away. Rebecca had strong ties to London, and she knew it well; perhaps that's why we connected. My English accent prevailed, though I'd lived in America for years. Rebecca sat me beside her best friend, Monica. Monica's blond hair swung in luxuriant curls to her shoulders, and every bit of her from eyebrows to fingertips was groomed to perfection. I wondered how she managed it.

Our coffee-time conversation soon gravitated toward ai-yis and stayed there. I listened and watched. Rebecca and Monica didn't say much, but the other three did, though everyone kept their voices down and said lots of "you-know-what-I-mean."

As I was leaving, Monica beckoned to me and asked almost in a whisper if I would like to join her and Rebecca shopping. She would let me know when her husband wasn't using their car. Embassy personnel had their own cars and drivers, but, when they shopped, my two new friends drove themselves.

"Ed, I met some neighbors today, embassy people," I said over dinner.

"Oh yeah?"

"Rebecca Young. We plan on going shopping."

"Know her husband."

"Would you like to get together with them?" I asked.

"I work with these people every day. That's enough for me." That said, he turned his attention to our old standby, tuna noodle casserole. "Want some ketchup?"

The following day Rebecca's invitation to her coffee came in the mail. The heavy parchment-type envelope was torn at the flap, and grease marred the picture on the card. I put it aside and waited for Ed to come home.

"Ed, look at this," I said, handing him the envelope.

"Yeh, it's been opened," he said. "I've heard horror stories about long delays and missing pages in reports."

"What about your mail?"

"Comes sealed on the inbound flights."
"Why would they bother with a card?" I asked.
"Nothing better to do?"
Hopeless. The man was hopeless!
There would, though, be a time in the future I would use the phone-bugging system to my advantage.

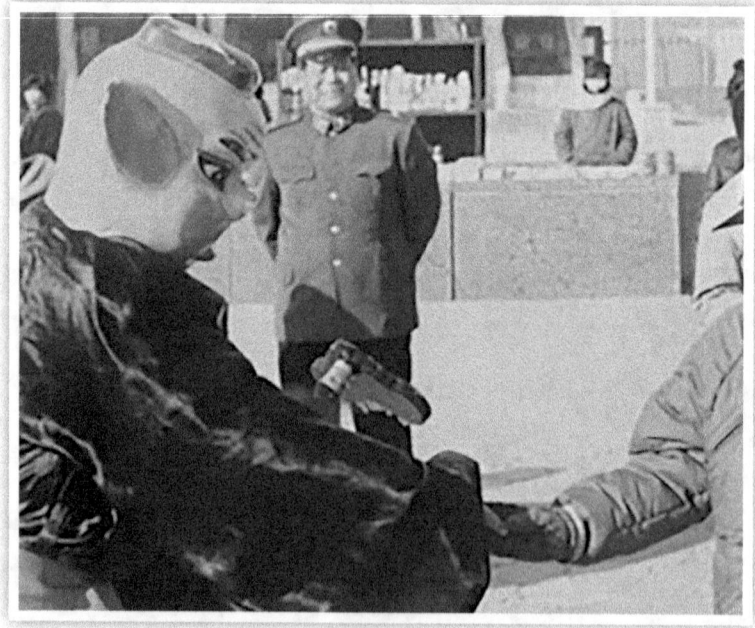

CHAPTER 7

TURN RIGHT AT THE CABBAGES

It's hard to take the road to Shu,
Harder than climbing up to the blue sky!
Hearing about it, people's faces
Grow pale and drawn with age.

From: **"The Hardship on the Road to Shu," Li Bai, c. 740

Rebecca said our first outing would be to the Drum Tower north of the Forbidden City and one of the markers to the original palace city. Off we set in Monica's large American sedan, with diplomatic license plates (which offered a bit of protection, I was told) and a skeletal, non scale map printed by the embassy. Street signs were scarce and written in Chinese characters, with some main streets written in Chinese and pinyin. All the signs were low and narrow, obviously for pedestrian and bicycle traffic.

The main road north was busy with pedicabs pulling two seater rickshaws, bikes with boxes of eggs stacked five feet high balanced over the back wheel; some carried live pigs or chickens or ducks wrapped in woven baskets and struggling to get free. Busy people, refusing to hurry, they pedaled at the same easy pace of a Sunday outing. Trucks spewed exhaust fumes and rattled along, some having traveled thousands of miles as evidenced by their mud-caked exteriors, and competed for space with long, accordion-centered busses. And there we were, buried in this no-lane traffic, looking much the same in a car as we did walking—foreign.

"Turn right by the cabbages," instructed Rebecca from the back. Cabbages? Yes, there they were: huge white cabbages stacked like bricks, and so high I was at a loss trying to visualize how they got there. They were free and ready for distribution by the group leader to the residents of that area. Cabbages were the mainstay of city dwellers' winter diet. They would be stored in stacks and last the entire season.

Beijing is laid out on a grid, like New York City, so it should be easy to find one's way (except for the directionally impaired, like me), but, once on the anonymous warren of side streets, one with too much going on, another deserted, distractions easily cause disorientation. It was when we passed the cabbages for the third time that we knew we were lost.

"Turn left," suggested Rebecca, uncertain this time. It was a sharp turn, and the street was wide enough for one car only. Tall brick walls edged the narrow pavement, broken by alleyways, *hutongs*, family compounds from before the revolution now divided into one-room homes accessed by these alleys. It probably went on forever, but we were stopped by a broken-down van, with no room to turn. By this time, Monica was becoming frazzled, but there was nothing for it, and, with Rebecca coaching her on, Monica drove her car in reverse all the way back to the cabbage turn. My hands were sweating for her, and I decided there and then I would never drive a car in Beijing.

It was the cabbages, Rebecca told us. They had put her off by one street. We tried again, successfully this time, and arrived at a large open space covered in rubble. Monica parked.

There were no shops that I could see. Once home to artisans and merchants catering to the emperor and his court, the area was in various stages of decay. I followed my new friends as they walked toward one of the original city walls. I had no idea what lay behind it, but, along its front, tiny shacks leaned for support, some raised up a step or two, ready for rain or snow. I saw not a lick of paint anywhere. It looked like Hobo Town.

Rebecca opened the door to the first shack, and a bell tinkled. Goosebumps of excitement crept up my spine. I smelled treasure! And, with the same degree of awe as when I'd visited my father at Christies in London, my eyes gathered in the bits and pieces filling every corner of this tiny dark space with one sweeping glance. Most of it was chipped porcelain, late Ching dynasty, but . . . there could be an undiscovered Ming vase in amongst the rubbish. My heart pounded, this time from excitement, the thrill of the chase, the best part of the hunt.

A stooped old man pushed himself through a ragged curtain and greeted us with little bows of welcome and a huge grin that showed off his few remaining teeth, stained brown from nicotine and *cha*. He wore the standard dull blue-gray jacket and pants, with a heavy black sweater underneath unraveling at his wrists. He looked so eager, so expectant, innocent as a babe. Smiling at us, he jabbed his crooked index finger toward the contents of a small glass case. I knew not to show interest too soon and, raising an eyebrow and pursing my lips, silently challenged him to show us more. It was very cold in his shop; oil was rationed, and there was no heater, no electric light either. He stamped feet dressed in canvas slippers and rubbed his rough, arthritic hands together, and the pressure built.

"*Qing ni kan-kan*," he said, and he went back behind the curtain and brought out a freestanding dressing table mirror, which he held carefully in his hands. The wooden frame was exquisitely carved. "*Taozi*," he said, proudly nodding his head at the round peaches carved in the wood. I caught a few words—"prosperous, long life," that's what he was trying to sell me, a guarantee of prosperity if I bought his mirror. The glass was blackened in parts where the silver had worn off, authenticating its age. I felt him lean toward me, saw his bent knuckles and crooked fingers. I thought of all the women who had gazed into the mirror's surface, perhaps on their wedding day, or dried the tears of a broken heart. I decided to make my purchase.

He told me the price. I looked appropriately shocked and told him, "*Tai gui le!*" We went around for a good fifteen minutes, and I bought it for one third of his original price. I knew immediately I had paid too much, but I didn't care. His eyes sparkled as he bowed us out through the flimsy door, smiling, waiving his hand in farewell. All that joy, I thought, for a mere eight dollars. It was years later, while unpacking at another overseas location, that I discovered my lucky *taozi* mirror was lopsided; one side of the stand had been deliberately sawn off, probably to cover some wood rot, leaving it leaning sadly to one side. And I smiled when I thought of my old friend and his crafty ways.

Wealth must spread. Can't give your money to only one shopkeeper—that was Rebecca's rule. You must buy from at least two to ward off the "green eye," so we stopped in all the shops, and Rebecca and Monica bought pieces of whatever they were collecting at the time.

"Ask him to write it down, Rebecca," Monica said when bargaining for a piece of old silver. She looked at me. "I lived in Russia and learnt Russian. Our term was two years, and we stayed ten. I refuse to learn Chinese."

Everywhere we went, heads turned and manners were forgotten as the locals stared at Monica. Her blond hair bounced at her shoulders, and her perfume left a trail. "They think she's a movie star," Rebecca explained.

We went to the Drum Tower often, and I learned to remember who was who. All the shopkeepers were the same indistinguishable age, friendly and spirited with wide, toothless smiles and crafty crinkled eyes and dyed-black hair. They had the same smell, too; dust and cigarette smoke were their perfume, but, like a fine porcelain vase, each one was unique in his own special way.

After a few trips, trust was established, and more treasures appeared from back spaces, some of which I had to hide on leaving, the items being in the "nonexport" category of antiquities, promising to get buyer and seller into trouble, even from nosey neighbors. We would buy another large item then, usually another mirror, as cover. And delicious shivers raced up my spine.

"Another mirror?" Ed asked after I bought my third.

"I needed to hide this piece of porcelain." I showed him the small Sung dynasty bowl incised with swirly clouds.

"It's so light. Here, hold it," I said, handing it to him.

"Take your word for it," he said, sipping his drink. "Looks imitation to me."

I didn't take the bait and walked to the kitchen for old newspapers. I was determined to ask for the car. I wanted to do my share of driving, though it would be Tzu Chow behind the wheel.

"Ed, can I use the jeep sometimes?"

"Nope. Company business only, Joan."

"Other wives do."

"That's their problem," he said. Arguing would be futile. His tone said so. I wrapped my new treasure in sheets of newspaper and put it in a closet in the den.

"What are you going to do with all this stuff?" he asked, changing the subject. I shrugged. I didn't want to think about that. Shopping was becoming my therapy. I was hooked on finding the hidden Ming vase, seduced by the bantering of old men.

There were plenty of hunting places in the city: rows of little shacks by the Bell Tower, south of the Drum Tower, government-run shops smelling of damp and wood rot, some mere warehouses for broken furniture that, under the hands of skilled workmen, could be put back together like new. All items at the government-run shops were expensive and paid for in FEC. There was no bargaining, no fun. But purchases came with a red wax chop, the only legal way to get certain pieces out of the country.

There were about three open markets on weekends, consisting of long make-do tables pushed together under green tarps. When Rebecca told me about them, I remembered how much Ed had enjoyed scouting the stalls in Portobello Road on our trips to London. He liked to look at old watches and compasses. We hadn't rowed in a few weeks, after I started shopping as a matter of fact. I felt magnanimous and wanted to share. Have fun browsing together, discussing the merits of innocuous things. Maybe have lunch somewhere.

"Come on, Ed," I said that evening. "You'll enjoy it, know you will."

"Okay. Saturday," he replied grudgingly.

Michael and Rose showed up, "What a coincidence," said Rose. Rose was originally from Chicago, and she and Michael were the only non-Chinese citizens working with Ed in Beijing.

"Ed, want to buy some sports shirts?" Michael asked. "Overruns from the factories. It's near the embassies."

My face flushed with annoyance. I wanted this to be *our* outing. But I couldn't say so, didn't want to appear the stuck-up wife, so I said nothing.

Back in the jeep we climbed, and Ed drove to a wide alley where tables were set up, row after row, and stacked with golf shirts, tee shirts, jeans. These vendors were well dressed, their eyes bold, their manner pushy, like their Hong Kong neighbors. I bought some jeans and a few shirts for Chris, then waited around while the other three walked up and down every table covered with almost identical merchandise. The longer I stood there, the angrier I became. I climbed in the jeep to wait, wishing I had the key and the courage to drive.

With bundles of stuff, Michael and Rose settled in the jeep. "If you want anything altered," Rose said, "I know a tailor. He lives near you. I'll draw a map. He's from the south, here without papers. He's very cheap. Don't know his name, though." Seeing as that was the first direct comment she'd ever made to me, I thanked her and put the note in my pocket.

The second time Rose and Michael showed up at the market, I greeted them with a cheerful hello, became absorbed in my surroundings, and strolled away to look for treasures buried in junk. The further I walked, the better I felt. I had experience in markets and felt quite at home, and it was great not to play tagalong while those two kissed their boss's arse.

"Find anything?" It was Ed. Alone. Rose and Michael didn't join us again, and I didn't ask Ed why or feel one bit guilty.

"There's a compass over on that table you might like. Come."

He picked it up. "German," he said, "probably military."

"I'll bargain for you," I told him, pleased I could show off my shopping language skills. Ed hadn't found it necessary to attempt the language, and ego prevented him from trying.

It was a tough buy. Having noticed Ed's huge signet ring, the vendor silently weighed the gold and measured the size of Ed's purse.

"They told me they know you're rich because you don't like to spend money," I told him as we walked away, compass in hand.

"Tell them my wife makes up for it," he laughed. The sound was rich, warm, friendly.

The markets were sweaty, crowded places frequented by local men and a few of us "big noses." Most of the items sold were western, remnants from the days before the Japanese occupation scattered and imprisoned the population.

Tables were semi specialized, old watches mixed with bits and pieces of broken silver chains, hair ornaments covered in lustrous blue kingfisher feathers magically adhered to their surface like cloisonné. Odds and ends of silk embroidery, panels off children's hats, embroidered edging from a lady's robe, ornate covers for the looking glasses I kept buying. I bought pieces of silver, mostly large, looped handmade chains and bobs once worn by men to hold toothpicks, ear picks, tweezers, and other mysteries for male grooming all destined for meltdown.

Most of the vendors in the open markets were younger and more aggressive than my old friends, not as cunning and definitely not as much fun to buy from, and I only went with Ed.

Every sale attracted a crowd. Buying and selling was considered a spectator sport, like a game of chess, or billiards, a bull fight, or a boxing match. Pressure built, and watchers took sides, usually the buyer's. They crowded close, breathing out stale cigarette smoke, their bodies emitting the sour smell of hard-earned sweat. They pushed closer, leaning in for the exchange of money, the "kill," vicariously spending money they didn't have. Once done, they made way for the buyer, happy grins on faces that could be interpreted for or against your bargaining power.

The Germans were zealous buyers of antiques, although they didn't play by the "*tai quai!*" rules and seemed satisfied with a mere 10 percent or so discount, which spoiled it for the rest of us, including the sellers. Bargaining was, after all, a battle of wits: the better the players, the longer the game, the more satisfying the outcome.

Ed began to enjoy these excursions, though his patience was limited. He was attracted to all things military or mechanical, no matter the state or condition. While picking things up and examining them was encouraged, taking too long to make a decision was not, not with these young men. Once you touched an object, the seller gave you his undivided attention, which meant he expected you to buy. He was a busy man, not like my friends at Hobo Town, where selling was performed as a leisurely art form. These young men had things to do, places to go, but

Ed couldn't be pushed. Rather than be pressured, he would walk away, and the novelty soon wore off. I thought of sharing my old Hobo Town friends with him but knew his large presence would scare them silly. So, our free-time excursions switched from flea markets to strolls in the parks or along the crowded streets, something we would never have done at home. We didn't need a reason or destination; just being out among our neighbors, who were living their lives, was enough. And we always ended our days with a feast from one of our favorite restaurants.

Rebecca and I were at the Bell Tower market keeping in touch with the latest finds. We were in the porcelain shop, an unpainted wooden shed like the rest, that specialized in pottery. A German couple stood looking at a tri-colored pot. "*Tang dy,*" assured the shopkeeper, making the piece anywhere from one thousand to thirteen hundred years old. They inspected it, put it down, walked a few steps, and whispered together. Taking advantage of our presence, the eager salesman showed it to me, hoping for a little competition.

I held it, weighed it, felt it, and said quietly, "*Fangza.*"

He looked horrified, hands to his face. "*Zhengde, zhengde,*" he repeated, "genuine, genuine," nervously glancing at the fishes he hoped to hook. I tried to hold back the smile that crept over my face.

Rebecca and I lazily walked up and down the maze of lanes, in and out of shops, and had decided to return home when in came the pottery shopkeeper. Baring his snaggled-tooth grin, he leaned close to me. "*Fangza.*" He smiled with his tobacco-breath whisper. We smiled together, like partners in on a scam.

These shrewd old men taught me how to bargain, how to call their bluff by pointing out the tiniest flaws—scratches in a piece of furniture, tiny chips in porcelain—and the evidence of imitations, each pair of eyes straining to see or not see what the fault might be. And so I became a collector.

CHAPTER 8

THE GOLDEN CHAIR

> We go to the Golden Palace;
> We set out the jade cups.
> We summon the honored guests
> To enter the Golden Gate.
>
> From: Anon., first century BC

Shopping and eating, in that order, had become my passions, so it was with pleasure that I answered Rebecca's call and agreed to join her for a little shopping at the Friendship Store. Always relieved to get out of the apartment, I didn't hesitate. It wasn't until we were in her car did she tell me our real destination. Mr. Huang, ex-coalminer now independent dealer, had invited us to a friend's apartment. "Couldn't tell you on the phone," she said. "They're bugged. The cars are checked daily, so we can talk here."

"Are you sure about the apartments?" I asked nervously, trying to think what I might have been overheard saying. Oh God! The rows with Ed. I bet they loved hearing those!

"It's quite common in diplomatic circles" was Rebecca's matter-of-fact response.

Probably not mine then, I thought, hopefully. We were in business, not government.

Mr. Huang had told Rebecca to go to a residential area just at the edge of the city, park on a certain side street, and wait to be picked up by Mr. Huang's friend. "No," responded Rebecca to my question, "don't believe I have met him. Wasn't given a name. It's better that way."

We drove through the old part of the city, then past rows and rows of high concrete blocks of identical apartment buildings, each numbered in huge red letters and looking as if it had been dropped on the dirt-covered roads by giant helicopters. The treeless streets were almost deserted, and, when we came to the numbered building of our meeting place, Rebecca parked tight against a low brick wall. We were to stay in the car and wait for our ride to pull up alongside. The minutes ticked by, and our excited chatter dried to nervous silence. It was cold in the car. The windows fogged up, and I began to wonder what we had set ourselves up for—but just then a dark, battered sedan pulled alongside— the driver pushed open the back door, and in we climbed, pulled our scarves around our faces, and slid down as low as possible in the seat. My heart beat a little faster.

Our driver turned many corners, though it didn't seem long before we pulled up behind another brick wall in front of an old three-story brick apartment building where a scrawny tree tipped its branches to the bare earth. Opening the car door, our driver motioned us to follow. We walked into an unlit corridor and climbed stained concrete stairs to the second floor. Two sharp knocks, and the apartment door opened.

A man in his early forties welcomed us. "*Qing jinlai*," he said, and into the gray room of the gray building we went. Two other men about his age were seated in the room, smoking hand-rolled cigarettes and dressed in ill-fitting Western suits, sans ties. They all looked as nervous as I felt.

"*Qing ni dzwo*," the taller of the two said, standing up and gesturing toward the now vacant chairs. We knew none of them.

"Where's Mr. Huang?" I whispered to Rebecca, who merely shrugged, as cool as ever.

Introductions were made, "Old Uncle," "Younger Brother," anonymous titles. Cigarettes were proffered and politely declined, to the relief of our hosts. They stood around, trying to look casual, one hand pressed into jacket pocket, the other holding soggy cigarette butts. My stomach tightened. Nobody, including us, knew where we were. These men weren't factory workers, nor were they educated; they were the new breed of entrepreneurs—dealing in . . . ? Ed would have a fit. . . . Good!

"*Ni xihuan cha ma?*" The offer of tea relaxed me. As I sipped the fine green *cha*, I looked discreetly around, and there, in the corner of the room, glowed *the* chair. A classic horseshoe-shaped armchair gleamed in the golden hues of *huang huali*, a wood found in Ming dynasty furniture from trees unique to China that are now endangered. This magnificent chair seemed lit from within as it waited for its owner, its curved arms worn thin in parts by generations of occupants whose silk-robed arms had graced its surface, their hands finding comfort in the chairs embrace. Twin copper bands wrapped around the thinnest parts gently supporting the open arms of this golden chair.

I walked toward the chair, ran my fingers along the smooth surface of the arms, saw the foot bar hollowed from supporting satin-shoed feet for four hundred years or more.

How I longed for that chair, but it was not to be. Our entrepreneurs were either honest or too clever to sell to me, saying they knew I would never get it out of the country.

Gradually, from a backroom came bits and pieces of furniture and porcelain. Rebecca bought a small bedtable, but nothing appealed to me, except an opium kit in an elaborately carved box. There were two pipes carved from ivory, tiny transparent china bowls, scales and pipe cleaners and things I couldn't name—all the paraphernalia used by the elite in the infamous opium parties of the age. The kit was a work of art, and I felt stupid explaining that, though beautiful, I didn't wish to own something that must have caused grief to its owner.

Time to leave, and I was leaving emptyhanded, since I couldn't have the chair and dumb ethics messed up my buying the opium kit. Just before he opened the door, the man who had shown me the opium kit reached into a cupboard and pulled out a small wooden object about the size of a walnut, intricately carved and hollow inside, used, he explained, as a finger drum by ladies when they prayed. "*Kang IIsi*," he told me, making it late seventeenth century. I doubted the authenticity of the period. He probably wanted me to know it was old—therefore expensive. He tapped the tiny drum. The sound it made was rich and clear. It was lovely.

"*Duoshao qian?*" I asked.

"*Zengpin.*" Gift, he said with a smile and placed it in my hand. I felt guilty, greedy, accepting this lovely gift when I thought I was about to be cheated.

"*Xie xie.*" I smiled, holding the treasure between my palms, hoping to communicate my gratitude.

"*Qing dzai lai,*" our nameless hosts invited, and we walked out the apartment, down the stairs, and into our host's car without seeing another soul. The ride back to Rebecca's car seemed so much shorter. It was a relief to hear the click of her door locks.

I looked at the tiny drum and smiled. "What an amazing afternoon, Rebecca."

"What if we were watched?" was her response as she fumbled for her keys. She turned her head quickly to look out the windows. It was her turn to feel uneasy—and all the way back to our apartments she kept checking the rearview mirror, vowing that would be our last trip into the unknown. We both knew it wouldn't.

I was relieved to find the apartment empty when I got back. I had that guilty feeling and knew Ai-yi would be able to tell by my flushed face, the dodginess in my eyes, that I'd been up to something. While I wasn't certain she would tell her leader, I kept my adventures to myself and hid the little treasures that might cause concern or compromise her in some way.

"What have you been up to today?" asked Ed when he came home.

"Had a great day shopping."

"Take your word for it," he said.

I decided not to tell Ed about our adventure. It would make a great story, but I knew he wouldn't understand why two adult women would drive off in a foreign city to meet men they didn't know. Besides, I reasoned, as long as peace reigned, he took little interest in what I did these days.

Early the next evening, I received a phone call from Mrs. Chang, obviously homesick for Beijing. She asked how things were going, and was I pleased with the repairs to the table? The table! I'd bought it while shopping with her over three months ago and had promptly forgotten about it. I was supposed to pick it up but couldn't remember the shop. Mrs. Chang gave me the name, and I scribbled something illegible down. The next morning, Ai-yi answered the doorbell to a bent old man carrying my table on his back. It was a small bed table, with three secret drawers.

I couldn't wait to tell Ed about the phone call and the magical appearance of the table. He didn't agree when I said, "This proves the phones are bugged."

"Coincidence," he said. "It's just your imagination, Joan."

"So how did the old man know where to deliver the table? And why now?" He raised an eyebrow and said not a word. I tossed my hair. I didn't care what he thought.

I knew.

I called Rebecca and invited her over, ostensibly to view my table but really to illustrate the bugged phones.

"Thought you might like to see these, now you're in the furniture business," Rebecca said as we sipped tea, and she passed me half a dozen xeroxed pages. "They're from a book about Chinese furniture by Gustaf Ecke. He's the leading authority, you know."

I looked at the pages, amazed at the amount of detail, even to the types of wood used, where it came from, the different ways of assembling furniture, and how much Gustaf Ecke admired the clean lines created by Ming dynasty cabinet makers. It was so detailed a quick glance didn't give me the answers I craved, except a desire for more.

"The book's at the Embassy, not allowed to borrow it, honey. It's one of a limited edition," she said in answer to my question. We poured over the pages, admiring the intricate details, the photographs and drawings. "There's my chair," I said. And there it was, the back rail and arms forming a semi-circle, getting lower toward the front, waiting to embrace its occupant.

"Looks like a blueprint for Ming furniture," I said. Years later, I was to meet Gustaf Ecke's widow in Hawaii. She was known as Betty then, but her Chinese name was Tseng Yu-ho, an artist in her own right. They had fled Beijing in 1949, leaving everything they owned behind, from furniture to a huge collection of classical Chinese books, sealed in cases, ready for shipping. They were somehow lost, never to be recovered, books on art and literature, a collector's dream, lost forever. The furniture had a happier ending. Knowing they needed to flee China, the Eckes found a buyer among the diplomatic community and sold their furniture before they left. Years later, the diplomat who had made the purchase contacted Gustaf and sold him back all of the furniture at the price he had sold it for.

Betty Ecke was a friend of a friend of mine and invited us for lunch. Once there, I got to see her magnificent four-poster bed made in golden *huang huali* and a long alter table in black *zitan*. There were other pieces there of course, but the magnificence of the bed and table overshadowed everything else.

I did tell Ed about the chair, actually, I showed him the pages Rebecca had left with me to study.

"This is the chair," I said. "My new mission."

"You have four already," he said. He was right, of course, but the others were dining room chairs in heavy carved rosewood. They matched a table I had bought earlier for our house in Hawaii.

"This one is special, though," I told him.

Ed laughed. "Knowing you, you'll find it," he said. And I did. Found two, but they were not Ming, just good copies and easy enough to get out of the country.

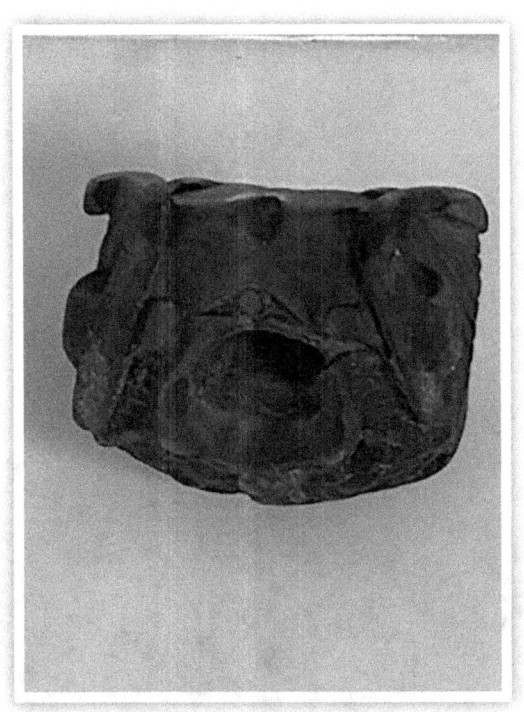

CHAPTER 9

BOOTS MADE FOR WALKING

The seams have come unstitched,
All falling apart, the leather is ruined.
Money wasted several times fixing them.

From: "Wearing Ruined Boots," anon.

Ed's friend, Joe, came up from Shanghai to do some shopping. Fluent in Mandarin, he had lived in Beijing for a few years before moving and knew all the best places on Wangfujing Road, where, he assured me, you could find anything. Great! I needed walking shoes. High heels weren't meant for these broken pavements.

We met at the Beijing Hotel, where Ed parked the jeep. Wangtujing ran alongside the building. The pavements were packed with families out for a Sunday stroll on a clear, crisp winter's day. While we saw no babies, there were plenty of toddlers carried in the arms or on the shoulders of their fathers, little bare bums peeking from the open seam in the back of their padded pants. A practical solution to potty training. Vendors temped all with the warm, rich winter smells of roasting chestnuts and sweet potatoes, cooked in old oil drums with holes punched in the sides. We bought sweet potatoes, and the skin from the sugary orange flesh stuck to the fingers of my wool gloves, and steam rose up into my nostrils, like the bouquet from a fine wine.

Joe pushed through the crowd and led us across the road to the Baihuo Dalou Department Store. Everywhere was packed, and we became part of the crowd, our identities temporarily hidden. Up to the second floor he led us. Empty counters covered in spread newspapers told potential buyers "*Maiyou*," we don't have, the most frequently heard word in shops and markets. There were shortages of everything. Today, though, shoes were in, attested to by the crowd packed around the counter. Two angry-looking women manned it, passing out shoes to be tried on, standing in place, and exchanging the "paid" slips for purchased shoes. Buying in local department stores involved a two-step process and queuing three times per purchase. There was no way we could get to the front, so Joe asked my size and converted it to metric while I chose a pair of brown calf-high boots displayed on the top shelf. Yelling across the frenzied crowd, he was able to get the attention of a saleswoman. The boots were passed back to us, over the heads of others in line. I tried them on, two-inch stacked heels, non-slip rubber soles, zippered sides, good leather. My aching feet thanked me. They cost four dollars and provided ten years of smart comfort.

It was still embarrassing to me when receiving special attention, though the Chinese took it for granted that we should. And there was never a feeling of resentment.

Joe wanted to take us to his favorite local restaurant, and he meant "local." Located on a side street, it was more like a coffee shop, too small to be considered a restaurant. There were about ten square tables, four chairs around each, all pushed close together. Cigarette smoke and steam rose in the air, and noisy chatter competed with banging dishes, making the space seem even smaller. The specialty of the house was *jiaozi*, meat-filled dumplings dipped in vinegar. We stood behind customers' chairs, the ones we thought were about to leave, and waited. I watched as the bare bones of pigs' feet were expertly spit on the table, no hands involved.

Joe ordered the dumplings and pickled pigs' feet, another specialty, served cold. The tablecloth was soiled by too many meals for one day, the dishes arrived chipped and cracked, the waiter's grubby thumb adding flavor, and the chopsticks, once lacquered, now exposed bare wood, which was wet. I watched Joe pour hot tea over his chopsticks and dry them on the tablecloth. Some other customers had done the same, and I followed suit—except I couldn't find a speck of clean tablecloth to wipe them on. My stomach churned, but I must eat at least two dumplings; not to do so would be rude. I gagged as I slipped the slippery ravioli-shaped dumplings into my mouth and tried not to think about the chopped-up meat filling. Ed and Joe had no problem at all with the meal, and they sucked on those pigs' feet like pros. I wasn't sure if that demonstrated their enjoyment or acts of bravado.

More shopping resulted in bamboo steamers, clay pots with glazed interiors, oven safe, and assorted kitchen knives.

We bought roasted chestnuts and shared the sweet, crumbly nuts from tiny paper bags. The sun was hidden in a haze of pink-orange and gray pollution by the time we started back, reminding me of foggy winter days in the London of my childhood, before the Clean Air Act banned coal-burning fires.

We went back to the flat, where I put on a pot of coffee and defrosted some brownies I had made earlier, and we relaxed in the warm apartment, away from the crowds and pollution.

While Joe was in his early thirties, younger than us, he entertained us with his tales of China. He had always wanted to see this amazing country and, after his arrival about ten years before, decided to stay.

"Had to learn the language," he said, "so I went to Taiwan first. They have language schools there aimed at foreigners. I had a dragon for a teacher, made me sit in the front of the class and treated me like I was a dunce. Would have given up otherwise, but I wanted to prove her wrong."

He worked as a translator for small export companies, wanted to get a permanent job. "Need to know I can pay the rent," he said. Ed used him sometimes, but he couldn't justify a full-time translator.

I gave him the leftover brownies, which, he assured me, were the first he had eaten in years, and off he went. Tomorrow he would be back in Shanghai.

"Really admire him," I told Ed. "Can't be easy living here on his own." While expats weren't uncommon, most worked for foreign companies and were married.

"There are a few single guys in Shanghai," Ed said. "It's easier there. Big Brother isn't watching you."

"I would really like to see Shanghai," I said. "I have all these romantic images in my head."

"The food there is great. About time I went down again. You can come along if you like."

"Fabulous! Can't wait."

CHAPTER 10

MARTIAL ARTS MASTERS

> Wu: Use courage to stop violence,
> But remember to use compassion to do the right thing.
> Shu: Use your skill to manage effectively.
> Always show concern for the vulnerable.
>
> From: A Wu Shu poem

Rebecca called. She had the car, which always presented a shopping opportunity. We were on a mission to find an antique shop Joe had mentioned during his visit. She drove around the abandoned streets until we both agreed there was no sign of the markers we looked for.

Pulling up to the curb, Rebecca said, "No point in going further. Shall we park and walk?"

The sun was low in the blue-gray sky, and the shadows long. There was a chill in the air, and I closed the snaps on my down coat. Our leather heels echoed on the cracked-slab pavement. I heard another sound, a hollow popping coming from the other side of the street.

"Ping pong?" I asked Rebecca.

"Let's see," she replied, and we walked toward the sound. It came from behind a brick wall. There was an opening without a door, and we walked quietly through it. Widely spaced benches created a center ring in which two elderly Chinese men were standing, both gray haired and very thin, one with a white doctor jacket, the other with a long white beard, dressed in a sweater unravelling at the waist, holes at the elbows, both wearing tai chi shoes. Six young men stood around them, hands in pockets, watching. Nobody seemed to notice our presence. We decided to join them.

Swords and poles and spears and cleavers leaned upright against a table, and a brazier glowed red as it held bars of iron. A placard stood high atop the facing wall.

"Martial arts school," Rebecca said in answer to my question.

The old man in the sweater held center stage, longbow in hand, a ping pong ball his arrow. He stood, ready to shoot at a ball held in a young man's teeth about forty feet away. With the grace of a ballet dancer, he crossed one leg behind the other and "curtsied," his knees almost touching the ground, his body perfectly balanced, the bow an extension of his arms as he pulled the string and took aim. The ball sped in front of us so fast its only evidence was the sound as it hit the stationary ball and sent it flying. Again and again he performed his moves. Sometimes the ball was held between index finger and thumb, sometimes chin and neck, but the result was always the same. No sounds other than those made by the balls could be heard, no questions asked, no comments made. I remembered my tai chi master. He didn't speak either. The student learns by observation and practice. Only when accomplished will the master move the hand up or down a fraction of an inch, push the toe in or out, silently, so the body remembers.

It was the white-jacket master's turn, and, with the side of his right hand, he demolished a solid rock the size of a man's head. Dust and shattered rock exploded and fell to the ground onto his long shadow.

We continued to watch them perform wonders in concentration and grace: piercing solid wood with red-hot iron rods, breaking a large brick resting on the raised legs of a young man with a swipe of the hand while the top brick stayed whole. And, as I gazed in fascination, Rebecca tapped her watch; it was almost 6:30. We left as unobserved we entered.

I wondered how to thank them for allowing us to watch, how to acknowledge their skills. This is the way we think in our Western world, while these masters of ancient arts were teachers and, as such, received the respect of their followers. Payment enough.

I had a lot to learn.

On our way back, Rebecca asked if Ed and I would like to join her and John for dinner at a Japanese restaurant the next evening. John would pick us up. I'd met John briefly at one of Rebecca's coffee mornings. Even if I hadn't known he was a diplomat, I would have guessed. He was a man comfortable in his own skin, gracious, just like Rebecca. Though in his late sixties, he had the lean body of a runner, with steel-gray hair and deep blue eyes that seemed always to be smiling. Ed knew John—the expat community was very tight—and I knew he would like Rebecca. His stepmother was from the south, and he had lived there for a while. And it would be a nice change from all the other dinners we had gone to, where nobody spoke English and I was the token female.

"Want to go?"

"Japanese food will be good for a change," he responded.

"I had no idea there would be a Japanese restaurant here."

"Surprised myself," he said, "with their history."

John parked in the secluded *hutong* outside the Baiyun Guesthouse. We entered the courtyard. It was so quiet, the only sound the splatter of a fountain in the center of the Chinese rock garden. The restaurant was part of the guesthouse complex where Chiang Kai-Shek lived when visiting Beijing, John told us.

Shoes off, we walked over tatami mats and sat on firm cushions at a table just a few inches from the floor.

"Are you ladies comfortable?" John asked as he took Rebecca's handbag. "I'll get you backrests," he decided.

I watched as John arranged Rebecca's backrest, noticed how gentle his touch was, the soft smile as he asked, "Is that okay?" The way she touched his hand in response.

The lighting came from oil lamps, soft and warm. The waitresses wore colorful kimonos and knelt to take our orders of vegetable tempura and sukiyaki. Ed ordered Saki; the rest of us kept to tea.

It was a lovely evening. Gentle noises filled the small restaurant. Service was quiet and unobtrusive, so unlike the Chinese banquets where the constant clatter of plates and bowls competed with earnest conversations and false laughs. How nice it is, I thought, that the husbands get along so well. Ed did have a few Western friends, but they were single.

"They're nice, aren't they?" I asked Ed when we arrived back at the apartment.

"If you like the dip types," he responded, pouring a glass of vodka.

Maybe it was seeing him sway while he swallowed more alcohol, maybe I was tired, I don't know what it was, but my face burned and my teeth clenched in anger. I wanted a fight! Not tonight, I told myself. He doesn't care tonight. I went to the guestroom and slammed the door. His snoring resounded throughout the apartment all night long. We never joined them for dinner again.

I made up the bed so Ai-yi wouldn't see. Must keep up appearances: my mother's motto.

And it hit me, just like that! The stories Ed's favorite aunt had told me about Ed's home life, how his father could be a raving, angry monster one minute, but, if someone came to the door, he would turn the anger off, become the mild-mannered, charming, caring husband and father he pretended to be. Keeping up appearances!

tai chi masters

Watch and learn

the Master breaks the rock in two

We left before the hot irons were used

CHAPTER 11

NIGHT NOISES

A gentle wind fans the calm night.
A bright moon shines on the high tower.
A voice whispers, but no one answers when I call.
A shadow stirs, but no one comes when I beckon.

From: "A Gentle Wind," Fu Hsüan, 217–278 (translated: Arthur Waley)

Ed was being wined and dined—spouses not included that night. Absorbed in a book, I hadn't noticed the night creep in. The apartment was so still, so quiet, a deep, uneasy quiet. I rearranged the silk cushions, pretending to find harmony in their rich colors. But the silence took over, ringing loudly in my ears. Nothing for it but bed I decided, and I was about to walk to the bedroom when I heard a soft scraping sound. I turned toward the front door, expecting it to open. It remained closed. I walked to the window in the den. The city below me was dark, the few streetlights hidden in filmy clouds of yellow pollution. Looking up, I jumped at my reflection peering at me from the window. I pulled the curtains closed.

The elevator operators were off duty from eleven at night until five in the morning. I looked at the clock, 11:25. Somebody might have entered the building.

There it is again! Definitely metallic. I jumped in bed, fully clothed, pulled the quilt up to my nose, held my breath, and listened. Cameras, that's what. Cameras moving back and forth on metal tracks monitoring the activities of every resident in this building. Mrs. Chang was right!

The scraping sound abruptly stopped. I listened harder—silence. My heart pounded; panic engulfed me. I wanted to run out the door to the corridor, down the stairs, and out onto the street. There was no one to call. It might be hours before Ed got home. It was the quiet sounds that had always terrified me. Not the crashing, shattering sound of exploding bombs, not the up and down scream of air raid sirens, but the soft click of a lock, the squeak of a floorboard . . . the whispers.

What was I doing there? China seemed like a good idea, exciting, an adventure, yet here I sat alone in this tower, waiting. Waiting for something sinister to seep through the walls, waiting to hear the whispers of the invisible men who watched. Waiting for Ed to come home, Ed with his professional life whizzing along, his social one too, I imagined. I'd been there almost four months with shopping my only outlet. Tears welled up, but I was skilled at holding them back.

In desperation, I ran to the bathroom, swallowed three antihistamine tablets, and buried myself back in bed, pillow gripped tight over my head.

I awoke groggy and late. Ed was up before me as usual, and I rushed to tell him about the night noises and the hidden cameras.

"Mrs. Chang's right," I said. "We're being watched." And I went over the night noises in detail.

"It's the pipes," he said. "Nothing works right here."

He sounded so certain, and his answer was plausible. I felt silly, clingy, like a child seeking attention. I decided to agree with him; it was easier that way. I didn't want a fight. Didn't want to tell him of the fear that rolled over me in cold waves, churning my stomach. Didn't want to go to that dark place where memories lie safe, buried.

But why did he need to negate everything I said?

The pressure of unspoken words knotted in my chest, and I swallowed what I wanted to say.

That night, I changed my clothes like a shy girl in a school locker room.

The noises stopped for a long time, and, when they started up again, Ed would hear them too.

Monica had told me about a shop on the main road that sold all kinds of porcelain goods, very cheap, *renminbi* prices, called Quingshanju Arts and Crafts Shop. It was a fairly bright day, and I decided to ask Ai-yi how I could get there on a bus. On a bus?! Ai-yi was horrified, told me it wasn't safe, that I would get lost, that I could get a taxi there, much safer. But I wanted the bus. I rode them all the time in London, and, being the helpful person she was, Ai-yi not only wrote the bus number, where to catch it, and the shops location, but she gave me the crumpled *renminbi* bills from the kitchen drawer to use as fare. She opened the door and saw me off with a worried face and a heavy sigh.

I felt like a naughty child, but that only added to the excitement, which increased when I easily found the bus stop and eventually climbed on the bus. It was standing room only—one of those large articulated busses that jerked their way around the main streets. All eyes were on me, the redheaded foreigner in a yellow coat. I looked for a place to stand and walked to the only empty space, which caused my fellow passengers to stare even harder, with alarm this time. An old man stood to let me sit. I thanked him and declined, then the bus started, and hands reached out to grab me. Seemed I was standing on the accordion section of the bus. Now I knew why it was empty. For the rest of my journey, all eyes stayed on me. What would happen to them if something happened to the crazy foreigner? I imagined them *sighing* in unison as I alighted.

The shop was clean and modern, filled with so much color I didn't know where to look first. I decided on the smaller pieces. There was a small vase in the shape of a bok choi that I knew would make a great napkin holder, ginger jars covered in painted flowers with animal-shaped handles, sugar and flour containers, thought I, and large blue-and-white fishbowls, waiting for silk flowers.

I chose two sets of ginger jars, one in blues, the other greens, and two bok choi vases, then walked over to the counter where the saleswoman waited. My language skills were pathetic, but, when it comes to buying and selling, there is an eagerness to communicate that surpasses all obstacles. Not only did I purchase these items; the saleswoman arranged a taxi to take me home.

I agreed with her *"Chin ni zailai."* I would be back Saturday, with Ed, for the fishbowls.

Ai-yi was waiting when I got home. She must have been looking out the window for me, as she was pleased I had come back in a taxi. As she fussed over my purchases, giving them a double wash and rinse, I thought what fun it would be to tell Ed about my day. I decided to fix a special meal and rummaged in the freezer hoping for something to cook. Cheese, a beginning, Italian sausages, getting better, leftover pasta sauce, jackpot!

"Great meal," Ed said.

"It'll cost yah."

"I have no doubt," he said with a smile.

So, I told him about the amazing porcelain shop and the two fishbowls that waited for us there. "I bought six items in that shop today, Ed, and the total cost was the equivalent of ten dollars."

"What, you can't afford antiques anymore?"

"Funny, but we can use these things."

"That's a relief," he joked. I knew what he meant. The antique pots were strictly ornamental. The chairs, well, they weren't particularly comfortable and were designed to be used with footstools, so even for Ed they were too high.

"I'll leave work early. Pick you up at around eleven."

Yes, a very successful day!

CHAPTER 12

LOST

> All alone in a strange land, a lonely stranger am I;
> Thoughts of my kindred redouble on every festive day.
> From afar I know, O brothers, where in the hills we'd be.
> Each wearing a spray of dogwood, all but the one away.
>
> From: "Thinking of my Brothers," Wang Wei, c.750
> (translated: Andrew W. F. Wong)

Ai-yi had left for the day when the phone rang. It was Ed; he said he'd be late... again! The third night this week, and it was only Wednesday! I'd used the last of the German sausages for today's meal, a casserole recipe given me by the top chef at the Lido that I'd spent most of the afternoon preparing. I had even made noodles to go with it, which amused Ai-yi enormously. Why make when I could buy? *But, Ai-yi, these are German noodles.* It didn't matter anyway. The meal was spoiled now. I shoved the uneaten food into the fridge, slammed the door shut, and, rushing around in my display of anger, stubbed my little toe on a kitchen chair. I hobbled back to the living room and checked my foot. The toe was beginning to swell. It matched my mood, red and angry So many small bones. So easy to break. I didn't care.

I rubbed the offended toe, debated an ice pack, and the silence became louder. The dark outside seeped in through the closed curtains.

The TV still didn't work, and I knew our few CDs by heart. I couldn't bear the thought of Johnny Denver singing "West Virginia" one more time, nor the thumping sound of Abba, not even the Beatles, my go-to guys. Forget about the calming effects of Mozart. Reading required too much concentration. My foot throbbed. I swallowed the nausea that comes with banged toes.

"Busy hands," Grandma used to say, as if keeping busy kept all the bad things at bay. I limped to the guest bedroom and pulled a bag from the closet. I'd brought a dozen or more skeins of wool with me to use on my extremely complicated knitting machine; now was the time to prepare the yarn. Using the backs of two dining chairs, I began to roll balls. I felt like the miller's daughter trying to spin gold out of straw. My arms ached from the effort, but I kept on winding, like a mechanical doll, mind blank, trying not to look at my watch.

I jumped when the key scraped in the lock. It was past midnight, and there he stood.

"You still up?" The stupid question was asked as he took off his shoes and hung up his heavy coat. I could smell tobacco and whiskey. What kind of work requires midnight meetings over whiskey? That's what I wanted to know. And Ed didn't even like whiskey!

"Why didn't you go to bed?" Maybe that question wasn't so stupid, but somehow the sound of it, the dismissal in the words, ignited such a rage in me that I wanted to tear his face apart. Force him to open his eyes, make him see me, hear me!

I threw a ball of wool at him and missed. He didn't even flinch. I watched as the ball rolled away, leaving a trail of yarn in its search for freedom. Scarlet wool on a gray carpet.

Ed had taken off his jacket, the cigarette stayed unlit in his hand, frozen.

Here we are, I thought, unable to share thoughts or feelings after all these years. What's the point? I went to the guest bedroom in impotent silence.

It was a miserable day. Thick gray smog blotted out the light. I decided to wind some more wool into balls. My head pounded, another migraine; it came on so suddenly all I could do was lie down on the settee where I sat. Ai-yi came over, her face troubled.

"*Toutong*," I whispered and put my hand over my right eye. She nodded her head and brought a blanket from the cupboard, which she gently placed over me.

"Tai Tai," I heard her whisper, "*chook.*" She sat a deep bowl of steaming rice gruel on the coffee table. A few snips of bright green chive floated on top. I was hungry and nauseated at the same time, but I dipped the china spoon into the bowl and took a sip. There was no flavor, just a smooth, thick sensation as the gruel slipped down my throat. It was comforting, like porridge on a cold morning or a cup of tea after a good cry.

"*Hau, hau,*" she repeated, pleased her patient responded to her care.

"Ai-yi, *xie xie.*" I swallowed about a third, and the nausea went away—just the pounding stayed—and I slept.

Ai-yi was still there when I awoke, long after her workday was through. I told her my headache had gone, that she should go home. I wanted to hug her for staying with me.

Worn out, I soaked in a hot bath and poured in rose bath salts to cover up the smell of the disinfectant recommended by Rebecca. "Showers are okay," she had told me. "But, when you take a bath, use this." She handed me a bottle of Dettol. I covered my nightgown with a new hand-painted silk robe and slipped my feet into embroidered silk slippers from the Friendship Store. The soft fabrics sat lightly on my body as if cushioned by a bubble of air. It was too early for bed, so I reclined in the large armchair, my legs propped up on the coffee table. Cooking was the last thing I wanted to think about—Ed could open a can of something. I just didn't care.

Balls of wool and piles of skeins covered the settee. I placed a skein over the backs of two chairs and started to wind another ball. It was dark by the time Ed's key turned in the lock.

"What's for dinner?" he asked, hanging up his coat and taking off his shoes.

"Haven't a clue," I responded.

He went into the kitchen and came back with a large glass of vodka. Ice clinked in the glass as he walked. He lit a cigarette.

"Would you please smoke in another room?" I asked. The smell of smoke made me nauseous and started up the ache in my head again.

"Sorry!" he snapped, thumping it out in the large glass ashtray.

"Why are you so nasty?" I asked him. "You know smoke gives me headaches."

His silence fueled my anger.

"What am I supposed to be doing here?" I stood up, demanding an answer, demanding a reaction. "I gave up everything! For what?"

His face reddened and seemed to swell. Slamming down his glass, he yelled, "Christ, what the hell's wrong with you?" Ed's voice and size intimidated a lot of people—that was part of his power in business—but not me, not then. At this point, nothing could frighten me. And the frustration and anger I'd felt for so long came pouring out of me in a scream. I had no idea of the depth of my feelings until I started. The words were clear, but I didn't hear them, my voice, my emotions, my body one entity, fighting to be noticed, to be heard.

My throat ached; my body shook. I sat back in the armchair, exhausted. Ed had been silent all this time. I looked at his face. His mouth was open. I couldn't look into his eyes.

"Maybe you should go back." His voice was low.

The words pierced deep. Give up? Admit defeat and give up everything I had hoped for, dreamed of . . . Our marriage? Chris would be upset; he'd know something was wrong. It didn't matter that I had a choice, unlike in my childhood when I could never go home . . . He doesn't want me, I thought.

The tears came. Ed had rarely seen me cry. My mother's words came to me: "You mustn't cry, Joanie. You must be good and brave." I'd done what she asked, but this time I had no control.

Ed walked toward me, extending his handkerchief. A peace offering. I reached toward it, and our hands touched. Every tiny hair on my body stood on end. Shivers raced up my back. My face flushed. My heart beat in my ears. He took my hand and gently pulled me to my feet and held me close. I smelled the aftershave I'd bought him. I felt the warmth of his chest, the beat of his heart under the palm of my hand. Bending his face toward mine, he kissed the top of my head, my eyelids, my tears, and my body trembled. Swinging me up into his arms, he carried me to the settee. He arranged silk cushions under my head and made sweet love to me, as if for the first time. And I didn't care who watched.

"This is the way we communicate," he said, smoothing my hair from my cheek. An uneasy feeling came over me, which I struggled to suppress.

CHAPTER 13

SHANGHAI

On this feast day the riverside is crowded with beautiful ladies.
Alluring yet remote, so provocative, so demure.
All finely formed, finely textured,
Dressed for this late spring outing in rich silks
Embroidered with peacocks and unicorns in gold and silver.

From: *"Ballad of Beautiful Ladies," Du Fu, c.753

"Like to go to Shanghai tomorrow?" Ed asked. He managed a branch office there and went every six weeks or so.

Shivers ran up my neck imagining this mysterious city, the home of Charlie Chan and other adventurous souls, once the center of sophistication and sin in the Orient and one of the world's largest cities.

"Fabulous! Love to."

"Good. Ken will take care of you. He's been in Shanghai for years."

We walked through the dreary airport and climbed on a UAL flight on its way to San Francisco via Shanghai and Tokyo. I had no idea the amount of tension held in my body until I sat in the immaculate first-class cabin and a smart blond stewardess looked me straight in the eyes, smiled, and asked if I would like a mimosa.

Time Magazine, Newsweek, The New Yorker, and *The New York Times* were just some of the reading materials brought to us for our choosing, all forbidden on the Earth under our wheels, and my muscles unknotted. I was back in the womb of the west.

Our flight was short, and, upon landing at Hongqiao Airport, every passenger disembarked to go through immigration clearance before the flight continued. Why the inconvenience nobody could tell me, but passengers from Beijing joined those from Shanghai. An old lady walked on her golden lily feet propped up by her cane and hobbled, slowly, painfully, along the glass-lined corridor. A glass-lined corridor! The windows not sparkling clean but clean enough. Glass looking out onto the runways, glass looking into the waiting area, glass-covered counters holding souvenirs for last-minute shoppers. This airport was bright, light, open.

Ken, the Shanghai manager, met us with handshakes and smiles. He and Ed were old friends, and Ed had talked about him during our flight. "Nice guy," he summed up. He was right; even though this was our first meeting, Ken felt like a best pal.

Ken guided us through the airport like diplomats. Every few steps, someone would greet him with a smile or a word—the pretty girls in their airport uniforms, smart, pert, flirty, baggage handlers unshaven, disheveled, customs agents in crumpled shirts, the toothless old man sweeping the floor, he treated them all the same, with a wave and a grin.

When I told him of the golden lily lady, he said he would have arranged for an immigration officer to go to her so she could stay on the plane. Yes, a nice guy, and I was impressed that a foreigner could have that much authority. Of course, I thought, Ken probably knows how many American cigarettes will buy what particular favor to oil the wheels of business. Also, in some strange way, he looked Chinese to me, with his tall slim frame, olive skin, and small features. Evidently, the Chinese thought so too, and, even though he admitted to speaking limited Cantonese, the people he met pretended to understand him. He'd clap a hand over a shoulder and try the words out, and even I could tell he was way out of tune.

"Ears shot," he told me. "Too many airplane engines. Can't hear the tones." There are eight official tones in Cantonese and four in Mandarin.

Ken's driver stood by the jeep, reclining, one leg crossed over the other, the inevitable cigarette stub in hand. He assumed that same know-it-all cocky attitude of Tzu Chow, streetwise and confident. Maybe that was a requirement for driving foreigners in these cities. His name was Chang Zhang, and, when introduced, he gave me a crooked, mischievous grin.

It was at least twenty degrees warmer in Shanghai, and the air was moist. We drove along roads edged in trees bearing the last of their rusted leaves. As we approached the city, I saw Western-style houses. Slightly decrepit and badly in need of paint, they still delighted me with their varied lines and tiled roofs. Once in the city, the old buildings leaned together along narrow streets as if competing for space. Most were two or three stories high and housed as many families as could be squeezed inside. Their overflow sat outside, preparing dark green vegetables, washing clothes in white enamel basins. No concrete box towers here.

Gutted fish hung from trees, waiting to dry out in the polluted air. Bamboo poles dressed in shirts and pants poked out of windows for the same purpose. Front doors opened to crowded dark passageways. And, unlike Beijing, the streets curved, and wiggly lanes trickled off the main road. The people looked different too, plumper. Neighbors gossiped, and young women dressed in Western clothes and wore makeup and high-heeled shoes, the tops of their knee-high stockings peeking out as they walked.

Chang Zhang pulled up to the brand-new Shanghai Hilton International, a five-star hotel with white marble floors and antique furniture in the lobby (with discreet "no-sit" signs). A grand piano stood in the cocktail lounge, and lush leather upholstered chairs waited for occupants to recline to music by Cole Porter, played softly from five in the evening until ten at night. A small willow-pattern-type bridge carved from the same white marble stretched over koi-filled ponds, separating the lobby from the restaurants and shops at the back. Shiny black river rocks formed curled shapes around the indoor garden.

A beautiful girl in a long cheongsam stood beside an equally beautiful young woman in a smart black suit. They bowed low and invited us to register in our room. We followed them to copper-covered elevator doors placed in copper-covered walls. Not a smudge could be seen, and

I saw our mirrored reflections with the lobby behind us shimmering like a mirage, just a little out of focus.

Fruit bowls and fresh flowers filled our room, and wine cooled in a bucket. As soon as the young women left, I walked around the suite. The bathroom was brighter than bright. Mirrors faced each other, and I saw my reflection reaching back to the beginning of time. Large, fluffy white bathrobes and slippers waited for us, and crisp white linen towels were placed alongside the bed to keep pampered Western feet from touching the wool carpet. I fell back on the bed and kicked my shoes in the air.

"Ed, I could stay here forever," I said.

"Good luck," he said, grinning. "I plan on leaving in two days."

It was easier to talk to him here, in this city. Beijing must be hard for him too; maybe that's why he was so closed down, drank too much.

"Why can't you work from here?" I asked.

"Be nice," he said, "but all the power's in Beijing. Can't get away from that."

Ken's office was in an old colonial apartment hotel not too far away, and we went to meet the staff. The building bore that dissipated look of buildings I'd seen in New Orleans' French Quarter, with lazy fans in high ceilings and wooden shutters filtering the light. I could feel the old energy of its decadent past vibrating through me and imagined the victims of the unsolved double murder prowling the squeaky corridors trying to get out. Ken was not as charmed as I, and he couldn't wait for his new offices in the Hilton lobby to be completed.

There were six employees, four local girls and two young American men. The girls smiled, told me how pretty I was. They loved the color of my hair—they would give me a Chinese name. Ed already had one: "Laoban," roughly translated as "top boss." First names have magical qualities and deep meaning in China, as they do in Hawaii. Mine turned out to be "Xie Qiao Shan," difficult to write, impossible for me to pronounce or remember, and roughly interpreted meant "coral bridge stretching under and over the oceans, connecting the lands." I smiled and thanked them and thought them so sweet, like unspoiled preteen girls.

They were very proud of their choice for my name, and, in excellent English, they pointed out that my hair was the color of red coral. I was from another land and obviously very friendly. They were certainly friendly, more so than Ed's employees in the Beijing office, who only nodded their heads when introduced.

"You're right," Ed said when I mentioned the difference. "Big Brother isn't watching here."

That night we three were to be guests of Mr. Shu, an important client. Ken decided to hire a taxi instead of using his driver and negotiated the roundtrip fare, with the promise of a big tip to take us back. Impossible to get cabs at night, he told us.

We arrived at a very large restaurant of private dining rooms. Up two flights of carpeted stairs we climbed to be greeted by our interpreter and Mr. Shu's interpreter waiting outside the door to our dining room. Mr. Shu stood as we entered and came around the table to shake hands. He walked with a slight limp, I noticed. He was a small man, shorter than I, with piercing black eyes set in a tranquil face and dressed in what looked like an expensive silk Hong Kong suit. His handshake was gentle, though his hand was rough and gnarled. His manner was gracious but not polished like Mr. Dzao's in Beijing.

The six of us arranged ourselves at the usual round table according to Mr. Shu's direction, though, no matter the shape, there is always a top and bottom; Mr. Shu sat at the top, and I sat across from him, with an interpreter on the right between Ed and Mr. Shu and the other on the left between him and Ken. Two shadowy figures stood in the corners of the room behind Mr. Shu, hands behind backs, legs astride, trying to blend into the walls. While I couldn't help but notice them, I acted like everyone else and pretended they weren't there.

Waiters dressed in white shirts and black slacks and ties stood waiting for Mr. Shu to give the order to serve. We were honored guests, our meal chosen to include rare specialties—in other words, all the things you find delicious to the palate and where it's best to remember that "ignorance is bliss."

Bottles of Mao Tai appeared, a clear drink more powerful than Russian vodka, and small shot glasses filled. With each dish—or, I found out to my horror, each compliment—it was custom to say, "*Ganbei,*" and throw the burning, bitter-tasting liquid down your throat. I couldn't insult this charming man by refusing his toast. Tomorrow would have to be a wasted day.

Mr. Shu talked through his interpreter the entire evening, as did we, though it was mostly polite food talk, with a little business subtly slipped in by Mr. Shu. I watched his eyes while we spoke and saw the quick shifts, and I knew he understood English. (It is not good business to let people know you understand their language, I discovered.) Having finished my eighth "*ganbei,*" a special dish was presented, presentation meaning a lot at a Chinese banquet. Large chunks of gray blubber appeared on a blue-and-white dish. "Very special," assured our interpreter, his smile tense. As with all the other dishes, I was served first, and I looked at that gray two-inch jelly placed on the clean plate in front of me and felt bile rise in my throat.

Taking a deep breath and holding my long white slippery chopsticks firmly in my right hand, I somehow managed to pick up the floppy flesh, pop the entire piece into my mouth, and swallow hard. Mr. Shu had been watching, and my expert handling of the sea slug—yes, sea slug—proved to warrant another "*ganbei.*" I held the glass, prepared to toss my head back, and, with that motion, knew by the spinning of the room that, if I drank it, I would die.

The great part of Chinese banquets is that, once the last dish is served, the meal is over. Hosts stand up, guests follow, thanks are exchanged, and everyone parts ways.

We walked down the stairs and out into the cold night air, eager to get into the taxi and back to the Hilton.

"Shouldn't have paid him," said Ken as he looked at the empty parking lot. And, arm in arm, heads lowered, we braced ourselves against the wind and walked as quickly as possible back to the comfort of the Hilton. I squeezed my escorts' arms, and Ken flexed his muscles in response. Maybe Ed didn't notice.

The only other people we passed were old men pushing wooden carts. "Night soil," Ken said. Human waste destined for the farms at the edge of the city. In spite of them, and the thoughts that came to mind, it was a refreshing walk that cleared my head. I began to believe Mao Tai was not as big a deal as people made out. Perhaps the Chinese wanted to justify the exorbitant price of a hundred dollars a bottle. The same as single malt whisky.

The bed was sumptuous, and I quickly fell asleep. But something awakened me during the night. I tried to look around. I couldn't see. Oh my God! Alcohol poisoning!

"Ed, I'm blind!" I cried as I fumbled my way to the bathroom. He sleeps like the dead and didn't stir. Reaching for the tap, I splashed cold water on my burning eyelids—they were swollen shut. I placed a wet washcloth on my lids and sat on the edge of the tub wondering if the hotel had a doctor. I took deliberate, long, slow breaths, and, as I relaxed, I felt something scratching my eye. In my drunken state, I'd forgotten to remove my contact lenses, and my green eyes were now red!

I awoke in the morning without the expected headache, though my eyes were still red. Other than being a little tired, I felt great, and my "blind" story was too good not to share, so I told Ed and enjoyed hearing his laughter.

"Mao Tai will get you," he said. "And they keep filling up your glass hoping to get you pissed. It's a game, Joanie."

Shanghai is famous among the Chinese for three things: its beautiful women, excellent tailors, and abundant, delicious food. The women wore long hair, and some perms bounced along the street, accentuating mascaraed eyes and rouged lips. Their clothes were modern and colorful, though mismatched, and only a few elderly citizens wore the dreaded monochrome Mao suits. They returned smiles too, sometimes with a hand raised to hide yellow teeth.

"Lack of calcium," Ken told me. "Kids don't get milk here." Later, Ai-yi told me the lack of enamel was due to too much penicillin.

The famous tailors we were to experience later in Beijing, and Ken did his best to demonstrate the quality of the food, first with lunch at the Peace Hotel.

This grand hotel sits at the foot of Nanjing Road, the wide main road cutting through the city, and faces the Bund, a tree-lined esplanade along the Huangpu River. Tall buildings run along either side of the hotel, leftovers from former Western powers. It looked very much like London's Embankment to me after the war, with that certain edge of neglect.

We entered the crowded lobby and maneuvered through the maze of dusty kiosks plunked there—they seemed to me an afterthought—to the hand-operated elevators.

Like the hotel's façade, the interior was gloomy, giving the impression it hadn't seen a fresh coat of paint or a vacuum cleaner since its construction in the 1920s. We rode up to the eighth floor, where resided one of the best restaurants in Shanghai. Walking on threadbare carpets, we followed the slim cheongsam-robed hostess to a table by a window made from small squares of leaded glass and pushed open toward the harbor. The table linen was shiny with starch, the table set with unchipped china. Chopsticks rested on the backs of white porcelain lions.

"Sit here, Joan," invited Ken, indicating the chair that would provide a view of the dining room and the busy river. A cool breeze brushed my face. The click-click of busy chopsticks made music, and the smell of food made me breathe deeply. It must have been this way sixty years ago, I thought.

"Hey, Ed," Ken joked, "Joan can really put 'em away." He was referring to the Mao Tais.

"Tell me."

"I was only trying to be polite," I said. "I didn't want to drink the awful stuff."

Ken grinned. "You didn't have to drink them, you know. You weren't expected to. Chinese women don't drink."

I looked at Ed. Why didn't he tell me!

"Don't look at me, Joan. Nobody forced you." He laughed and patted my arm, and I joined in the joke.

Ken offered to do the ordering, and the dishes came, and, with each, dish a clean plate: fresh prawns with sugary walnuts, tiny emerald-green bok choi, winter melon soup served from the melon shell, an assortment of dim sum, my favorite being sweet rice with shrimp in lotus leaves. The food in Shanghai was lighter, fresher, and tastier than that in Beijing, and young waitresses moved quietly and placed dishes on the table with a smile.

The conversation was business, as usual, and I gazed out the window and at the other diners, but my attention was peaked when Mr. Shu's name came up.

"Wants more space, Ed," Ken was saying.

"Ken, what do you know about Mr. Shu?" I asked.

He told me that Mr. Shu was abandoned at age five. "Has a clubfoot," he continued, "considered a waste to feed a cripple. Lived off garbage and slept in alleys, so the story goes."

I wanted to know more about him, how he survived, how an uneducated street urchin become an industrial tycoon . . . why he needed bodyguards. Ken shook his head. "Don't know." I had heard the Chinese have secret lives, and their ability to keep secrets is renowned, and, while my curiosity wasn't satisfied, I was still impressed with Mr. Shu's courage and success.

"Good, eh?" Ken asked when the meal was finally over.

"Great," Ed agreed. "Now I need to walk it off."

We climbed six more floors to the aged copper-peaked rooftop and patios where westerners once dined. To get there, we walked along corridors, passed through double doors like six-sided telephone kiosks, with illuminated dome-shaped ceilings made from frosted glass and decorated in delicate copper lines emulating a spider's web. I stood in its center and, with my head thrown back, turned in a circle, feeling like Alice.

Rich mahogany paneled the walls. Shell-shaped glass sconces holding dead flies and twenty-watt bulbs barely lit our way through the hazy corridors. Art deco abounded, providing a peep into another time, another world.

From the green copper roof, we could see the harbor spread out before us, a busy place with cargo ships and small boats bobbing on the choppy water. Flags cracked around us in the cold wind off the East China Sea. My hair danced around my face.

"It's wonderful, Ken," I told him. "I feel anything is possible in this city."

"You're right," he said, and the beginning of an idea formed before I came to China began to sprout wings.

That evening we dined in one of the Hilton's eight restaurants. They were all outrageously expensive, equivalent to a meal in any Hilton. Meals in the Chinese restaurant were the highest.

The chef was making Shanghai noodles, the specialty of the house. Dressed in a Western chef's coat and hat, a tall Chinese man proceeded to toss a ball of dough from one hand to the other, magically producing unbelievably long strings of white ribbon.

"Like pulling taffy," Ed said.

The noodles were made to order and cooked at our table. They were light and luscious and reminded me of the pasta the children helped me make when they were young.

Ed extended his belly and smiled. "Can't stay here much longer, Ken."

"Let's go for a stroll, walk it off a bit."

The area around the hotel was tree lined and mostly residential. The occasional bicycle glided by, but we saw few people and heard not a sound.

"I've got something special to show you," said Ken as we turned a corner—and, on our right, the expected walls of a building disappeared, and we saw straight into a Chinese version of Dante's *Inferno*.

"It's a bean curd factory," he said, smiling, satisfied he'd shocked us.

Massive iron cauldrons boiled over open-flamed fires. Men and women stood on stools around them, eyes barley level with the top, stirring the steaming contents with long wooden paddles.

"They work at night," Ken said. "Even in winter, it's as hot as hell in here." And he proceeded to enter the factory. We followed and were greeted with smiles and greetings of welcome from the sweating workers. The main light came from the fires; a few low-watt light bulbs hung from the high ceiling. I winced at all the accidents just waiting to happen with naked flames and scalding liquids.

The leader, a chubby middle-aged woman, her hair tied back with a red scarf, beckoned to us. We crossed the ash-covered floor, past the boiling cauldrons, to a long, narrow table. Off-white material was being rolled flat by hand, sliced into squares, and stacked for packing. Our hostess walked up to the table and picked up three slices, one for each, and gestured at us to eat.

"This is the cream," said Ken as he and Ed chewed.

Not impressed, I looked at the tasteless wrinkled square placed in my palm. I saw her dirty hands, the dirt embedded under her nails, the dirty floor, the unwashed wooden rolling table, and I shuddered. Then I looked at her eager face and the expectant faces of the men halted in rolling the bean curd. I realized she had given us a special treat. I nibbled a corner and bit into rubber.

"*Hau chi*," I lied.

Saying our goodbyes, we left them happily working. I carried my nibbled square back to the hotel and threw it in the copper waste bin in front of the spotless elevators. I didn't want the workers to see it in the gutter.

"What an amazing day, Ed," I said as we settled down for the night.

"On your own tomorrow," he replied. "Work to do."

And I wondered what tomorrow would bring.

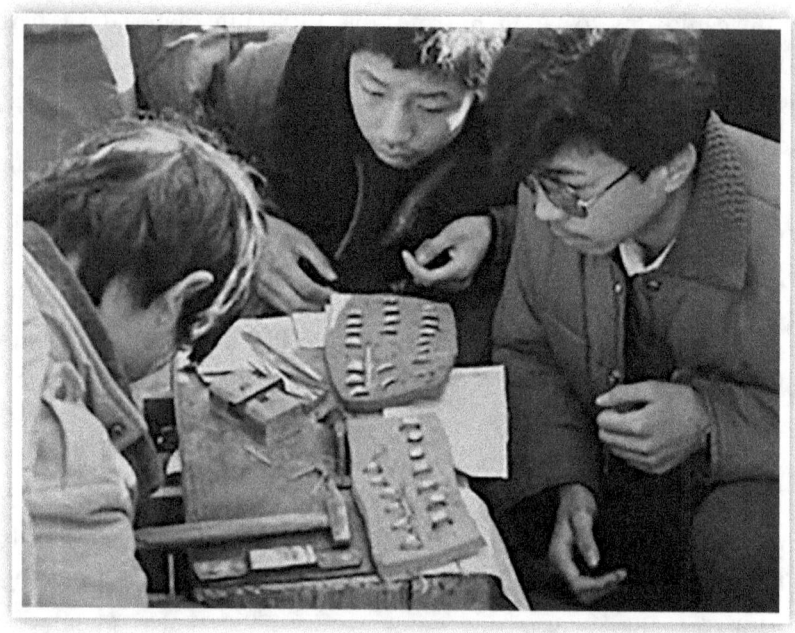

CHAPTER 14

THE NINE DRAGON PLATE

When the dragon comes, ah!
The wind stirs and sighs.
Paper money thrown, ah!
Silk umbrellas waved.
When the dragon goes, ah!
The wind also—still.
Incense-fire dies, ah!
And vessels are cold.

From: "The Dragon in the Black Pool," Po Chui, c.830, *Rainy Day Poems*

Ed was in the shower when the phone rang. It was Ken.
"Hey, Joan, want to see some sights?"
"Yes. Great."
"Come to the office with Ed."

Chang Zhang was waiting for us outside the lobby. Like many buildings designed for westerners in China, the Hilton was off limits to local Chinese, unless they worked there of course. I wondered how they felt about this exclusion and if Mr. Shu would be turned away.

Ed pushed some money into my hands with a "Don't spend it all in one place," and I was ready.

My destination was Yu Yuan, the Garden of Happiness, in the old part of town. Chang Zhang would drive me there and pick me up at three. Chang Zhang grinned and nodded his head at Ken's question—yes, he understood. Ming Dao, the girl who headed my "christening" event, put her hands on her hips and said something that wiped the grin off his face. He nodded meekly. Another Ai-yi in the making.

"It's a great place. She can't get lost, Ed," Ken said. "There's shops and restaurants around the garden, Joan. And go inside the teahouse. It's famous."

"Here," Ed said, "you'd better take some extra money." He handed me another wad of notes. It didn't matter that I had my own money; he wanted me to have a good time.

"Any shopping requests?"

"Wouldn't dare. Enjoy yourself."

Ed closed the door of the jeep and flashed me a smile. He was generous to a fault, gave gifts without keeping score, sometimes leaving us short, but he gave from the heart. I knew that, and, whenever his dark moods brought me down, I'd remind myself, "He's generous."

That was the oldest bridge that connected us.

Trees joined arms across the narrow streets, and old shanties looked bright under their whitewash and thatched roofs. Chang Zhang pulled up in a large parking area where trucks and bicycles were parked willy-nilly, just the same way they behaved on the roads.

Chang Zhang opened my door and grinned. "*San,*" I told him, three fingers tapping the face of my watch.

"*Shi, san,*" he replied, jumping into the car and reversing into a vegetable cart.

I hurried away. "Whenever there's a potential confrontation, leave quietly and unobserved. Cardinal rule," Rebecca had advised me.

I followed the crowd of chatting Chinese toward what appeared to be an opening in a high brick wall. Inside, the buildings were close together, about two stories high. Faded red paint and gilded New Year good fortune stickers from decades past peeled off the walls. I looked up to the sky, and tiled roofs met my gaze, turned up at the corners like giant hats. Dragons adorned the peaks, daring any misfortune to try and enter these auspicious buildings. I went into a shop selling embroidered linen. No lights brightened the room, but it wasn't gloomy. Wide floorboards were hills and valleys and squeaked with each footfall.

This little town within a city dated back to the mid-sixteenth century and had survived wars and revolutions. Every corner I turned in this rabbit warren of alleys opened to shops filled with Chinese lanterns, carved walking sticks, sweet bean sticky buns, sugared nuts, dried sweet plums, and salted lemons, all teaming with noisy people. Restaurants occupied most of the second floors, their windows pushed wide open. The smell of sweet pork and roasted chestnuts surrounded me. My enchantment was broken by the sickening sound of people coughing deeply and gurgling phlegm in their throats before dramatically spitting out the results. To stop my stomach cringing, I began a rating system. "That was an eight or a nine," I'd think. Old men rated higher than old women.

A pot of tea Ken had said, and I started to seek the teahouse. I wondered if there were toilets, preferably Western, and, as if in answer to my question, raw sewage came spewing out of a pipe from the second floor of a building right in front of me onto the pathway, where it sought a drain. I put my hand to my mouth, held my breath, and quickly turned another corner. I'm going to be sick, I thought. Maybe this wasn't such a great idea. Then I saw it: the Willow Pattern.

Huge stone dragons hid the small lake spanned by a zigzag bridge and draped in willow trees. Teahouses built like gazebos faced the lake and pavilions, and a huge rockery garden surrounded the ornate bridge. It took my breath away with its quiet beauty.

I walked the zigzag bridge with its low ornate balustrade toward the pavilion teahouse on the lake. Its very shape said, "Slow down, enjoy the moment." Goldfish swam leisurely in the murky water, heads breaking the surface in idle curiosity, looking at the foreign woman in her bright clothes.

My Mandarin was of no use here, and smiles and gestures were the means of communication. I was seated at a table for four next to long shutters open to the lake. The heavy carved wooden table glowed, not from varnish but from age. Wooden floors, flat, dusty, worn, told their own story. Generations had walked these boards. I looked around; generations still did. I felt alone for the first time that day, not because I was the only foreigner but because I was a woman, by herself.

The waitress took my order. I wanted green tea and pointed to the green in my paisley-print skirt. The tea came in a tiny teapot made of red clay decorated with lines incised in the sides, the tiny cup translucent white porcelain. Sugared peanuts and small rice crackers were placed alongside with chopsticks. I poured the tea, admired its clear color, inhaled the steam rising up to the ceiling, and took a sip—fragrant and delicate right down to the last tiny cupful.

I looked up at the high ceiling, at the wooden beams carved and painted in faded flowers and fruit and bats, symbols of long life and happiness. This had been a private home at one time, a tranquil haven for its elderly occupant. I wanted to stay, but an hour had passed without my knowing it.

I was lost. I'd been so involved with the surroundings I hadn't paid attention to landmarks. There were no signs. They wouldn't be in English anyway. I knew I always get lost and always find my way, but this time someone was waiting for me, and I began to worry—that is, until my nose caught the whiff of sewage. That's where I turned, toward it this time.

Pedicabs waited for fares outside the gate but no Chang Zhang. It was five past three. I waited another five minutes, feeling awkward at the looks strangers gave me, looks they might give a lost child, wondering if they should intervene. Look busy, I told myself, and I walked across the road to another line of neat shops. Treasures filled their windows: ink stones carved in the shape of lotus blossoms, calligraphy brushes made of fox hair, and little red clay tea pots. I stepped down into the teapot shop and was met by a thin elderly man who greeted me in perfect English.

"Good day, madam." He smiled and invited me to sit on a carved high-backed chair. My feet hurt from the rough stone pavements, and I was grateful for the rest. Tea was offered, but I didn't want to further challenge my bladder, so I declined.

"These teapots are lovely," I said.

"Let me show you." He arranged an assortment in clay pots from golden yellow to rich umber on the table beside me. They were more delicate than those in the teashop. I picked up one in the shape of a pumpkin, its handle the vine. It was like holding warm air in my hand, that same feeling I'd experienced when holding antique porcelain.

"Very old," he told me. "Yixing teapots come in many colors. The clay varies so."

I knew I was holding a treasure. Underneath, I saw a chop. "Is this the artist?" I asked.

"Yes," he replied, and he continued on to tell me he dealt in antique Yixing teapots made by famous artists. "Very collectible." He told me what to look for: the delicacy of line, the smoothness of clay. "Never buy with a crack, not even as fine as hair. Value drops to less than half." I knew nothing about this lovely material or how to buy it, how to bargain for a fair price, and, sighing, I put it down. Something told me I couldn't afford it. He went into the backroom behind the inevitable curtain and brought out one so small, so fine, I knew I was being shown the best.

"Ming," he told me, "very rare." It was lovely, and I listened to this gracious man tell its story.

It was getting dark. I looked at my watch, almost five o'clock.

"Come again, madam," he said, smiling. He opened the door as I hurried out.

Chang Zhang pulled up as I walked out of the shop. His hair was standing on end, his shirt hanging out of his pants, the cigarette clenched in his lips aiming up at the sky. He looked around, worried, not his usual cocky self. He was late and knew he was in for it. And he'd lost Laoban's wife!

His face lit up when he saw me. He spat out his cigarette and walked toward me, patting his hair and pushing in his shirt, lips twitching in a nervous smile. I got into the back of the car without a word. I wanted to tell him not to worry but knew better than to encourage bad behavior.

We arrived back at Ken's office at 5:30. Ming Dao came outside to meet us and shamed Chang Zhang, so he hung his head like a scolded child. Ken wasn't too pleased either. "Eh," he said, pointing to his gold Rolex, "three o/clock!" He made a growl-like sound and turned to me.

"Sorry, Joan, hope you're okay."

"Had a great time. I saw the Willow Pattern in living color." That's exactly what it was, Ken told me. The gardens were the inspiration for the blue-and-white pattern on the large platter holding my mother's delicious leg of lamb, sometimes roast beef, every Sunday.

The following day I went shopping again. This time, Chang Zhang stayed as close as a guide dog. We went to antique shops, little kiosks set up along tree-filled lanes, junk and treasures assured equal space. I saw a tricolored antique porcelain platter, nine dragons, five on top, four underneath. It was in perfect condition. I looked at the markings, late Ching dynasty. I wanted that platter, and the bargaining began.

Chang Zhan heard the prices. "Too much," he told me. He started to walk away, beckoning me to follow. Tact was required. Ken had told him to take care of me this time, and to Chang Zhang taking care of me included taking care of my money.

"This is the perfect plate for spaghetti," I told him as I handed over the money. I winced when I saw him swagger along, my new treasure tucked casually under his arm.

Early next morning, we left Shanghai for Beijing. Ken and the airport staff waved and smiled at us from the sun-filled lobby, and we climbed on board and settled down for the three-hour flight. I looked at Ed, ready to share some of my Shanghai adventures. His lower jaw grated back and forth. My body tensed.

Beijing Airport was wrapped in its usual flat gray shroud. Spitting in public was against the law here, so maybe smiling was too.

On our next trip to Shanghai, Ken had a surprise. "Local art school, they're having an open house with the teachers demonstrating and selling their work. Like to go?"

Would I!

Just that week I'd been looking around the apartment and wondering what else I could do to warm it up, make it more personal. Paintings would do it perfectly!

The '80s saw a tremendous increase in the number of artists in China, and the art scene was big in Shanghai. So, off we three went to the very impressive art college. There were at least three floors, though I didn't make it any higher, so there might have been more, and there were four classrooms per floor.

Most of the work displayed was modern in style, safe subjects, nothing to cause controversy. There were a couple of traditional artists who painted with care and focus, their work depicting classical scenes of birds and fish and mountains. The end result was both delicate and realistic but seemed a bit too controlled for my taste. Ed took a liking to a painting of a yellow bird sitting amongst what looked to me like the fronds of a banana tree. It was so unlike him, with its delicate lines, sweet almost, but he said he felt sorry for the artist; that's why he bought it.

It was a kind gesture, and I saw what Ed meant. The artist was extremely thin, his black suit too large for him, his white shirt collar nowhere near his neck as he stood alone, unlike the other artists who drew small groups. This was Ed at his best, his compassionate, generous self. And, at times like this, I could forgive him almost anything.

I gravitated toward the more modern style, which, in my very limited art world knowledge, were bold depictions of landscapes, presented like a more sophisticated rendition of peasant paintings, which I also collected but much later. That trip, we managed to take home six paintings. These provided fun over the following two weeks as I set about arranging and rearranging them on the dull gray walls of the apartment. Fun for me, not so much for Ed, who did all the work, with lots of sighs and "What difference does a damn inch make?" and "Are you sure *this* time?" Though he did grudgingly agree that the end result was worth it.

We went to Shanghai for a few days almost every month, and the contrast between the sparkling energy of Shanghai and the tense, cold flatness of Beijing became more apparent with each trip. I was reminded of those terrifying pressure cookers, the way you have to let the steam escape before opening the pot. That's what Shanghai did for Ed and me; it seemed to give us a reprieve from the pressures we brought with us.

CHAPTER 15

POTTED PALMS AND GOLDFISH BOWLS

> In the Royal City spring is almost over: Tinkle, Tinkle—the coaches and
>   horsemen pass.
> We tell each other, "This is the peony season,"
> And follow with the crowd that goes to the Flower Market.
> Cheap and dear—no uniform price.
> The cost of the plant depends on the number of blossoms.
> For the fine flower, a hundred pieces of damask.
> For the cheap flower, five bits of silk.
>
>   From: "The Flower Market," Po Chui, c. 820 (translated: Arthur Waley)

November, and outside the dirt-stained bedroom window I saw the sun, or what I knew to be the sun, looking like a ten-watt light bulb peeking out from a frosted shade. It was only three in the afternoon, yet the sky was dark and heavy, filled with Gobi Desert sand swirling around, up and down, playing with the heavy industrial pollution from the coal-burning factories. Resting my hand on the window ledge, I felt the perpetual grit oozing between the tiny spaces like sand in an hourglass or some insidious monster. My skin screamed for moisture. Over the past twenty-odd years, it had adjusted very nicely, *thank you*, to the pampering of Hawaii's moist, never-ending summers, and, while I knew we were lucky to have central heating, I couldn't open a door without getting an electric shock. And my hair! While a perm seemed like a good idea back home, the dry climate of Beijing gave my hair the freedom to fly just anywhere it wanted. Not a good look.

Sunday came, and off to the old Jianguo Hotel lobby we went to sip coffee and listen to Straus waltzes. To complete the atmosphere of old-world charm, potted palms interspersed with the small round tables.

"Plants would do it," I said to Ed.

That next Saturday afternoon, we drove to a large plant shop that resembled a combination glass house and steam room. Heavy plastic sheets served as doors, and the concrete floor was wet from leaking hoses. Atop oil-burning stoves, huge kettles boiled away for the occasional cup of cha but primarily to create moisture. Palms reached up to the glass ceiling alongside bonsai trees content in their tiny gardens.

A tall thin man with white hair and a scant, pointed beard walked toward us. He was dressed in a long navy-blue gown, hands clasped together, hidden in his long sleeves, his feet encased in white socks inside black canvas shoes. He bowed and beamed his welcome, offering us tiny cups of tea. Of course, what he was looking at were foreigners with more money than sense who would buy plants to put in their too-hot apartments, causing them to die, requiring more plants to replace them, and so it would continue throughout the winter months. It took a second return trip for me to realize this. The first time we were just impressed with his friendliness and the inventory of palms and aspidistras. He didn't own the shop; it was a government store, which he was running. This meant too that we would have to use "clean" money, FEC, to make our purchases, which increased the price four times over.

We bought four tall Areca palms in black plastic tubs and a beautiful bonsai planted on a hill in a black earthenware dish. It was this little world that took me back the first time. It was obviously not pleased at the change in environment and decided to die. I felt such guilt at the thought of this ancient, tiny tree killed by my hands that I took it back and apologized profusely for my cruelty. By now, I knew his name, Mr. Wi, and he smiled and told me not to worry, and he sold me another plant and a little ceramic spray bottle. I believe I bought the same plants once every two months, recycled and made healthy by Mr. Wi.

The palms thrived in the living room in front of the patio doors and were watered every other day by Ai-yi. It still wasn't enough. My nose bled, and my skin rebelled. I looked at the largest of the blue-and-white fishbowls I'd bought from the Qingshanju Arts and Crafts shop. I had filled it with silk lotus blossoms, which seemed a good idea at the time. But it needed fish, and they, like me, required water.

Early Sunday morning, I convinced Ed to take me to the Guan Yuan Fish and Bird market. "I hear it's very interesting, and we can buy a fish," I said. He sighed.

Ed parked the jeep on the main road, and we walked down narrow *hutongs* toward the market. Cold as it was, the place teamed with life. A barber set up shop alongside a wall, where he shaved heads and faces with an open-blade razor sharpened on a wide leather strap, his white enamel bowl covered in soapy froth and flecks of black whiskers. Little children swaddled against the cold trotted alongside parents, the opening in the back of their pants occasionally revealing little pink bums. The most fascinating sight of all was "the dentist." His antique dentist chair was positioned in the middle of the lane; his patient meekly reclined in the cracked leather seat, and the dentist operated his drill by stepping on a pedal with his right foot, up and down, hands busy in the client's mouth. The slow, whining screech put my teeth on edge. This spectacle was of huge interest and attracted an audience. The poor patient, a prisoner. I quickly looked away toward the smell of chestnuts and sweet potatoes roasting in metal barrels. I breathed in their flavors.

"Like a sweet potato?" Ed asked. He bought two and peeled back the paper-thin crinkled skin to reveal the soft golden flesh of the potato and handed one to me.

"Delicious," I told him, watching the steam rise in the air. I pulled gloved fingers away from the sticky treat to reveal more potato. Somehow, the sweet potatoes made me feel less conspicuous. Munching on the potato became the equalizer, and the large dark-haired man in his black leather jacket and the small red-haired woman in the yellow coat belonged at least for that shared moment.

Turning a corner, we entered the small crowded market. It was really a group of tents set up on hard-packed earth. Old men crowded around songbirds, thrushes, canaries, mynahs, and the sweet Beijing robins, and admired carved bamboo cages and tiny porcelain food and water bowls. Jars of long fat worms and live grasshoppers waited to be purchased as a special treat for a beloved bird. Vendors dressed in dark gray unisex Mao suits stood by their goods, stamping their feet and alternately clapping their hands and blowing on fingers poking out from chopped woolen gloves. The fish vendors guarded their pets placed in bowls on the ground from the pushing crowd. There was no color there at all except the bright blue trim on the white enamel bowls, in which swam tiny fish. I wondered vaguely how the fish felt about the cold or if they even felt it.

"Ed, let's choose a fish," I said. "We can put her in the fishbowl." He gave me a quick sideways look, and I gave him an innocent smile.

"You and animals," he said and obligingly walked with me to the nearest vendor, a tiny round woman with the wrinkled face of an apple doll and one large front tooth that she flashed at us.

The old woman had twenty of these bowls, each with differently sized fishes separated by breed. I knew I wanted the goldfish with the huge tail that fanned out like a peacock—I'd seen them at the Fangshan Restaurant—and pointed to the bowl. The old lady started jabbering away: my choice of fish was definitely inferior. I should buy the orange-and-white fishes, very strong. They looked like carp to me. The old lady was convinced she was doing the foreigner a favor, and the only way I could get my fish was to compromise. One of each. Then the old woman performed what appeared to be the impossible; she folded in half, over the mass of padding in her jacket and pants, scooped up an aggressive-looking sharp-nosed orange-and-white fish, and plunked it in a small plastic bag, along with my choice of goldfish, which she assured me was sluggish and weak. I smiled and shrugged, and she shook her head and tutted, then threw in a bag of small blood-red wiggly worms—free.

Home we went with Wanda and Dorothy, and into the blue-and-white china bowl they swam. Ed had to feed them the icky worms until we found fish flakes at the Holiday Inn Lido.

I'd never before thought of fish as pets, but I'd watch my tiny fish swim in their porcelain palace and relax to their elegant moves, just as I had with my dogs and cats and horses. In Beijing, pets were an oddity. You'd see the odd mangy dog slinking around, head lowered, tail between its legs, hiding from the butcher, but never a cat, and birds in cages were the coveted domain of old men. I don't remember seeing them fly free in the city, only migratory birds flying in formation. Somebody had told that all the grass had been torn up during Mao's time to help get rid of diseases. The end result was hard-packed earth everywhere, except in parks, where clumps of grass struggled to survive, and no food supply for wild birds. So, Wanda and Dorothy were admired and fussed over, their water changed every Saturday by Ed. The bowl was heavy when empty, and, even though Ed was a powerful man, carrying the sloshing bowl into and out of the bathroom was no easy feat. I'd stay quietly out of the way, holding the jar with Wanda and Dorothy, waiting. Ed did certain things for me without question, and I was always pleasantly surprised. He once told friends, "Everything in the house is ours, except the garbage, which is mine."

As our pets grew, their personalities formed in the shape of their bodies. Dorothy, sharp nosed and quick, looking more like a shark than a goldfish, swam in spurts of speed and at feeding time torpedoed Wanda's round underbelly with her sharp nose. While Wanda floated about like a dowager duchess, round and gentle, her huge eyes looked forward out of her round face, her golden tail fluttering about her, silk chiffon in a breeze.

Like all the odd things we accumulated, Ai-yi made no comment. She observed, curiosity on her face, but the only remarks she made were about my abundant wardrobe and the number of dishes we used, then I would hear her mumble, *"Hen duo, hen duo dongxi."* It wasn't a complaint, and definitely not envy, more amazement at how much we needed.

One day, while I stood in the kitchen waiting for our drinking water to boil (ten minutes, per Ai-yi), I asked her about her kitchen. Her kitchen was so small, she said, that only one shelf and one person fit. She told me that she and her husband had *"yige wanze, yige beidze, yige kuaize,"* raising her index finger with each for emphasis. But she smiled with pride when she told me of her two gas burners. I thought how simple life would be if we owned only one bowl, one cup, one set of cutlery each, and the impossibility of it.

Thanksgiving would be here soon, then Christmas. Family time. Time for school breaks. Time to go home. I left for Hawaii that week. I'd be back between the holidays, I told Ed. It wasn't like we weren't used to this conflict between work and play. Now it seemed the pull was even greater for me to leave Beijing: Chris, of course, holidays, birthdays, my mother's poor health. I spent hours in Japan at Narita Airport waiting for the next flight to Honolulu, New York, London. Sometimes the wait seemed so long I gave up caring if I left. And this time I wondered if it would be better for all of us if I remained in Hawaii. I could get another job, be closer to my children, give up this endless struggle to sort out my marriage.

So far, my being with Ed hadn't been the magical fix I had thought it would be. There were times when I asked myself what did I really want. We had a life here, went out more often than ever, and the trips to Shanghai, the banquets, seemed to provide enough of a distraction to offer a sense of promise. But I still had no idea how to get through to Ed. Sometimes I wondered if he was capable of any feelings at all—except anger, of course, that he was master of. Anger boiled within him ready to surface, waiting to be vented. It was his default emotion. I could see it in the set of his jaw, the flush of his face, the narrowing of his eyes.

In any case, I decided to talk to Christopher's doctor that trip. He had a new one now. After his diagnosis, three years too late in my estimation, I no longer trusted his first doctor and gathered the names of four highly respected psychiatrists, two women, two men, for him to choose from. Chris saw each of them and chose the oldest man. Maybe because he was Anglo-Irish like me and reminded Chris of our annual trips to London, where he claimed "Nothing bad ever happens." Whatever the reason, it was a good match.

While doctors in general keep mum on anyone over eighteen's medical condition, I found that his psychiatrist would answer any questions

I asked. We were a team, I thought, and I trusted him. So, I asked what sort of impact a divorce would have on Chris. He didn't hesitate. "As long as you stay in his life, none. Chris pulls from your strength." While I didn't quite know what that meant, I felt a surge of relief. If it told me anything, it said that Chris was strong. Much stronger than I had thought!

But I wasn't quite ready to give up yet. And I thought of the treasure hunts with those crafty old men, China's rich culture that seemed to wrap itself around me, hot sweet potatoes, my bizarre sense of freedom in that oppressed society . . . Ai-yi, my new friends . . .

Tzu Chow met me at customs and this time rushed me through. He must have oiled the gates in advance. I looked around for Ed and saw him by the exit talking to Michael. I thought for a moment Michael would ride back with us and was relieved when he turned and walked away.

"How was it?" Ed asked.

"Great, the children are fine. Enjoying school from the sounds of it."

"Good."

I held my hand carry out to him.

"What's in here?" he asked, weighing the bag in his hand. "The kitchen sink?"

I laughed. "Almost."

We climbed into the jeep and started the bumpy ride home. Ed's hand lay on the seat next to me, and I placed mine around his palm and gently squeezed. I felt his arm stiffen and his hand slowly, deliberately pull away from mine. I busied myself searching my handbag for a lipstick I didn't need.

Back at the apartment, Ed helped unpack the inevitable cigarettes and the cheeses, canned tuna, corned beef, lamb, Italian sausages, and steaks I'd wrapped in layers of newspapers and plastic, then packed in dry ice, hoping I wouldn't get stuck at an airport somewhere and land up, as Ken had, with rotten, stinking meat and a dead giveaway to customs or, worse, be arrested as a murder suspect.

"Do you think you can make it back for Christmas?" Ed had just finished one of the steaks. A good time to ask, I thought. We had always made a big event out of Christmas, with the tallest Douglas fir we could fit in the house, ornaments that had become a treasured collection, roast leg of lamb with all the extras, Christmas cake, Christmas pudding and Christmas crackers, the ones that make a bang and contain silly hats, ridiculous jokes, little presents that I'd bring back after visiting my mother. I remember asking Ed about his childhood Christmas memories. "Church twice and roast turkey." That was it, no warm memories of decorating a tree, of playing board games with his sisters and brothers. Just another day but with turkey.

"Christ, I don't know what I'm doing next week, let alone next month," he said, pushing his plate back on the table. His face seemed to swell; his eyes bulged as if something was trying to escape. My stomach muscles tensed. I felt the hair on my neck bristle, the all-too-familiar feelings of fight or flight. I stood up and slowly moved the plates to the sink and began rinsing them off.

"Ai-yi will do that," Ed said, then, "She's been using the back shower."

"What? She probably doesn't have one of her own," I said, shaking my head in annoyance, wondering why it mattered and what that had to do with Christmas.

"She should ask!"

"She doesn't speak English. Anyway, nobody uses it."

He pushed back his chair, ready to stand. I was too tired for an extended discussion about Ai-yi. She did so much for us: ironing sharp creases in Ed's jeans, slapping and pushing our sweaters into shape as they dried. Why be so petty about the shower? I left the room before he could answer and went into the back bathroom. Ai-yi's small towel hung from the rack, worn thin, like those of my childhood. I placed soft pink towels next to it, hoping she would use them. She never did.

Ed was pouring a drink when I came out. He rarely drank after a meal.

"Anything wrong?" I looked at him, waiting for an answer.

"Everything's fine. You'd better get some rest," he said. He picked up his book from the coffee table and sat in his favorite chair.

The days dragged by. I saw Ed for dinner and morning coffee. Our conversations were equally brief.

"How was your day?" I would ask when he came home.

"Same old," he'd answer, throwing his briefcase down and heading for the bottle.

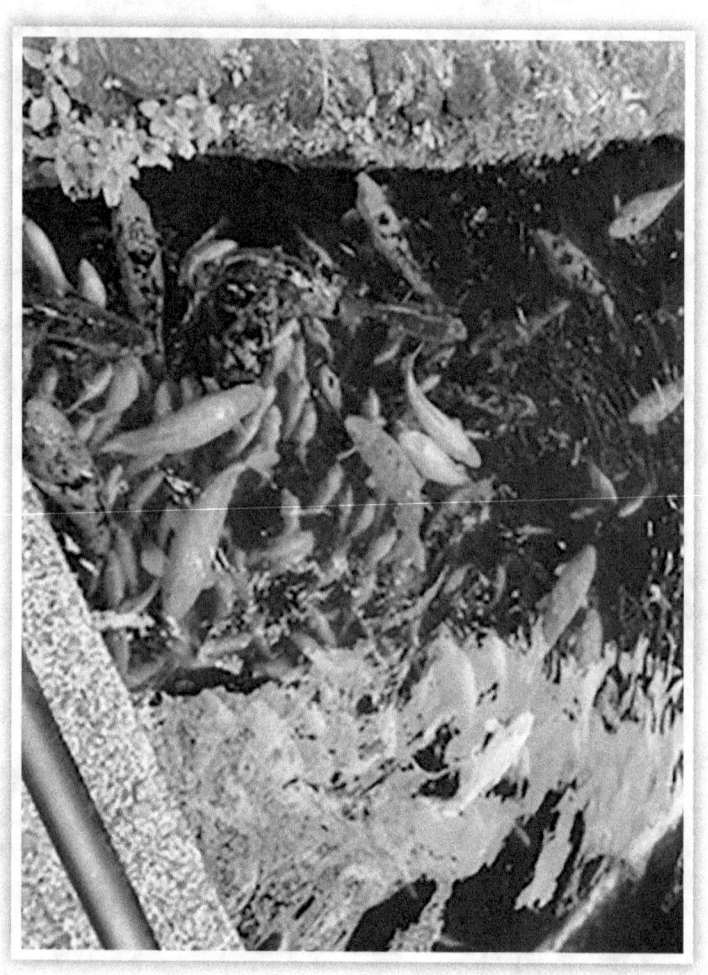

CHAPTER 16

HONG KONG

Hundreds of houses, thousands of houses, like a chess-board.
The twelve streets like a field planted with rows of cabbage.
In the distance perceptible, dim, din,
The fire of approaching dawn;
And a single row of stars lying to the west of the Five Gates.

From: *"Climbing the High Terrace," Du Fu, c. 755

Rebecca was away for an extended holiday in Virginia, and, except for walks in Ritan Park, I didn't feel like doing anything. Even if I did, the thought of walking for miles in the cold, filthy air was more than I wanted to consider. And when the usually weekly migraine struck, it was almost a relief to have an excuse to stay in the flat.

"Meeting in Hong Kong next week,", wives are invited," Ed said. "Wives are invited." We'd been to Hong Kong often and had always had a good time.

"Great. What's it about?"

"The usual. The clowns from home office want to use up their expense money for the year and put on a show. They don't even know what time it is here."

That was true enough. Many nights I'd jump out of bed when the phone rang, thinking it was one of the children in trouble; it had always been the "home office."

One of Hong Kong's greatest thrills was flying into and out of the airport. Kai Tak Airport was plonked right in the center of overcrowded Kowloon, rather like the grand railroad stations in the world's largest cities.

The usual message crackled over the intercom, and we all obligingly buckled up and got ready for landing. We started our descent, then the plane banked at an impossible angle, made a sharp turn, and the cabin became quiet, as if all the passengers were holding their unified breath. Then I saw them, mountains on three sides as the pilot aimed toward the twin mountains through which we had to pass. I felt I could reach out and touch them we were so close. Then there, right beneath us, was the dense hodgepodge that was Kowloon. We skimmed rooftops, barely missing the television antennas that covered them, and descended onto the tarmac, and, as we taxied past, I could see inside the crusty windows of the concrete cells occupied by laborers lucky enough to find space. Traffic rushed by us, the runway just another lane. It was a thrilling entrance to an intriguing city, and, as far as I was concerned, Kai Tak earned its status as one of the world's most dangerous airports.

Blindfolded I would have known where I was. The stench from the bay smothered everything in an overwhelming mix of pollution from the factories, legal and illegal, and sewage, turning Hong Kong's name "Fragrant Harbor" into a bad joke.

We stayed at the Sheraton, four expat managers and three times as many vice presidents. One other wife was there, Peggy from Taiwan. We met Peggy and husband Tom in the lobby before dinner. Ed knew Tom well and greeted him with "Meet my beautiful, wonderful wife." Ed hadn't referred to me like that in years, and I was taken by surprise, left a little uncomfortable even. Peggy was about my age, tall with short blond hair. She was very down to earth and felt like a long-lost buddy. We agreed to explore this unique place together the following day.

Peggy and I met in the lobby, and off we set from the immaculate Sheraton Hotel along scruffy, thriving Nathan Road and its blazing jewelry shops and their huge turbaned Indian guards standing outside, rifles at the ready—our destination, Hong Kong Island, our goal Tsim Sha Tsui and the Star Ferry pier.

We climbed over cabbage leaves and rubbish cluttering the pavements and stepped wide over water thrown by shopkeepers into the street. The air was hot and humid. Every building supplied its own unique scent to the bouquet of exhaust fumes and sweating bodies, but, in spite of the heat and hurrying crowds, the city pulsated with enthusiasm and energy as if all the Chinatowns of the world were concentrated in this one spot.

The sound of a departing ferry horn hurried us along. Neither one of us knew why; it's just what everyone does, rather like rushing to get onto a tube or train. There would be others, but the urge was too strong to resist.

We climbed on board. Deckhands, who wore white sailor suits and silly little flat hats, ribbons down the back, freed us from our mooring, and off we went. There was always a breeze on the water, which was very welcome, as was the occasional spray. "Keep your mouth closed,' Peggy joked. The ride took about twenty minutes and provided views, not only of Hong Kong's magnificent skyline but other boats in busy Victoria harbor: sampans, moving slowly, steered by old women standing straight, looking elegant in their long black pajamas and big straw hats, green jade bracelets sliding up and down their skinny arms as they used long poles to navigate passengers to floating fish restaurants, little girls in uniforms to and from school, and the Yau Ma Tei boat people, who walked from boat to boat to visit one another and shop. They earned their living as fishermen, selling their catch to restaurants, some of them floating restaurants in the harbor. They seldom walked on land.

We took a taxi to Hollywood Road, visited their famous antique shops ranging from tiny and cheap to select and expensive. We didn't buy anything. We had a better and definitely cheaper market in Shanghai. The hills in this area are steep and many, some with crude steps, and each level space held an opportunity for a seller of souvenirs or workmen to set up shop. There was a knife sharpener, a basket weaver, and a furniture maker. He was my favorite, and Peggy and I stood watching as this skinny old man in a wifebeater t-shirt shaped lengths of wood into curves, probably for the backs of a horseshoe-shaped chair, using a boiling kettle of steam and a bowl of cold water. It was like watching a magician turn a bunch of tired paper flowers into a white dove.

Right at the top of the latest hill we had climbed was the Man Mo Buddhist temple. It was surprisingly small and very dark, the dark emphasized by smoke from huge vats of josh sticks filling every corner of the tiny space. There was nothing serene about this temple; it was alive with paper ornaments hanging from the ornately painted ceiling, prayers written on strips of paper, fruit and rice piled on dishes, vases of silk flowers, burning candles of various lengths, and large, old-fashioned Christmas tree lights. There was a constant flow of worshippers rushing in and out, taking time only to light their josh sticks and say a few prayers.

By now it was lunch time, and Peggy suggested fish and chips, which were to be found at Stanley Market, located on the south side of the island.

"Shall we get a bus or taxi to Stanley?" Peggy asked. "They would have given us a car if we'd asked. I get to use ours all the time."

"You use the car?" I asked.

"Of course. Don't you? Wives can use it if it's not needed for business. Tell Ed not to be so stingy." Blood rushed to my face. I shut my mouth tight and told myself I didn't care.

We decided on the bus, a red double decker straight off the streets of London. We sat upstairs, first row so as to enjoy the view.

"I don't believe this bus has springs," moaned Peggy. I clung to the seat, trying not to bounce on my friend or, worse, onto the floor.

The road followed the rocky, winding coastline, and, between breaks in the lush vegetation, we could see the South China Sea way below us, waiting for the unexpected. Low-hanging branches from trees beat the bus as it passed. At times, it seemed we would just topple over and roll down to the waiting sea. We decided on a taxi back. If we survived.

My first impression of Stanley was how non-Chinese it looked. Buildings were painted, colorful awnings stood over doorways, and street signs were in English. Once at the market, we were faced with a warren of narrow lanes. There was a map of sorts, but, as the alleys were nameless, it wasn't much help. "Head toward the ocean," Peggy said.

Clothes and embroidered table linen, leather goods, and electronics squeezed together under tarpaulin-draped alleys, overruns from the factories nearby waiting for buyers. We shopped, then kept walking to the original little fishing village of Stanley. And there it was, a quiet oasis looking out onto calm ocean waters. It was such a contrast to everything we had experienced so far that day, and there we sat, at an outside table looking through trees at the deep blue ocean, where we enjoyed a greasy lunch of fried fish and chips and warm soda, among other expats, mostly Brits.

We dined en masse for the two nights we were there, and I always felt on these occasions that I was an employee.

"The boss wants us to sit next to him tonight," Ed said. "He'd like to know about Beijing."

"Gosh, I'd much rather sit with Peggy and Tom. They're so nice."

"So would I," he replied.

Ed held my arm as we walked into the bar, then placed his hand around my waist. It felt as if I belonged there.

"This is my wife," he said to those I hadn't yet met and some I had. I didn't mind. I enjoyed the attention, sharing jokes, feeling protected, pretty. He could be so charming, his smile leading the way. Just like when we first met all those years ago.

Ed sat me next to the huge senior vice president, the only really important man there.

"Watch out for Joan," Ed told him. "She'll con you out of anything."

He smiled when he said it, but his remark stung. Pretending not to hear, I asked our host if he'd been to Beijing.

"It's an amazing city," I told him. "Amazing food too, from all the provinces."

"Driver's good, Joan? Knows his way around?" he asked. I didn't know how to answer and looked at Ed. I watched his face for a reaction. He turned away.

"What about the water. Same as here?"

"Worse," I said. "We can't get bottled. I believe that's why the Chinese drink so much tea."

He liked that and gave out a loud belly laugh, and I presumed I'd passed the interview. It was like a game, everyone playing their roles: the very important vice president in charge of pencil sharpeners, the extremely competent expat manager and his charming wife, a nice couple, well matched. And the not-so-happy, looking for a weakness they could turn to their advantage: a promotion, perhaps a transfer to a bigger station . . .

But, in spite of the stuffiness of people who had never lived outside their comfortable cocoons of air conditioners and immediate gratification, it was good to hear English and laughter and eat Western food. I considered the boring conversations and interrogations a small price to pay.

Back in our room, I stood in front of Ed. "What's this about the jeep?" I asked. "Why did you tell me I couldn't use it?"

"News to me," he responded. He usually watched his drinking on business occasions, but he'd had a few before dinner, and I decided not to push him. Knowing I could use the jeep was enough for now. Wounded pride would have to wait.

Peggy and I said our goodbyes in the hotel lobby. "Next time I'll visit you," she said. That was the first of many trips we enjoyed together.

Our flight didn't leave until much later, so Ed and I set off for the Ocean Terminal with its amazing assortment of shops and restaurants. I'd brought some peasant paintings with me and wanted to get them framed at an art store there. We left them while we went for lunch at our favorite dim sum restaurant. The space was enormous and noisy as servers navigated steaming carts around tables, calling out their specialties while customers vied for their attention. There were no reservations taken and nobody to seat you; the trick was to stand behind people already eating and, as soon as they finished, jump into their chairs. Despite of the chaos, the system worked, and we had yet to see a fight over territory. And the food—the best of the best!

On the flight back to Beijing, I remembered the first time we took the children to Hong Kong. Shanty towns made from cardboard and rotten wood clung to the cliffs, home to illegal Chinese immigrants, escapees from communism. One electric cord strung up and down the mountains fed the single electric bulbs at each shack, which twinkled in the dark, giving the illusion of a cozy, magical place. Like Jack's beanstalk, it grew out of control. Illegal factories provided work; noodle factories provided food. Tt was a world unto itself. Most of them were gone now. But there were still enough left.

"Do you remember how much fun the children had on Lantau Island?" I asked Ed. He was flicking through a magazine and devouring a cigarette. He didn't answer, and I left him to it and thought of our seven-year-old daughter, blond wavy hair down to her waist, bargaining for fans and Christopher's quiet observation of everything. Trips to exotic places were one way we could spend time together. The other was on our annual visits to London to see my parents, though for the past six years Ed had declined to come with us.

"I travel enough for work," he'd say when reminded. "Hate flying. You go with the kids."

"It's not the same without you," I'd protest. Every year we went through the same discussion, and every year the children and I went without him.

CHAPTER 17

THE INTERPRETER

Behind vermillion portals meat is left to rot,
While out in the streets starving people are frozen to death.
Prosperity and decay, so distant, yet so near.
Distressing—what more need be said?

From: *"Thoughts on the Way From the Capital to Fengxian," Du Fu, 755

Hong Kong's thriving entrepreneurship had energized me. I took out my shoeboxes of silver and jade pieces picked up on our Saturday excursions. Some were quite beautiful: the chi lings, mother and child sitting on silver lions, hammered scenes of gardens and birds with tiny bells hanging in varied lengths, some gilt covered, jade peaches and abstract animals. They would make lovely necklaces, attached to cords with the intricate knots used as fasteners on cheongsams.

As soon as Rebecca returned, I invited her for tea at my apartment.

"Rebecca, I need to find someone who can make those knots they use for the cheongsams."

"You mean at the costume factory? You'll never find anyone," she said. "They won't let you inside the workrooms."

Rebecca was right. I needed an interpreter to look official. I called Kathy.

It was through Kathy that I met Justine. We arranged to meet for coffee at the Jianguo Hotel. A tall slim young woman was waiting outside. She was a student at Beijing University, and her English was perfect.

"I need an interpreter," I told her, "someone who can source things for me."

"Perhaps I have a friend who can help," Justine said. "I don't have much free time. I can show you around some factories if you like. I have contacts."

Sometimes people come into your life and you feel an immediate connection. That's what happened with Justine and me. Over the next few weeks, we went by taxi to factories in the city, and I saw cheap copies of Tang dynasty pottery lined up in untidy rows, exquisite silk flowers in magnificent disarray, small shops making satin-covered boxes, wig shops, tea shops, and all the while we exchanged easy chatter.

The more we saw of each other, the more personal our conversations became. Justine wanted to know about the Christian faith. What made people believe in an afterlife? Did Christianity encourage people to be kind? Why do we have pets? I'd taken religion for granted, and she made me think. I shared my personal views, based loosely on my Catholic upbringing. Then, one day, our dialogue took a different tack. We were driving in a taxi and had just passed the railroad station. Men and women, their possessions in cloth bundles, cluttered the pavements outside, waiting for trains that were never on time and tickets that were hard to come by.

"When I was sent away on the train," she began, her voice soft, her speech slow, "I was excited at first. I was with a friend from school. We were taken to a farmhouse in the north. A two-room farmhouse. Eight adults lived there, men and women. Intellectuals. Nobody knew how to cook or clean. They fought over schedules and screamed insults if someone burnt the food. It was rationed. There was no meat." She stared out the window so I couldn't see her face.

"Dignified adults changed in front of me and banged their bowls on the table and cursed whoever cooked." She shuddered. "We tried to grow our own vegetables but knew nothing of the land."

I wanted to put my arm around her shoulders, comfort her in some way.

"We wore rags. It was so cold."

Her delicate, beautiful face was white, her hands clenched together, as she sat upright in the taxi as if hearing her own story for the first time. I held my breath, waiting for her to continue.

"How old were you?" I asked.

"Fourteen. That's why I'm older than most at university. I was away four years."

"Why were you sent away?" A distant memory stirred of the train that took me to my own forced evacuation.

"My father was a suspect of the communists. My parents were imprisoned, and I was sent away to be 'reeducated'."

"I'm so sorry." I took a deep breath, holding back tears.

"We had to collect 'night soil' for the farmers. The peasants humiliated us."

I stared at her hands. Her knuckles were white.

"I still wake up screaming," she said.

I couldn't ask her any more. I couldn't say a word. Justine had confided her story to me, and I understood about nightmares that never go away.

"Rest, Joan," she said. She leaned back against the seat of the taxi and closed her eyes.

She came to the apartment for tea after our outings. Ai-yi wasn't friendly toward her, not the way she was to Rebecca or Kathy. I was annoyed when I had to ask for tea the second time.

"Be careful, Joan," Ed said when I told him of Justine's internment.

"What of? She did nothing wrong."

"Just be careful, that's all."

"She's very smart," I insisted. "And I like her." Ed raised an eyebrow in response.

He of all people should have understood how innocent people get trapped. His sister had told me years ago about their miserable childhood with a violent, abusive father, the two years all three of them had been placed in an orphanage after their parents' divorce, how an aunt had wanted to take them home with her but their father wouldn't allow it. Ed must have been nine at the time. I'd tried to talk to Ed about it, gently, without probing, but he never answered my questions, not even

"What did you like most as a child?" We never talked of our childhoods, either of us. That was our common thread, the pain, the isolation, the secrets, the lies.

I dreamt I was flying, pushing the ceiling up with my outstretched arms, trying to stay clear of soldiers invading my room with their bayonets and swords. I heard myself scream and sat up in bed, sweating in the cold. I reached out to Ed. He was still asleep. Nothing disturbed him.

The next time I saw Justine was when she took me to a wig factory. It wasn't a successful meeting. I wanted to know where the hair came from—actually, whether it was legally obtained, (I'd heard some horror stories)—and didn't get an answer.

Justine leaned back in the taxi and closed her eyes. She looked so tired, like she had just finished a marathon.

"Do you have time for lunch?" I asked.

"Yes, but I need to do something first," she said, "at the CITIC building." There was someone waiting for her there. The someone turned out to be a beautiful little girl, about seven or eight, accompanied by an older Chinese woman.

"My daughter," Justine said. "I have to give my mother-in-law something."

I sat in the taxi and watched the warm hugs between mother and daughter and the exchange between the two women. It didn't take but a few minutes, and I watched the little girl, standing so tentatively, waving her mother goodbye.

"Her father and I are divorced," she told me. "His mother takes care of our daughter. I don't get to see her very often."

We rode the rest of the way in silence. I knew I'd just witnessed something deeply personal and had no idea what to say.

We stopped at the Jianguo Hotel for lunch. It was always quiet there, a good place to relax. Our table was in a corner, and palms blocked off the other diners, not that there were many. We were served tea and placed our orders for lunch.

"How's school?" I asked, an innocuous topic.

"I'm under a deadline," she said, and she went on to tell me of her plans to go to the US to complete her PhD and that she had a sponsor. And here I am, I thought, wasting her time by introducing me to prospective business interest I'll probably never follow through with.

"I won't have much time starting next month, but I have a friend. He's a fellow student. His name is Ernie." We agreed to have Ernie stop by with Justine Wednesday afternoon after Ai-yi left.

"You've come such a long way since your internment. Your parents must be very proud."

Somehow, maybe the quiet restaurant or the warmth from the delicious food, Justine felt comfortable enough to tell me about her parents.

They were intellectuals and were persecuted, so they escaped to Taiwan. The Chinese government soon saw the errors in their plan and appealed to all those who had joined Chiang Kai-shek to come back to China, promising them a return to normal. No punishment. Their lives restored.

"They lied, of course," she continued. Her parents were imprisoned, and, while her mother was eventually released, her father died the day before his release came.

"I've told my mother about you, Joan. She would enjoy meeting you."

And my mind struggled to grasp what I'd just heard, to understand the sheer devastation of their lives. Her family's life story was beyond my experiences. It was with a heavy heart that I said goodbye that day.

We did meet her mother, Ed and I. Justine's mother was an older version of herself, tall and elegant, with sad dark eyes in a thin face. Her English was perfect, her manner gentle. "Please call me May," she said.

The first time, Justine invited us to a restaurant that we hadn't seen before. We were treated to a banquet, a feast, which must have cost a small fortune. I noticed the staff seemed almost hostile as they served us and tried to figure out why. Ed and I talked about it later; he had noticed it too. "Yep," he said, "they either know who she is or hate foreigners."

It was dark by the time we left. There were no taxis, and Ed insisted on driving May home. We drove nearly empty roads to one of those monstrous concrete apartment bloks.

"Please come in," May said. "Join me for a cup of tea."

Into the dark lobby we walked to be met by the standard traction elevator operated by the typical stern-faced woman. She stared at Ed and me and gave a narrow-eyed look at May as we grated our way slowly up to the tenth floor.

May's apartment boasted one bedroom, a kitchen alcove with a two-burner stove, and an entry room arranged for guests, with a small settee and two kitchen chairs. The asphalt tiles were cracked, some missing, but May did have a bathroom. The whole place would have fit easily into the open sitting-dining room of our apartment.

May served us tea in Western cups and little sesame seed biscuits, and the conversation gravitated to Justine.

"Poor child," May said. "She had a terrible time while we were in prison. I just wish she could relax a little, enjoy life. We never know..."

"I agree," I said. "That's what all parents want for their children, to be safe and happy."

We left May and, after waiting ages for the elevator, made our way home.

"May's apartment is a special one," I said to Ed. "Her compensation for all that was taken from them."

"I know," he said. "Poor woman."

We did meet again, this time at our apartment on a Saturday afternoon, May and Justine and my new interpreter, Shan Shan, and her daughter, Little Snow, and husband. Ai-Yi made her special *jiaozi* and Ed bought up Jianguo's patisserie.

While Ai-Yi didn't join us, she seemed very pleased at all the compliments her dumplings earned and enjoyed the laughter we shared that day.

Though Justine and I occasionally got together, it was considered unwise for Chinese nationals to form personal friendships with foreigners, and that was the last time we saw May.

CHAPTER 18

CHINESE OPERA

There was a beautiful lady, Madame Gongsun,
Whose sword dance drew people from all quarters.
They packed the house, and as they watched, quite stunned,
Heaven and earth seemed to move to her rhythms.
Dazzling as the nine suns shot down by the legendary archer,
Agile as the gods careering in the clouds on their dragons,
Coming on as the thunderous drums fell silent,
Ending in a pose serene as the light on peaceful waters.

From: *"On Seeing Madame Gongsun's Pupil Perform the Sword Dance," Du Fu, 767

Rebecca called—would I like to go to the Chinese opera costume shop? To tell the truth, I was always ready to go anywhere, anytime. The costume shop was located in the Qianmen area of the city, directly south of the Forbidden City, very crowded and no parking. Taxis were available from hotels only, so I called Ed and asked if I could use Tzu Chow for a few hours.

"What for?"

"Rebecca and I want to go shopping. She can't drive today."

"It's a company car," he said.

I wasn't going to give up, so I stated my case: Rebecca always drove; it would only take an hour total. And what about his driving the Changs around? And Lilly Chang had told me she used Tzu Chow to drive her shopping. What about the fish? "He's just sitting around," I said. "What's the big deal? Besides," I added, "Peggy does it." Ed sighed.

Tzu Chow dropped us outside the front door of the costume shop. He'd come back in an hour.

Wooden pallets piled high with bolts of silk stood at odd angles on the cobblestone pavement outside. Old men bent double under their loads while carrying bundles through the swinging doors.

"This way," Rebecca said, walking around the corner to another entrance. Grimy glass panels filled in the top half of the door, wild painted posters promoting the next event spread across layers of happenings long past covering the walls on either side.

Bells rang when the sticky door yielded to Rebecca's push. Even in the typical dim lighting, the costume shop gleamed and glittered with swords and helmets, satin costumes covered in embroidery, trimmed in gold cord that hung on the walls and lined shelves in vibrant colors from emerald green to Schiaparelli's shocking pink. Hats with five-foot-long pheasant feathers stood ready for the White Snake, and masks, hideous and handsome looked down on us. Dainty embroidered satin slippers in every color of the rainbow, their sides black to make the foot appear smaller, waited to be tried on.

"Rebecca, I want some of everything," I said. I tried on two pairs of slippers, turquoise and imperial yellow. Their soles were rubber, designed for performers doing their impossible jumps. The masks were striking. I bought three masks for Ed's office: red, black, and white. "Each color represents a human emotion," Rebecca told me. "Red for loyalty, black for ferocity, and white for treachery."

Rebecca was there for a fitting of her cheongsam. I made my purchases and followed her up the stairs to the factory. Tables lined up in rows vibrated with the sound of sewing machines. The smell of machine oil hung in the air. How could these women create such intricate details in this dingy factory with its forty-watt bulbs, I wondered.

"It's lovely," I told her as she spun around. "The work is so fine, and those knots are just what I'm looking for." I continued looking at the intricate weave of silk cord for the frog openings and the exquisite knots used instead of buttons.

"It's my fourth fitting," she told me. "They kept insisting it fit when it was obvious it didn't. They actually fixed it this time."

"I need to get to know this Knot Lady."

"They won't let you talk to her, you know," she said. But I was determined.

This was a government-owned shop, I found out, and, like all government-owned shops, the management staff were indifferent and uncooperative. There was no point in asking, not right now. But I knew there must be a way. Here the best jobs were given to the well connected. They kept themselves apart from the actual workers and controlled who they spoke to and what they did. It was so in the Friendship Stores, too. Ed scornfully called the young girls "princesses." He didn't take kindly to being ignored when there he stood, FEC in hand.

When Ed arrived home from work that evening, I told him about the costume shop.

"I've bought some masks for your office wall," I told him, unwrapping the brown-paper packing.

"I wondered were to get those," he said. "I can get tickets for the opera if you'd like." I assured him I would. He obtained tickets for Friday night's performance.

Over the next two days, I read all I could on Peking Opera, which wasn't enough to satisfy my curiosity and, as I later found out, nowhere near did it justice. Friday evening, I was ready early and preened away, waiting.

"Something came up." It was Ed, on the phone. "You remember Joe, the young guy in Shanghai?" he asked. "You two can go together. He loves it. He'll pick you up."

I don't want to go with a stranger, I yearned to tell him. I want to go with you. I wanted to yell my disappointment and decline to go. I held my breath. Maybe I was being unreasonable. This was a difficult country to work in; things did "come up" all the time. Maybe Joe did want to go.

"I really hoped we'd go together" was all I could say.

"Not tonight, maybe later" was his hurried response.

Joe picked me up, and off we drove in the jeep. He was just a few years older than my son. Traffic was very heavy, and he swore in Mandarin and thumped the horn. He's stuck too, taking out the boss's wife, I thought, embarrassed for us both. My attempt at small talk dried up.

Once inside the large dingy theater, I became absorbed in my surroundings. I was surprised to see such a large audience, men mostly; it was almost a full house. Musicians were arranged in a group on the far right of the stage, partially hidden by a screen. Chinese characters were displayed on a scroll-like screen on the left for the audience to follow. The orchestra struck up. Impossibly high sounds scratched from string instruments, drums roared, cymbals crashed, the performers entered, and the theater came to life.

"It's the Monkey King," Joe said, "Chinese myth."

The Monkey King appeared in his scarlet and gold costume, the colors of the sun, two long pheasant feathers attached to his hat. His face was elaborately painted in red and gold, depicting a monkey mask. He fought with sword and arrow, leaping over his enemies' heads in a slow, graceful aerial flight. While on the ground, he fought like a kung fu master.

I watched and listened, fascinated by sights and sounds I'd never seen or even imagined before: vocal sounds higher than a Western tenor or soprano, costumes so ornate I wondered how the performers could do their amazing acrobatics, choreography so abstract the dramatic effect was overwhelming, faces painted like the masks I'd bought Ed, each a work of art.

Chinese, being a tonal language, makes singing a challenge, listening an art form in itself. The audience stamped feet and yelled their approval when a singer held a note, high and impossibly long. I noticed the men sitting in front of me shake their heads rapidly from side to side, tossing the sound around in their ears, like a sommelier tasting a superb glass of wine, swirling it around his palette before swallowing.

The audience was slow and ungenerous with their applause, except for the note held and suspended, the end result being the note became buried in their cheers. The most noise was made toward a man sitting in front of us. I could smell this awful rotting odor, like gorgonzola cheese gone bad, and wondered what it was until my neighbors yelled at him to put his shoes back on.

It was over much too soon, and I sat there made immobile by what I had seen and heard. The audience, however, left quickly, like at a Chinese banquet.

"The leading lady would like to meet you," Joe told me. I was dizzy from the avalanche of sensations and wondered if I could remember how to say "hello."

The dressing rooms were crowded with costumes on racks, spears and swords and amazing hats. Pots of colored grease paint and powder lay open on narrow shelves in front of dusty mirrors.

The star dressed with everyone else and walked toward me as we entered. She was so tiny, inches below my five feet two, lean and muscular like a gymnast, with a wide, bright smile. I judged her to be around her midforties and marveled at the acrobatics she had just performed.

We exchanged greetings, and I told her how I admired her obvious talent. She replied that I was small enough and could be trained to perform too, and, as if to prove it, she threw her long spear to me, which I caught in my hand.

"*Ching ni dzai lai*," she invited as I left. I assured her I would.

When Joe dropped me off, we were both more relaxed. "Glad you had a good time," he told me.

Ed was already in the apartment, reading a magazine and sipping a vodka martini.

"It was fabulous," I told him. "My ears are still ringing."

"Thought you'd like it," he replied.

"Got to go backstage, too." I told him of the amazing costumes, the makeup and skill of the performers. It was then that I realized there was very little scenery on stage, only items necessary in telling the story, like the large rock the Monkey King used as a prop, a few cardboard trees. I hadn't noticed the sparseness at the time.

I changed into my bathrobe, made a pot of red tea, and curled up on one of the two settees, eager to share my experience.

"Joe said tickets are hard to get for foreigners."

"It's all *guanxi*," Ed replied, rubbing his thumb against fingers, and he went on to explain the Chinese system of "gratitude" for past or future favors. With his job, Ed was in a position to help a lot of people and built up a lot of favors, few of which he exercised.

"Why didn't you want to go?" I asked. I knew it had been his choice. He had a habit of last-minute no shows.

"Just tired, I guess."

"I had hoped we'd do things together," I said. "And I think you would've enjoyed it."

"Maybe next time." I bit back my "I doubt it."

Ed went to bed before me that night. I couldn't shake off the excitement of the evening. It was as if I'd sprouted another head.

Two weeks later I was to go again, with Ed this time. A real surprise! We were to see *The White Snake,* which was to be televised. This time the opera house was full, and television cameras blocked the aisles.

"Why such a big deal, Ed?" I asked as we were seated. He told me the principal male role was to be played by a man just released from prison. He'd been the most famous opera singer in China.

"Forty years, political prisoner." I was silenced by the thought of it, as well as the fact that we had to seem neutral.

I knew who he was as soon as he entered the stage, not by the audience—they were their usual stoic selves—but by the fact that he was dressed in a long brown robe and wore no makeup. Then he sang and held a sound so long I breathed for him, and the audience cheered, then stopped to see if the note still held true, then cheered again. It seemed like an impossible feat, to hold a single note for such a long time, without taking a breath. Like everything in China, the best was without comparison.

We went backstage together. The famous guest singer had left, but I met the lovely woman again. She and I talked about children this time, and she told me her son played a wind instrument in the orchestra. It was her husband who owed Ed the favors; that's how he managed to get the tickets impossible for most foreigners to buy.

"I swear you're part Chinese," Ed said on the way home. He'd said that in Hawaii too when I'd eat my weight in dim sum and look funn noodles.

Chinese Opera

CHAPTER 19

SHAN SHAN AND THE KNOT LADY

Sewing thread in hand, the loving mother;
Clothes for the son to wear, her traveling son.
On and on she sews, his leaving now nears;
Stitch on stitch, she fears—a delayed reunion.

From: **"The Absent Traveler," Meng Jiao, 751–814

The dull winter dragged on. Once or twice a week, Rebecca, Monica, and I went on our shopping adventures or joined each other for tea. Ed and I fell into our "truce" mode and continued with Sundays at the Jinguo, grocery shopping at the Holiday Inn, staying for a meal, but we were living on the outside of Chinese society looking in. I wanted to get below the surface, see everyday life, absorb and be absorbed by it. Alone in my restlessness, I decided to continue my search for an employee of my own, someone who would be comfortable with me. English language required.

Kathy introduced me to the perfect person, Shan Shan. Kathy brough her to the flat for an interview. While reserved, Shan Shan wasn't shy, and she offered her services as interpreter and guide. Great! Her language skills were perfect, her manner confident. Smaller than me by a few inches, her hair was cut in the usual bob, but on her it looked stylish. Her clothes were smart, and she wore pink lipstick. Shan Shan presented herself as a completely independent, self-sufficient, thoroughly modern young woman.

"I can work three half days or one and a half full days each week," she said. I didn't really have a plan, but her directness forced me into one: one full and one-half day for a whopping twenty US dollars a month.

Shan Shan could start the next day. What to do? Jewelry! All the bits and pieces I had purchased at the markets would look wonderful attached to those rolled silk cords I'd seen in Hong Kong. All I needed was to find someone adept at making the frog knots used on cheongsams. The best place to get one made? Off to the Peking Opera Costume factory—but first some fabric.

Shan Shan and I caught a taxi to Qianmenwai Dajie, a crowded narrow street of small shops and lots of character. The two-story fabric shop stood set back from the street; its steps, steep and narrow, rose from the broken pavement to the front entrance. Porters squeezed by us, pallets holding bolts of cloth strapped to their backs, and wooden floorboards creaked in protest as we eased our way around counters and shelves overflowing with fabrics. The word "haberdashery" came to mind, and I saw in this ancient shop of absolute chaos a scene that matched the chopped-up sound of the word.

I chose one-yard cuts of silk in jewel-like tones, ropes of cord in matching colors and thread, destined for the necklaces I wanted made. Selections made, my money was transported along thin cables stretched out over the heads of other customers. The change and receipt came whizzing back the same way.

The costume shop was nearby. I opened the door and froze on the spot, as I once again tried to take in the abundance of color and costumes, my eyes and mind trying to process the contents crammed into every nook and cranny of this small space, leaving me speechless. Swords and spears, wigs and beards hung randomly around the small room. A magical space. Another day I would be back again buying these glorious costumes and more shoes and hats, but today we were sent upstairs to the dressmaker.

Shan Shan was successful in obtaining the Knot Lady's address, though it wasn't easy, and it took three separate visits and the purchase of lots of embroidered slippers and a made-to-order cheongsam for me before a scrap of paper was discretely placed in her hand. This was a government factory. Watched over for breakers of rules. Socializing with foreigners was discouraged.

"She lives in a *hutong* behind the factory," Shan Shan told me, and we made plans to meet at the apartment the following Saturday.

Time to look at my treasures: small silver-gilded locks and depictions in silver of the Eight Immortals, silver lions with moveable legs and eyes that once pulled closed sheer bed curtains on four-poster beds, pieces of jade carved into the shapes of auspicious signs, cameos of engraved amber that once adorned silk robes, gilded hair ornaments embossed with birds and blossoms. Every piece I touched made my head buzz with excitement. From yards of silk, I cut two swatches for each piece, one for the cord, the other for the clasps, and drew a rough sketch showing the length of the completed piece, and into plastic lunch bags they went. One piece per bag. That first day, I would take just five to be worked on, a test.

That night, over luscious dumplings at Ritan, I asked Ed if he thought it would be okay for Ai-yi to see what I was doing.

"Don't know," he said, lighting a cigarette.

I didn't know either, so I decided to keep my little enterprise from her for the moment. It was the same with Tzu Chow—not that he might get into trouble, he was just too nosey and a known gossip, so I used him to get to the Beijing Hotel where I could easily hire a taxi. Only on innocuous journeys did he drive us.

Saturday morning, I could barely contain my excitement while I waited for Ai-yi to leave, but Shan Shan arrived early.

Ai-yi opened the door, and, with a brief word of thanks, Shan Shan strode right in as if at home. Those two will get on fine, I thought.

Once in the taxi, I opened my large handbag and pulled out a prototype for the necklaces and the five pieces ready for assembly. It was

Shan Shan's job to write instructions on each slip of paper. This she did as we bumped along the road to the alley next to the costume factory. Time to switch to a smaller mode of transportation.

"I'll get a pedicab. Please stand back out of sight." I obliged and watched Shan Shan negotiate. Her hands moved energetically until she got her price.

I climbed up and sat on the cracked red plastic-covered seat followed by Shan Shan. The operator turned to look at me, and I saw his thin face, his watery eyes. He was old, his body worn thin like his shabby clothes and cloth shoes.

"*Jipo, jipo,*" urged Shan Shan, and the old man leaned his body forward and stood hard on the pedals. I sat back in the seat and tried to hide behind the arm of the shade.

Traveling the narrow maze of *hutongs,* we arrived at an earth-packed alley.

"He'll wait for us," Shan Shan told me. "I won't pay him until we go back."

Formerly a family compound, additional single-story structures built onto existing walls out of rocks and bricks formed two straight lines in what had been an open courtyard. We walked along a narrow alley that was swept clean. A little girl sat on a small white enameled potty; two old ladies sat on stools snapping green beans. They all pretended not to see us. Doors were open along the solid walls, which faced each other. Eyeless houses with open mouths. I resisted the temptation to peek inside.

We walked to what had been the original main house, now converted, like the rest, into one-room apartments. Everywhere, the earth was swept clean. I could see the brush marks raking the earth in front of us. The Knot Lady was waiting. Short and chubby, her soft face flushed, she stood at her open door.

"*Ching, gin lai,*" she invited, and into her home we ventured.

One naked light bulb hung from the ceiling. A small refrigerator placed next to the table covered in a white crocheted cloth was their only display of luxury. Two gas jet burners served as a stove and were placed on a small doorless cupboard in which a few dishes and a wok were stored. A single bed lined one wall, on which reclined a middle-aged man, crippled from an industrial accident. Crutches resided on the floor beside him. He smiled his welcome.

This was their home, one room, neat and clean—their water, like their neighbors', collected from taps outside . . . their lavatory, I found out later, consisted of buckets, the "night soil" collected on flat wheelbarrows before dawn and taken to nearby farms for fertilizer.

The Knot Lady invited us to sit at her glass-covered table. There wasn't a mark on it. Tea was offered and the steaming golden liquid poured from a rose-patterned thermos into unmatched cups. Shan Shan did all the talking, but the Knot Lady kept looking at me.

"Does she understand?" I asked. Shan Shan assured me she did.

Then Shan Shan talked fees. *Furen* would pay twenty *renminbi* (the equivalent of fifty cents) for each perfect piece. Shan Shan had argued that was too much money—I could pay five and she'd be happy—but, after meeting this quiet woman, I felt good about holding the price. The Knot Lady walked to her wall calendar—the red rose picture was the only decoration in the room—and pointed to a date.

"That's when we come back," said Shan Shan.

Her work was beautiful. We made one trip there a week to drop off and pick up. Soon, she had her son, a schoolteacher who lived next door, help with the manufacturing. Shan Shan kept the per-piece price lower than I wanted, but I gave a bonus when the work was impeccable, and Shan Shan tried to keep a balance by having, in her estimation, inferior work redone free of cost. While I would've done the same in England or America, it was hard here; the money was nothing for the intricate work, and they had so little. Even so, our Knot Lady was able to purchase a new bed for her husband and eventually a television set.

It was a rainy Saturday, and, while pleased at the prospect of cleaner air, the rain made traffic a nightmare and pedicab-cabs hard to find. Shan Shan stopped an old man, shoulders covered in plastic, and bargained with him to take us to our Knot Lady and back. Pleased with her negotiating skills, she told me the fare; it was too low. The old man bent over the handlebars and forced the pedals down; his shoes were sodden canvas, his efforts immense.

Today, our Knot Lady had prepared a snack for us, rice with a piece of flavored meat inside, wrapped and steamed in a wide green leaf tied neatly with fine string. It reminded me of the lau lau popular in Hawaii. While I knew I wouldn't eat it, I was touched by her generosity and remembered my grandma telling me, "Poor people are always kind. They know how hard life can be."

We returned to the sodden old man, and still the neighbors ignored us. The old man was waiting. He had covered our seat with his sheet of plastic and pulled the shade up. I noticed his right leg was at least three inches shorter than his left, and, through his soaking wet shirt, I could see his shoulder blades sharp through the cloth.

More guilt. I told Shan Shan to give him his original asking price for our fare, not the lower one she had negotiated, along with the precious rice. "We shall give him one thing," she said. "With one, he is happy. If we give him two things, he will want more." We gave him the bundles of rice.

But, when I got out, I slipped him a few soiled notes and smiled at Shan Shan's look of disapproval.

On my Christmas trip home, I'd found a market for the necklaces, a posh shop in one of the exclusive hotels in Waikiki, and arranged for a broker to handle the small shipments. The little kitchen factory would be kept busy.

"Her son is helping her full time now," Shan Shan told me. I was pleased to hear it and eager to restart our weekly pedicab trips to the Knot Lady's home and see the abandoned trinkets turned into works of art.

"You are a woman of the world," Shan Shan told me as Tzu Chow drove us to the Beijing Hotel. "You shouldn't ride in a pedicab."

"It's fun," I told her. "And I feel less conspicuous in the *hutongs*." She couldn't disagree with that.

By now, I felt quite comfortable sitting back while a skinny old man pulled me along. He was earning a living, and I was helping him; besides, it had been the same for centuries, and it really was fun. The pace was slow, and I could see the surroundings in detail, unlike the blurred view through a glass window in a speeding car. I could feel the road beneath the thin tires too; every crack, every pothole, reminded me of where I was. Rainy days were my favorite, when the hood wrapped itself around me and I could hear the rain tap, tap, tap on its roof and see it bounce off the driver's waterproof cape.

That Saturday evening, Ed wanted to know what I had been up to. I went into the back bedroom and showed him the necklaces our Knot Lady had created.

"Making a few bob on these," I said.

I showed him the broken pieces we'd picked up at the flea markets, now transformed into something lovely.

"Nice," he said.

"Yes, very satisfying."

"When do the markets open again?"

"Why? You missing the excitement?"

"Something to do, I guess."

"Springtime, I think. Not long to wait." Hobo Town was open, but I still had concerns showing up with Ed. My old friends, I knew, would be intimidated. Best keep that shopping experience with us three girls.

CHAPTER 20

THE BROTHERS HU

*How wretched it is that I who love old things am born so late;
Faced with them I find the tears go rolling down my face.*

From: ** "The Rocks on the Mountain," Han Yu, 768–825

Once started, I felt compelled to keep the Knot Lady supplied with work, which required a new source for bobs.

"Know just the place," Rebecca said when I asked. "The brothers Hu."

Rebecca drove. "I don't mind," she told me. "It's better to keep things to ourselves." With no embassy connections, I had become Rebecca's shopping companion. Long-term foreign residents kept quiet about what they bought and downright secretive about their sources.

The brothers Hu worked with their uncle, Old Mr. Hu, in a smart shop near the embassies. Behind their walls could be heard the rhythmic hammering of metal, men beating shapes into silver and tooling patterns to form the base and sides of ceramic shard boxes.

"They're amazing," I said upon seeing the jewel colored porcelain boxes covering a corner of the room, each box shaped and sized to set off the broken pieces of what once was a magnificent vase.

"Made from broken treasures. Everyone's doing it now, but the Hus were first. That's why the government gave them this shop."

Old Mr. Hu wore a long blue coat with matching skull cap. His round shiny face spoke of "prosperity." The Hu brothers, on the other hand, looked like tall skinny scarecrows. Their Western suits were too tight to button and short in the sleeves, as if shrunk in the wash, their hair stood on end, and their whiskery chins wanted shaving. They were all very friendly and, like the old men in the markets, carried an air of crafty, innocent naiveté. I remembered my grandmother telling me, "It's no good getting old unless you get crafty." It was only now that I understood what she meant.

Glass cabinets hung on the walls of their shop, and glass case counters covered two sides of the bright room. My eyes caught what I wanted right away: antique hair ornaments made from semi-precious stones arranged like apple blossoms, pieces of jade, amber beads from Tibet, embossed silver lock charms made to protect their wearer from evil spirts or other misfortune, some engraved with Chinese symbols promising good luck, longevity, and high rank.

This being a government shop, prices were supposed to be fixed and paid for in FEC, but, by the look of the Hu brothers, I guessed there was some flexibility. No market tactics here, though; feigned interest and diversion to something else was the key—the more diversions, the better. I even bought an antique cloisonné pipe—I had no idea how it was smoked but thought Ed might like it—and some of the beautiful shard boxes. Numbers were written on pieces of paper, the buyer and seller taking a respectful time to review the other's offer before making a counter. The final price was never spoken. Old Mr. Hu handled the money, and the Hu brothers opened the doors for us as Old Mr. Hu bowed us out, and we left, treasures in hand. I couldn't wait to get back to the flat and enjoy experiencing again the pleasure these vibrant pieces of porcelain gave. I decided I would give them each names reflecting the story they told: Mother Riding Chi Lin with Precious Son, Court Ladies in the Palace Garden, Two Immortals on Mount Penglai, the Golden Dragon's Tail, Peasant Boy with Oxen in blue . . .

"Wonder where they get the shards from, Rebecca?"

Rebecca proceeded to tell me that, during the Cultural Revolution, Mao demanded a total break from the decadent past and ordered raids on temples and homes to destroy collections of porcelain and art. "At least, that's what Old Mr. Hu told me. He said some of these treasures came from the Imperial Palace, which I doubt, but they could be from private collections."

Giving a second life to these wonderful works of art was a comforting thought.

The street was wide, the trees on either side tall and stately even stripped of leaves. It was a glorious sunny winter day, and we walked slowly to Rebecca's car. A horse and cart came trotting toward us. How small Chinese horses are, I thought, then he stopped. The driver hit its skinny haunches, but the horse didn't budge. He got down from the cart and pulled on the reigns, and I saw the horse's legs slide open on either side. I saw his ribs, his spine, the sores on his shoulders, the dark terror in his eyes. His legs were splayed open. He couldn't move.

"Oh God, Rebecca," I said, bile filling my throat. "He's going to die, right there. He's going to die. What can I do?"

"Keep walking, honey," said Rebecca, her voice calm. "It's not the same with them, you know."

We drove back to the apartments in silence. I declined tea. I wanted to be alone. Ai-yi had left for the day, and I paced the apartment. I couldn't sit still. The look in that horse's eyes haunted me. He couldn't cry out his agony, his fear, like a dog or cat or human. He was alone in his terror. I ran to the bathroom and vomited, climbed into bed, and closed my eyes tight.

"Have a headache?" Ed asked. The room was dark.

"Yes," I lied. I watched him take off his jacket.

"Get you anything?" he asked.

"No, thanks. Ed, I saw a horse today. He was pulling a cart. It was too heavy, and he just stopped, and his legs splayed out. What do you think happened to him?"

Ed was hanging his tie in the closet.

"Need to find a tailor," he said. "Should've had more suits made in Hong Kong." He looked toward me. "Horses are like cabbages here," he said and left the room.

Somebody else had told me the same thing, "They treat people like animals and animals like vegetables," but I didn't want to hear it. I needed to forget the haunting terror in that horse's eyes.

Ed's amazing snore kept me awake. There was no escaping it; he made the bed vibrate with every exhale. Try as I might, I could still see that poor, terrified animal every time I closed my eyes. Then, out of nowhere, the memory of a huge black thoroughbred mare came to me. I saw her as if it were that day again, galloping down the hill toward me, her mane and tail streaming behind her, the Earth vibrating under my feet. I remembered my terror as I stood, frozen in place, as she slowed to a trot and stopped in front of me. I saw her blow through her wide wet nostrils and felt her graceful movement as she wrapped her magnificent head around my skinny shoulders and nibbled the back of my dress with her lips. I remembered the warmth of her body sticky against my face, the sweet scent of her, her gentleness, her power. I had felt my heart open that day and love flood inside me, filling me, fulfilling the unrealized dream of what it would be like when I finally met my family again. The dream that had comforted me through five years of war. I wept until I fell asleep.

CHAPTER 21

THE FORBIDDEN CITY

I still remember the imperial presence at the South Park,
Everything glowing with his splendor;
The Most Valued Concubine in the same carriage;
Bow-bearing maids of honor riding ahead on white horses golden bridled,
Suddenly leaning back in their saddles and shooting into the clouds,
A couple of flying birds falling,
The Lady laughing, her eyes sparking.
Where are they now?

From: *"Riverside Lament," Du Fu, 757

Just down the street from our apartment, the Forbidden City stood in fascinating magnificence while I impatiently waited for Ed to make time for a day out together. It was Sunday. The sun shone clear in a powder blue sky, a great day to be outside.

"Ed, how about the Forbidden City today?"

I heard his sigh before his "Okay."

Ed drove the jeep and sneaked in a parking space outside the Beijing Hotel. We'd done it before, and evidently the attendant decided to turn his head when the foreigners parked.

The air was crisp, and, for once, pollution didn't burn my throat. Ed bought a bag of roasted chestnuts that we shared, peeled skins placed back in the bag. Families passed us, children sitting on their father's shoulders, wearing bright clothes and eating treats . . . the treasured only child.

We had been there before, the four of us. That was the month Ed was offered the position. "See what your family think first," his boss had said. It was a very rushed trip. We managed a glimpse of the Great Wall, the Ming Tombs, and the Forbidden City. It was January, extremely cold, and of course Chris and Lisa found it all very exciting. It wasn't much warmer now.

Shadows of the outer wall angled their way along the pavement. Bricks painted a flat red stood where they had for over five hundred years. I read they were made of white lime and glutinous rice, the cement from glutinous rice and egg whites. A massive portrait of Mao dominated the wall, his round face smiling benignly like a happy buddha, the lucky mole on his chin prominent.

Ed bought our tickets, and over the high threshold we stepped into a dark room where sentries once stood, over flag stones, across a low white marble bridge carved in dragon shapes, up stone stairs, and through another set of gates into a huge expanse of a courtyard.

There were no trees, not a blade of grass, not a weed, just stark white paving stones, and everywhere red walls edged in ornate balustrades carved from white marble and bright yellow ceramic-tiled roofs that gleamed gold in the pale sunlight. A few Chinese visitors stood in the courtyard, but they did little to fill the space, which was designed, I read later, to accommodate ninety thousand people. The silence was tangible, as if the walls, buildings, the very ground, were holding their breath, waiting to come to life again. Like an abandoned movie set. It was a place of whispers.

With no guide or map, walking in a straight line seemed appropriate, so we headed for the first building, *Taihedian*, the Hall of Supreme Harmony, at least that's what our seven-hundred-page China Guidebook had told us. We had left it on the coffee table; it was too bulky to carry. We climbed stairs and entered the enormous room. Dust hung in the air. The only light preceded us through the door and tried to come in from a few opaque windows; the combined effect was like walking through a dry mist on a winter's day. Wooden columns, like leafless trees, reached up to the ceiling. Once covered in carpets, they were now bare. The throne stood on a podium, behind it a screen with imperial five-clawed dragons.

"Nine," I said to Ed. "There are nine dragons."

"Are you sure?" he teased.

Ignoring him, I looked around. The entire building was made from wood. Ceilings and pillars painted with dragons. I tried to imagine it a century ago. It would have been alive then, with color and people and music. Now it looked sad, neglected, not a bit like I'd imagined it to be. But then my expectations were based on the palaces of Europe.

It was almost as cold inside as out. "How do you think they heated this place?" I asked. The palaces and castles of Europe had enormous fireplaces in all the rooms.

"Maybe they used those hot water flasks," he joked.

I pinched his arm; he smiled down at me. And I wondered where this smile retreated to on those days Ed was his moody self, the Mr. Hyde of his current Dr. Jekyll. What was the secret switch that lightened his mood? Did he even know himself?

We walked through courtyards, past huge martial lions, climbed marble stairs, and entered rooms until my mind was numb from so much space, so many dragons, so much mystery.

Two and a half hours later we still hadn't seen it all. Ed reminded me there were over nine thousand rooms. My feet hurt; it was getting colder.

"Want to go back?" Ed asked, and, for once, I was willing to leave without completing a tour. It's just down the street, I thought. We'll be back again. And so it was. With every business associate of Ed's who came to town, every friend, we went to the Forbidden City. Often, I would take the wives of visiting VIPs while the men had their meetings. I never got used to my disappointment at not seeing candles and lamps lit, smelling incense, looking at furniture, porcelain, settings replicating how it once was in all its magnificent glory. And I never got to see it all.

We three on the Great Wall

The Ming Tombs

Chris Lisa and me climbing the Great Wall

CHAPTER 22

HARBIN ICE AND SNOW FESTIVAL

Fox-fur coats are not warm enough,
Brocade quilts are too thin.
The general cannot manage to flex his bow of inlaid horn;
The protector general wears his iron mail against the cold.
The desert is covered everywhere with hundreds of feet of ice,
And gloomy clouds hang dim and dark,
Solid for thousands of miles.

From: **"Song of White Snow," Cen Shen, c. 750

"Want to go to Harbin?" Ed asked over dinner. I'd fixed a rich red sauce for our pasta. Ed preferred to eat in now, and the ferocious gas burners didn't intimidate me quite so much, though I still managed to burn my share of meals.

"Where is it?"

"Up north, near the Russian border. Heavy industry area."

It didn't sound very appealing, freezing weather in a polluted city, until Ed told me there was an ice festival with competitions for ice sculptors from around the world. That's all the information he was given, an ice festival.

"It's a PR trip. Got conned into it," he told me.
"Sounds like fun."

When the time came, Ed had exhausted every possible means of getting out of it. He was an honored guest and couldn't refuse. He was not happy!

We climbed into a minibus with four tour guides and one driver. Ed's face had the stony look of someone ready to have all his teeth pulled with no anesthetic. He sat down heavily in the row across from me and lit a cigarette. I saw the quick look exchanged by our guides. It was polite to offer cigarettes here, and Ed was usually generous, but he put the pack deliberately back in his pocket. The disappointed guides lit up their foul-smelling Chinese brand. The van, its windows frozen shut, soon filled up with cigarette smoke, and I wished I had a cigar.

It was impossible to talk over the noise of the van, and I soon gave up trying. Even if Ed heard me, his expression told me he wouldn't listen, and I needed all my energy to stay warm. The van's heating system either wasn't working or couldn't keep out the cold. We sat bundled up, hats low, scarves high. My feet froze from the ice-cold floor. Windows iced up on the inside, and, every once in a while, I'd clear a space and peek out to see the same white expanse without definition or contrast. Every so often, the driver pulled over, and a cold burst of air entered the van as he left to scrap ice off the windshield. I folded my hands under my arms, but still my fingers burned with cold. After about four hours, the van came to a shuddery stop. We've arrived, I thought, with a sigh of relief.

"Lunch time," announced a guide. They'd given up talking to us after the first half hour. Either Ed's mood was catching or they didn't want to be on the trip either. Gray snow frozen solid greeted my rubber-soled boots. We were in a small town, its one-story buildings slapped together, pavements and roads the same height, the same color, the same texture. It reminded me of a ghost town we'd visited in Colorado on vacation. Yellow roads instead of gray, high blue skies replaced by low gray clouds, but it had the same empty feeling. The only traffic was a donkey, a rice sack thrown over its furry coat, slowly pulling a flat cart.

"Where is lunch, and where are we?" I asked Ed through stiff, frozen lips.

"Hell if I know."

"Little problem, sir," the chosen messenger said to Ed. "We have a small mechanical issue. Just five minutes."

Ed and I stood in the middle of the empty street, stamping our feet. Ed thumped his hands around his body, hands too cold to light a cigarette. There was no lunch, no toilets either, and no point in getting angry. We were all stuck, and to have a fit would cause us to lose face, and loss of face equaled loss of power.

Back in the van, we were given a red rose thermos of tea. The liquid was still piping hot.

"They do one thing right," Ed said as he handed me a cup. "They make a great thermos."

We bumped along icy roads until I turned numb.

"This is where we stay tonight," said our guide. We had pulled up at a low signless building, and I forced stiff limbs to follow him. "Food is served in this building," he said. "You sleep in that one. Good night." He indicated another building about forty feet away and hurriedly left us to it. Smart man.

Ed ground his jaw. "Nobody told me about this," he said. "We were supposed to go straight to Harbin."

The dining hall was empty, void of light, of color. Bare wooden tables formed straight lines, chairs on either side. An unpleasant, unrecognizable smell hung in the cold air. I heard footsteps, and a young girl came from the back and nervously pointed to a table.

"Let's eat," said Ed, and we sat down. There was no menu; hot tea, a large bottle of beer, cold pickled cabbage, and noodles in a broth were bought to us from another building containing the kitchen.

"This must be it," I said, almost relieved I didn't have to make a decision.

"It's cold," Ed said, beckoning to our waitress. She stood in front of him, hands clasped in front of her, dark eyes pleading with me from her round baby face.

"Ed, she's only a girl, Lisa's age. You're scaring her." I put my hand on his arm. "Please," I said.

"All right, Joan," he replied through clenched teeth.

We finished our cold noodles and crossed the freezing compound to the sleeping quarters. It wasn't much warmer inside. The same young girl was waiting for us and led us silently to our room where our bags had been placed. Two metal cots stood against the walls. No curtains hung on the high windows, no carpets on the brown asphalt-tiled floor. We had a bathroom, but our hot water came in a thermos. My teeth hurt when I brushed them. My fingers felt brittle enough to break.

"I've never been so cold, Ed."

He looked for a radiator and found a pipe going from ceiling to floor. "Stone cold," he said.

I pulled back the covers on the bed under the window. The linen looked as if it had been ironed, but huge black marks covered the pillowcase.

"They look like footprints," I said. "I can't sleep in this. Somebody's used it. Unless they climbed in through the window." I took a hasty glance at the narrow window above the bed. It was possible . . .

I brought the girl back to our room and showed her the filthy pillowcase. She looked quickly at me with her frightened eyes. I smiled and handed her the pillow; she brought back another only slightly cleaner.

"Ed, I'm so cold," I told him as he was climbing into his cot. I'd left my thermal underwear on under my PJs, and two pairs of socks covered my feet and a wool cap my head, but still my teeth chattered.

"Here," he said, placing his coat and mine on top of the covers.

"Thank you, sweetie," I said. A gush of warmth filled me, not from the covers but from the gesture.

Cold hard-boiled eggs and rice gruel were served as breakfast, then we were off. I looked at the buildings as we left, a single-story compound dropped in the middle of nowhere.

By the time we arrived at our destination, all I could think about was the journey back. Our guides began to do their job again, wiping windows with coat sleeves and showing us the sights. Huge black buildings with massif chimneys belching thick smoke into the dark sky stood all around us. How could they have any kind of festival in this place?

"This doesn't look like China, Ed."

"Take my word for it, it is."

This time our hotel was a modern concrete building with stained red carpets covering the floors and bright gold dragons painted on the walls. Central heating worked, and hot water flowed in the shower. I stood in the steamy tub, defrosting.

"I feel like I'm in a shabby version of Las Vegas," I whispered to Ed, who was way beyond being amused.

After a substantial meal and a few bottles of local beer, Ed was ready to see the festival. By this time, it was early evening. Colored electric lights lit our way to Zhaolin Park.

Artists were still chipping at their work. Families, round and padded in coats and hats, held on to one another as they walked the clear ice floors of palaces and bridges, past dragons and demons. I grabbed Ed's sleeve to keep from falling. My face tingled with the cold, and my nose froze. There was no wind, and, even though it must have been around minus-twenty degrees Celsius, I forgot the cold.

"It really is amazing," I said as we walked into a crystal palace. Colored lights shone on and through the ice, bringing out shapes that shined like precious jewels. Even the ice under our feet sparkled with lights buried within it. The smell of roasting chestnuts filled the air. Horse-pulled troikas waited for fares.

"Ed, let's go for a ride," I suggested, hand on the side of a troika. He reluctantly climbed into the seat next to me. He didn't like horses, and, no matter how much Lisa protested, his description of them as "big and stupid" held firm.

The driver cracked his whip, and we sailed over the frozen lake. Boys jumped on the back, yelling their joy at the free ride, their laughter joining the chiming of little bells. I snuggled tight into Ed, hummed "Laura's Tune" from *Doctor Zhivago*. His body was stiff, unyielding. He didn't smile.

"The only thing that spoils this is the thought of driving back," I told him casually as I pulled away.

"Don't worry," he said. "We'll do it my way this time."

Back at the hotel, Ed found our guides. "No stopping on the way back. I don't care what time we leave here, but no stopping."

They tried to explain that the stop was necessary due to slow traffic, the mechanical problem. It was unfortunate, unscheduled, and, yes, we go straight back. It took over thirteen hours of bone shaking, freezing discomfort.

"The things I do for this company," Ed said, kicking the bags into our apartment.

Warm air greeted us. Wanda and Dorothy swam in their blue-and-white bowl. The palms wore shiny green leaves. Not a speck of dust could be seen, and the only smell was of lavender furniture polish, the same brand my mother used.

I soaked in a hot bath while Ed heated canned tomato soup. We sat in our oversized royal-blue terrycloth robes around the white kitchen table, copper pots gleaming warm in the yellow light.

"This is the best part of the trip," I said.

"You're right. Remind me not to go on any more."

We laughed together for the first time in ages.

CHAPTER 23

MR. HUANG

Businessmen boast of their skill and cunning,
But in philosophy they are like little children.
Bragging to each other of successful depredations,
They neglect to consider the ultimate fate of the body.

From: "Businessmen," Chen Tzu-ang, c. 680 (translated: Arthur Waley)

"Joan, can you go shopping with me?" It was Monica. It must be something special, I thought. My two friends kept their sources secret from each other. "I'll drive," she added.

She started the car, and we slowly pulled away. "Let's go to see Mr. Huang. You haven't met him, have you?" Her blond hair swished over her shoulders as she looked at me. Her coat was navy-blue cashmere, fitted. There was a pale-blue silk scarf around her neck. She does look like a movie star, I observed.

"I need an interpreter," she said, and I was happy to show off. "But first I need to check something out. They swept the car yesterday, so we should be okay."

"What do you mean?" I asked, confused. I knew diplomatic cars were checked for listening devices, but that was the norm.

"I'm being followed." And, as if to emphasize the fact, Monica looked over both shoulders as she drove

"What? Why?"

Monica parked outside Ritan Park. We walked along the narrow lane surrounded by bare earth and skeletal trees. "Here," she said and sat on one of the wooden benches.

"What are we doing?" I asked.

"Wait, I'll show you." We sat there in the cold, stretching the bonds of friendship. I was about to stand up when Monica put her hand on my arm. "Don't look now," she whispered, "but there's a man over there pretending to read a paper."

Humoring my friend, I looked around casually, or so I thought, and saw a man dressed in a thick black overcoat wearing a scarf high around his neck sitting on a bench to the right of us.

"He looks Western." I told her.

"He is. CIA. They have listening devices." She picked at the seams on her leather gloves and stood up. "Let's walk." She put her arm in mine, and we slowly continued our walk along the path. Monica talked loudly about the rag dolls she wanted manufactured, how difficult it was to get into the factories, the import/export restrictions. She tried so hard to look unconcerned she looked guilty of something dark and sinister. It felt so melodramatic I had to hold back the urge to giggle.

"You're the only one I can tell," she said, touching my arm. "I had an affair with a secret agent in Russia," she confessed. "Fred was away. Mongolia." The significance of this escaped me, but then I wasn't a diplomat's wife, so I listened without comment.

"I've been followed ever since. I met him at a party. He just came after me. He was so handsome, so masculine, just gorgeous, and I got swept away. We met in his hotel room. It was so exciting. Now this." Her voice was clipped, as if time was limited and we were about to be arrested.

I quickly turned back to look at the man in the scarf. He was putting the paper in a rubbish bin.

"He looks Russian to me," I said.

She didn't hear me and continued with her worries. "I don't love Fred, you know. In fact, he repulses me, reminds me of his icky mother. But if he found out . . ." She shuddered. "His career."

We kept walking until she said, "There's another up ahead. Let's get back in the car." There was another man up ahead, dressed in an overcoat and hat. Her concerns were real; in fact, her anxiety was catching, and I found myself looking over my shoulders, the tiny hairs on my neck raised.

"I just had to tell someone," she said. "I thought I was going crazy, but you saw them too, didn't you?"

"Yes," I admitted. "I saw two Western men, but the Russians come here a lot, Monica. They're always in the restaurant."

"I know the signs," she said. "This man is close to the top. He's in on all the meetings."

She started the car and pulled away slowly.

"Let's go see Mr. Huang."

I wonder how the Russians had treated her. She had lived in Moscow while her husband traveled across the country, doing his "boring job," as she put it. And her son was away at school. "Ten years of solitary confinement," she'd said. Ed and I had visited Russia in the '70s. I remember it was a grim place, inhospitable even. We went with a select group to promote the birth of tourism, but KGB people followed us, and guards handed out hotel room keys on each floor. I could understand how living under that oppressive society for so long would make any hint of romance seem like a reprieve, a welcome change from loneliness and isolation, and how it could make someone paranoid.

"How can I help you, Monica?"

"You already have," she told me with her beautiful smile. That was the last time Monica mentioned her ex-lover or her fear of being followed.

Mr. Huang's business was in the dank cellar of his home. The walls and floor were damp, and the smell of rot filled the air, so I tried not to breathe. I heard a child's cough, a bronchial sound, deep and thick.

"He worked in the coal mines," Monica told me as we walked down the stairs. If she hadn't told me, I would have guessed. Mr. Huang's skin was embedded with coal dust that would never scrub away. His hands were calloused, and he leaned to one side due to a leg that had been crushed in the explosion that had left him unemployed. He was so thin a strong wind would have challenged his ability to stand. I suppose he couldn't be more than forty, but he looked ancient, as if the life had been sucked out of him. There was none of the cunning in him of our regulars, and I felt obliged to buy an ornately carved late Ching dynasty rosewood table that I didn't need and didn't really like.

"I really want chairs," I told him in Mandarin. "Captain hat chairs." He assured me he would be on the lookout. In the meantime, he would deliver the table.

Two days later, Ai-yi opened the door to Mr. Huang, who was bent double under the weight of the rosewood table on his back. Her face showed disapproval of this scruffy man making a delivery to *Furen's* penthouse apartment. Obviously, the elevator operators thought the same; they had made him walk up to the sixteenth floor and back down again.

He placed the unwanted table in the den, and I gave him the rest of his money enclosed in an envelope to disguise the exchange. I was paying him in *renminbi*.

About a week later, Monica called to say he had four chairs to match the table, would I like them? Four of anything was hard to come by, I'd found, and I agreed to see them.

Twice more Mr. Huang stopped by the apartment. The last time he brought another dining table and two captain hat chairs. They were rubbish wood and poorly carved, but he'd lugged them up the stairs to the sixteenth floor on his back, two trips. The elevator operators still wouldn't let him ride—I couldn't have him carry them back down.

Ai-yi showed her displeasure by making him leave the furniture in the hall. As she closed the door, I saw her lean forward and talk to him. I don't know what she said, but he never came back.

By now I had collected two horseshoe-back chairs, as well as the six from Mr. Huang, and two long narrow altar tables. These were of fine hard wood and bought through government-sponsored shops.

"What the hell are these for?" Ed asked when the last lot of chairs was delivered. "You can't sit on them." It was true; they were all uncomfortable. Designed to be used with footstools, they were too high even for him. But beautiful they were, no doubt about that.

"I keep looking for the perfect chair," I told him, "The one that got away."

"Okay, Joan," he said. "Got to hand it to you, though, it looks better in here." Ed liked watching me fuss around the place, moving a vase from one spot to the next, standing back to see the effect. "It doesn't take much, does it?" he'd say, meaning how these senseless activities pleased me.

"Have to give up soon," I said. "Running out of space."

"Knowing you, you'll find room," he said with a smile.

CHAPTER 24

THE HUNDRED-DOLLAR SUITS

Kind sir, I urge you not to cherish a gown with golden threads;
I urge you instead to cherish in full these youthful days of yours.
When flowers bloom you should break them off
Break them off when you can;
Don't wait till the flowers have gone
To break off a branch in vain.

From: **"A Gown with Golden Threads,"
Du Qiuniang, c. 825, female poet

"Found you a tailor. Rebecca's used him," I announced to Ed on the phone. "We can shop for fabric if you like."

"Great. See you at the Friendship Store after work?"

"Yep, I need a walk."

We met on the second floor of the huge department store, where bolts of wool were piled high on tables and shelves. Fiber content was woven in the edges, ready for export. Strict quotas controlled the market, and some of the fabric had been waiting a long time.

"Cashmere wool blend is nice, Ed, though it doesn't wear well."

"What the hell? At these prices, I can't go wrong."

We bought enough for two suits.

The tailor came to our apartment for fittings in the evenings, after Ai-ye had left for the day. I watched him measure Ed, mark the fabric with French chalk, and pin here and there, pulling the fabric into place.

"Knows what he's doing, I think," I responded to Ed's question. The second fitting needed closer supervision.

"Sleeves too short," I told him. "Trousers too. Must leave enough length to break at the ankle." Tailoring required a new set of language skills from me, and, though he nodded and smiled his understanding, I wished Ai-ye were there.

That was the first of Ed's "hundred-dollar suits."

"Hell, not bad for a hundred bucks," he said when he tried on the finished product. He stood in front of the full-length mirror in the bedroom and looked at the suit from every angle.

"Jacket could be a bit longer," I told him, warming up to all the other things that were wrong with the awful saggy suit.

"What do you mean? It's fine, just needs pressing."

I opened the jacket buttons and pulled on the hem. It was too short. In fact, the pants were still too short too. And something was funny about the shoulders.

"Feels good on, great fabric," he said, preening. I thought of the fable "The Emperor's New Clothes" and bit my lip to hold back giggles. Ed had a great sense of humor, but laughing at himself wasn't something he could do. I'd have to find another way to keep him from wearing that suit.

"It creases too much," he said after wearing it once. I hid it in the back of the closet.

He was on his fifth suit. "What's wrong with this one?"

"Not bad." It was the best of the lot, a beautiful gray wool with blue pinstripes that complimented his olive skin and silver sideburns. I buttoned it up, smoothed the labels with my palms, and felt his muscular chest and the warmth of his body through the fine wool.

"This one might work," I said. "I think it's just the lining. There's that man Pearl mentioned ages ago, the one without papers. I think I can find him."

"Okay. Worth a try," he said. And I wrapped up the suit for the next day.

Early that afternoon, I walked along the same pockmarked alley behind the market that had seemed so empty to me a few months ago. This time, I was on the narrow packed-earth pavement hoping I wouldn't fall down to the road two feet below. I kept my gaze forward, resisting the temptation to peek inside the occasional tiny windows set haphazardly in plaster walls. I wanted the house with the green door. Tree roots pushed the earth up, making the narrow space even harder to negotiate, and the rotting trunk of a large tree seemed to break between the walls of the space with the green door. Two crooked steps led up to the threshold. I knocked softly, and the door was opened by a young woman, her high cheekbones accentuating wide eyes.

This wasn't my first experience with a private home, but I stood back, not sure if I should enter, could enter. It was so dark inside. A huge black potbellied stove stood cold next to the door. Two cutting tables piled with fabric were alongside two walls and a single bed against another, on which sat the tailor in a shabby black suit, blanket pulled up across his lap. A young man stood at an ironing board pressing a garment with a wet cloth. I heard the iron spit when it touched the damp, smelled the singeing cloth and, to my horror, something else coming from the man on the bed. I held my breath, turned my head, and hurriedly placed the suit jacket on the table, then, like everyone else in the room, I pretended not to notice what was going on.

My nameless tailor was young, tall, and painfully thin. His nails were long and his hands unwashed. I wanted to leave, run from the clutter and smells and poverty. Too many memories tried to surface at once. I shook them away and turned my attention to the tailor. I had come to him, and this was his home. So, I showed him what I wanted, and he drew a sketch for my approval. He spoke a dialect I didn't understand, so we nodded our agreement. As I left, I saw his battered treadle sewing machine.

Once outside, I breathed in the air. Shivers ran over my body, and I swallowed hard on the lump in my throat. I'd have to go back there and pick up the jacket in two days' time. I braced myself for that day.

I didn't tell Ai-yi where I had gone, Shan Shan either; they wouldn't approve. Besides, the poor man would get in trouble if he was found out, maybe separated from his family. Since they were from another province, they didn't qualify for local benefits and consequentially relied on his work as a tailor to survive.

Two days later, I knocked again on the green door and entered the tiny, crowded space. The jacket was ready, the workmanship so fine. Barely visible handmade stitches held the lining right where it should be. I smiled my approval and paid his fee, one dollar in *renminbi* and a little extra.

"Found your Shanghai tailor," I told Ed when he came in from work. "Need to get this drycleaned before you try it on. Don't ask me why." I smiled and raised my eyebrows.

"That's right," Ed said when I told him about the tailor's lack of travel permits. "I have to get permits every time an employee wants to travel."

"What about emergencies?"

"Makes no difference if you're dying," he said. "Can't move without papers. That's the way it is."

"Tell me more," I prompted.

"What do you want to know?" I didn't have just one question. I didn't know what I wanted exactly, and, in that pause, Ed picked up his drink and returned to his book. I went to the bathroom and soaked in a hot bath smelling of disinfectant and roses.

CHAPTER 25

TIBET

The high tower is a hundred feet tall,
From here one's hand could pluck the stars.
I do not dare to speak in a loud voice,
I fear to disturb the people in heaven.

From: **"Staying the Night at a Mountain Temple," Li Bai, c. 740

"Hey, Joan, planned that trip yet?" It was Ken on the phone with a reminder of my casually mentioned desire to see Tibet. His call, and the thought of seeing Tibet, came as a welcome break to the monotonous winter. He could make the plans, he told me, under Ed's name. "We can get permits easy that way," he said. I had yet to mention the trip to Ed, so planning was required.

I went to the Friendship Store looking for books on the mysterious country I'd always wanted to visit. While there were a few on the various provinces, the only reference to Tibet was a short section in a book covering China's Northeast, added as a sort of afterthought. While disappointed, I hurried home to read about this amazing place high in the Himalayans and drool over the spectacular photos.

With Ed's reluctance to travel, I would have to set the scene, so that evening I used up the last of the Italian sausages and slow cooked a red pasta sauce. The apartment soon filled with the smells of comfort food and sunny climes.

"Smells great," Ed said, heading for the pot and a spoonful of sauce. Cooking pasta sauce was one of the competitive games we played, with Ed insisting his was better than mine and the children playing along with the popular vote of the day.

We sat in the cozy kitchen, copper pots gleaming, chasing away the gloom outside the windows. And, with a bottle of wine and our abundant meal, I watched Ed finish two huge bowls of pasta and devour all three sausages.

"Great meal," he said, pushing away from the table and leaning back in his chair. I took a chance that my timing was right.

"Ed, I'd love to go to Tibet. Ken said he and Olivia would join us. What do you think?" He didn't answer. "I'd really like to go," I added.

"Why should I want to go there?" he asked. This was the question I had read up for, and I told him of the marvels of the Potala Palace and the beautiful countryside high in the mountains.

"Besides," I said when he still didn't answer, "you deserve a break. It'll be fun."

"You go."

"It won't be the same without you," I told him. "Just think about it, there's no rush." Leave it open, I thought, let it grow on him.

"Think I need reinforcements," I told Ken when he called again. "You know how Ed hates to travel."

Between the two of us and Ken's traveling companion, Olivia, Ed ran out of excuses. He liked Olivia, as did I; our English backgrounds gave us a lot in common. Olivia worked as an interpreter for an international company and had lived in Beijing for years, and, while her work schedule kept her busy, we made time for the occasional cuppa. A phone call was in order, a united front was required, and Olivia and I agreed to meet for lunch at the excellent Chinese restaurant in the CITIC building to go over the plans. Ed liked the food there.

"I had it typed, Ed. It just covers Lhasa," Olivia said, handing him two sheets of paper.

"I'll have my friends at CITS take care of it," he said, folding the pages in half. "They owe me some favors." As easy as that, I thought.

"Are you happy now?" Ed asked me as we walked to the jeep.

"Thanks, Ed. It'll be great." I put my arm through his.

Travel permits and airplane tickets and the necessary permissions took several weeks to process, and, during that time, I packed and re-packed for a week away without laundry facilities.

"Take only what you can carry," Ed had warned. Seeing as I weighed less than the clothing I needed, I pared it down to the basics and decided we'd take one suitcase that Ed could carry. Shoes, it always boiled down to shoes. Ed's size thirteen took up so much room! I sat on the lid trying to get the locks to touch.

"Tai Tai," said Ai-yi, gently waving me away. She knelt on the floor, took every item out of the beaten-up case, and slowly, methodically packed it again. My mother could do that, pack the most impossible amounts of stuff neatly into a small space. I just didn't have the patience.

"Come every other day, just to feed the fish," I told Ai-yi when we left the apartment.

"Tai Tai, *meiguanxi*," she told me, don't worry.

The four of us sat swaddled in down-filled coats and cashmere scarves in the enormous barren waiting room at the domestic terminal. Olivia sat serenely, gloved hands in her lap, as if she were in a first-class lounge.

I looked around for gates. There were none. All planes were boarded on the runways—and, from the sounds of the echoing overlapping announcements, more than one at a time. The crowds and noises reminded me of London railway stations during summer holidays: frazzled people, ragged announcements.

Blackboards listing flights in English and Chinese hung in one corner of the room. Most of the departure times were blank. Our fellow passengers came prepared for a long wait with hot thermos bottles at the ready. We were expecting our usual on-time departure and watched as people first nibbled on snacks then their lunch. Ed's cigarette stubs joined the peanut shells left by our neighbors on the dirty floor. We waited two hours before our flight was called, and all that time I waited for Ed to change his mind.

"Stay close," Ken told us as we walked down the stairs and onto the runways. A half dozen planes were parked like busses in a bus station, and passengers scurried to the one they hoped was theirs, looking at numbers painted on airplane tails.

Passengers pushed their way up the steps behind us and into the cabin. They crammed plastic bags under seats and into already packed overhead compartments. Seats weren't assigned except for the first two rows, where seat backs were covered with lace doilies.

"No first class, eh?" Ed said. "Except for cadres."

Most of the seat backs were folded against the seats. I thought they were all broken until Ed pulled one into place. The seat's metal braces poked at me through thin padding.

"I can't fasten my seat belt," I told Ed, who was squashed in beside me. He tried to shorten it and gave up.

"Hell, if this goes down, you won't need a belt."

When the engine revved up, I understood what he meant. The plane rattled. I could see the overhead bins shake. I held my hands over my ears, hoping to drown out the ear-piercing noise from the propeller-driven engines.

"Hey, Ed," Ken said from the row behind us, "think they have any FAA agents on board?"

Once airborne, the penetrating noise turned into a loud, vibrating drone. Stewardesses paraded the aisles as if modeling their uniforms and handed out canned sodas and white-boxed lunches tied in string that they threw onto open trays or laps.

"Chinese princesses," Ed said, pointing with his thumb.

I opened the box looking for something edible and found a shriveled chicken drumstick, a white roll, and something else wrapped in clear plastic. I drank the soda.

"Do you want this?" I asked Ed. "Looks good."

"That's all right, Joan, got plenty here." We both shoved the boxed food into the seat pockets.

"I need the loo, Ed." He stood up to let me pass, and I bounced along the aisle toward the back. The door of the lavatory flapped open and closed, and I pushed inside the small space. I don't know if it was the foul smell or the huge painted footprints on the wet floor showing which way to stand, but I did an about turn and walked back. The crowded plane was thick with smoke, and everything seemed to be moving. I grabbed the back of a seat and felt it move forward onto its passenger.

"*Duibuqi*," I said, apologizing, trying to smile. We four were the only foreigners on the flight, the only people dressed in winter clothes. Announcements were made in Chinese only, and the plane was falling apart.

"Find it?" Ed asked.

"It's nasty back there. I'll wait." It couldn't be that much longer before we changed flights, I reasoned to myself. The plane rattled on. My seat shook. One of the overhead bins opened; bags spilled out. I held the armrests tight. We shouldn't travel together, I thought. What if anything happens? What about the children?

"Ed, how safe is air travel here?"

"Too late to think of that now. Just remember the pilot wants to live as much as you do."

"Thanks," I said, patting his arm.

As the plane landed, the back of my seat folded forward as it tried to crush me. Passengers eager to disembark stood up while we taxied, getting their bundles and bags together, falling into one another. They all carried their little white-boxed lunches with them, strings still in place. I hid mine deeper in the seat pocket.

We waited for the plane to empty before we climbed down the shaky steps onto the runway. The air was clean, and I took in a deep breath. Olivia walked up beside me and put her arm in mine.

"Good to get some air," she said. "I'm so glad Ken doesn't smoke."

"Yes. Wish Ed didn't," I told her. We had placed bets that Ed, because of his smoking, would peter out first in the high altitude of Lhasa.

"Makes my lungs strong," he had bragged while we all jeered.

"One down, one to go," Ken announced as we walked toward our next plane. It was very small. A man in mechanics overalls walked from underneath it, pushing a wheelbarrow that held an airplane tire, its core showing.

"Look at the threads on that," Ken said, pointing to the tire.

"Be thankful we have one good one," Ed said.

Apart from us, there were only two other passengers. Officials by the way they dressed. We sat across from each other on the plane, our backs against the windows like paratroopers ready for a drop. The stewardess gave us each a cedar wood fan in a little box.

"New Chinese air conditioning," said Ken, flicking his fan open. But it was winter!

I stood on the steps leading from the plane and blinked in the piercingly bright light. I breathed in pure, crisp air. The golden earth undulated around me, draping itself over mountain peaks decorated with colored prayer flags dancing in the wind. I felt I could touch the bright blue sky.

"I've never seen such a clear sky," I said to anyone who would listen.

Two Chinese guides, one male, one female, waited for us and exchanged formal greetings in perfect English. Very politely, we were told not to go out without the car and driver, or them, for our own protection. We might get lost. We might get ill. We might fall off the mountain???

A minibus waited, and in we climbed. We were staying at the Holiday Inn in Lhasa, and, even though I knew the Holiday Inn Lido in Beijing was smart, in this mystical place I would have preferred a name that didn't conjure up Route 66.

The bus bounced along unpaved roads past cairns, stones piled high by pilgrims, and ropes of colored prayer flags sending their messages of hope up to the heavens.

"No photographs please," announced the chief guide to Ken, who had his camera at the ready. If she hadn't said anything, I might not have noticed the guns aimed at the monastery. As it was, my attention riveted to scars on the earth-colored building crumbling in the intense light and the machine guns anchored to the ground around it. I looked at Ed; he shrugged.

Our hotel was a one-story building placed on the side of a barren hill. It reminded me of a prefabricated building, like the ones built to house victims of bombings after the war, temporary, shoddy. Ceilings hung low over filthy carpets, and the floor-to-ceiling glass windows in our room looked like a car windshield after days of traveling through swamp and desert. Twin beds, a nightstand between them, a low table, and two folding chairs furnished the room. Bedcovers lay crumpled over sagging beds, and two oxygen cylinders and a thermos of tea replaced the fruit and wine that usually greeted us.

"Rest today," our guide said. "Climatize first." They would be back in the morning.

Ed unlocked our case and started to unpack. "Don't know where you want these," he said, putting my sweaters on a bed.

"Anywhere," I told him. My body felt heavy like it does when climbing out of a swimming pool after a long swim, and I was too tired to move, to speak.

Ken came knocking at our door, bottles of beer in hand. "My bed collapsed," he said, "put my back out again." He limped over to the other chair and eased his tall frame down.

The room turned black. A dull knife stabbed viciously into my head, nausea overwhelmed me, and I ran into the bathroom and threw up.

"What's that about cigarettes?" Ed asked, inhaling.

I was beyond caring about a stupid bet, and Ken refused to pay attention.

"It's the altitude, Joan," he told me. "Use the oxygen."

A flexible plastic tube was wound around the gauge of the tank. I wondered how many nostrils it had entered. As repulsive as the idea seemed, I put the tube into my nose, held the other nostril closed, and inhaled. That, combined with a cup of hot herbal tea, was the means by which I got through the excruciating migraines that ended each amazing day.

Our guides were waiting in the lobby to take us on tour. We didn't go far and soon stopped at the square in front of a temple known as the holiest place in Lhasa, the Jokhang Temple. Here we could go alone if we wanted, which we did.

We climbed out of the bus, Ken and Ed with cameras hanging around their necks, standing out in the crowd of scarecrow men and hollow-faced women dressed in long dark coats, "chubas," the women's costumes highlighted here and there with exquisite embroidery and turquoise jewelry. Hands reached up around us; open palms displayed pieces of turquoise, silver prayer boxes, nothing at all. Olivia shoved her hands deep in her pockets and climbed back into the bus. Eager faces looked at me. Hands touched my shoulders, my sleeves. Gentle, welcoming touches, soft words uttered from lined faces, tired eyes shining with warmth. Women with babies tied to their backs walked toward me, turned to show me their beautiful children.

I read the Tibetan people bathe three times in their lives, at birth, marriage, and death, but, while their clothes were stained and worn, they didn't smell of poverty. They had no odor at all. I was completely surrounded, no idea how to get free, and for a moment thought of joining Olivia, then our guide walked in front of me, uttering harsh words, dispersing the crowd, who quietly moved away.

Pilgrims walked the square with beggars. The women's hair, smooth and shiny with yak butter, hung behind them in thin, unraveling braids. Their bony hands rotated prayer wheels as they hummed sacred mantras while they shuffled along, shadows of one another. This was their journey of a lifetime, taking them months to reach this sacred place by foot or, I noticed, prostration. Some led white sheep with red dots painted on their tight, matted curls, sacred sheep brought along for blessings.

Flat carts selling potatoes, radishes, turnips, scarves, and pieces of jewelry lined the parameters of the square, and in an open space a crowd of men hovered around a young girl. Her skin was satin smooth, her body frail. Chunks of turquoise and amber and coral were braided into her hair. H, her many layered embroidered skirts touched her ankles. Don't sell your jewelry, I thought. I'd noticed some pieces on the carts, the centuries-old heirlooms now just baubles.

People threw money on the scarf at the girl's feet. The crowd made space for us, but a feeling of dread came over me.

"Ed, I'm going to see if Olivia's okay," I told him. He followed me. Only Ken stayed.

"I don't like crowds, and they're so dirty," Olivia said.

"Walk with us," I told her.

"Come on, Olivia," Ed said. "You can't sit here all day."

Ken came toward us, his face white.

"You know what that girl did?" he asked. "She cut through her arm. She held a dagger and shoved it through her arm, then picked up the money."

"God," I said, and a shudder rushed over me. How desperate she must be. What will she need to do next? Why did nobody stop her?

We walked into the temple courtyard and joined pilgrims traveling a path followed with devotion for a thousand years. Potatoes and radishes, barley and yak butter were placed on ledges in the courtyard, offerings from the faithful of food they couldn't really spare. Stone pots crammed with incense sticks sent straight spirals of vapor into the sky; their fragrance filled the air. Crimson-robed monks, linked together by a continuous cord, sat cross-legged in prayer, chanting mantras, ringing bells. This was a sacred place, not a tourist destination. I quietly put my camera away.

"*Tashi delek*," a woman whispered to me. I looked at her face etched in lines of worry and as bronzed as the earth around us. She smiled, showing her few blackened teeth. "*Tashi delek*," said another, touching the sleeve of my coat. Others joined in and brushed their hands along my sleeves. They crowded around me. Not Ed or Ken or Olivia. I felt trapped, uneasy. I looked at Olivia. "What are they saying?" I asked.

"Probably 'hello.'"

I returned their smiles and repeated their words, and they allowed me to look into their eyes. And I saw women I had thought old were probably years younger than I.

We followed pilgrims into each room. Smoldering candles barely lit our way. Ceilings disappeared. Gold-draped Buddhas, sleeping, standing, sitting, some covered in jewels, appeared to hover on the thick air around us. Vibrant murals hid on walls, their intensity dulled by centuries of smoke. I walked slowly, and, without a mantra of my own, listened to the murmurs reverently repeated around me like the hum of a thousand bees. I felt the stone floor beneath my feet, smooth and concave in places from the millions who had walked before me. I felt dizzy from the altitude and the sweet, heady smell of incense.

The others waited for me outside in the stinging light.

"Thought we'd lost you," Ed said.

I watched the pilgrims walk past. They no longer looked tired and downtrodden. Hope glowed in their eyes and softened the lines around their mouths.

"This is a magical place," I told Ed. "Let's bring the children here."

He didn't respond, which meant "count me out."

We walked back toward the square. Adobe-type buildings, the color of earth, with tiny windows and thick walls, enclosed it on three sides. Alleys poked at its center like spokes on a wheel, and down some of the alleys the carts continued, displaying carpets and jewelry from Nepal.

"Ed, Rebecca wants me to find her a carpet with frog feet on it," I said, turning down an alley. "She said I'll know what she means when I see it."

"We're not supposed to be here, Joan," Ed admonished, looking around for the guides. I followed his gaze and saw Chinese soldiers in crumpled uniforms trying to blend into the shadows. They didn't want to be seen, and I obliged by ignoring them. Alongside a crumbling wall, I found what I was looking for, carpets hanging like washing on a line.

Ken and Olivia followed us, collars up, hands in pockets.

"This must be it," I said pointing to a small peach-colored prayer rug with deep blue patterns in either corner shaped like the bony toes of a frog or an x-ray of an outstretched hand. I walked over to the rug and looked at the backing. The wool was thick and died with berries and herbs, the colors dulled by a layer of yak butter and smoke. I looked at the vendor. He was Chinese, not Tibetan. I still wanted the rug, for myself now, not for Rebecca. Maybe I could find another for her.

"Keep it if you want it," said Ed. "I'll be over there." He walked toward Ken and Olivia and left me to bargain. I had no idea what the rug was worth but went on the premise I could get at least fifty percent off, more if I bought the saddle rugs alongside it.

"How are you going to get those back?" Ed asked, looking at the two bundles tied in string.

"Can't they go as baggage?"

He sighed and grabbed the saddle rugs while I picked up the prayer rug.

"Thank you, sweetie," I said, smiling at him.

I bought some of the silver tooled prayer boxes, those with turquoise and coral imbedded in the metal, and turquoise, coral, and honey-amber beads. Tibetan men worked the jewelry stalls, and, when I turned away with my purchases, women came up to me with treasures in hand. The look on their faces urged me to buy. I hadn't come prepared to buy anything except Rebecca's carpet. But then I had no idea there would be so much beauty waiting for a second chance, and there was no way I could refuse their earnest gestures. Ed obligingly emptied his pockets, and sales were made. No bargaining this time.

On the way back to the bus, I heard people whisper unintelligible sounds as we passed. They didn't look at us as they spoke.

"What are they saying?" I asked.

"They want a picture of the Dalai Lama," Ken said.

"Too late to worry about that now," said Ed when I told him. I remembered a holy picture of Jesus dressed in white sitting on a golden throne in a blue sky. Angels flew around Him; children reached up to Him. The nun told me the gold writing said, "Suffer little children to come unto me." It was so peaceful to look at, so beautiful, so comforting.

Virtual prisoners of our hotel, Ken and Olivia came to our room, bottles of beer and boiled peanuts in hand. The smell of yak butter oozed from the rugs, and the thought of eating anything churned my stomach. I sat on the bed breathing oxygen through the tube and was relieved when they all left for dinner in the coffee shop and I could lie down in the dark.

"Get you anything?" It was Ed, standing beside me as he turned on the bedside lamp. "You have to eat something." I settled for a granola bar and hot tea. Ed turned out the light, and we sat by the window watching stars sparkle in the abundantly clear night sky.

"Remember the planetarium?" I asked.

"God, that was a long time ago," he answered.

Our son was a baby then, and Ed earned extra money by reading the shows at the planetarium. Sometimes Chris and I would sit under the huge banyan tree where doves and pigeons hunted; sometimes we went inside to listen to Ed's deep, rich voice. Either way, it was a day together. I turned my head to look at him. His cigarette glowed red in the dark as he inhaled, but I couldn't see his face.

Our destination was the Potala Palace. Olivia and I sat together on the bus while Ken and Ed each had a row to themselves.

Olivia took out her compact and patted her nose. "You look ready for a day at the office," I told her. "How do you do it?" She confessed that she brought her electric curlers with her, but that only accounted for her neat black hair. Her silver-gray down-filled coat, her black scarf, and her leather boots spoke city. By contrast, my yellow coat was getting grubby, and my red hair blew around my head in wild abandon, along with my long beige scarf. Maybe that's why people touched me and not Olivia, I thought. I remind them of the Earth.

"For pictures," our guide told us as the driver parked beside a lake.

I squinted against the glare and looked in amazement at the whitewashed palace layering the hills until it stopped, its roof golden against the blue sky. The reflection of it all looked up at us from the still waters of the pristine lake, glorious, like a double rainbow. Prayer flags, shredded by the dry wind, flapped around us.

"Takes my breath away," I sighed.

We climbed back in the bus and were deposited at the foot of stone steps that led up to the palace. They appeared to go on forever. After a very brief introduction, namely the number of rooms in the White Palace, "over one thousand," we were assured, our guides returned to the bus, leaving us to explore on our own. Ed led the way, and we started our slow climb up the uneven steps. Monks passed us, dressed in their scarlet robes and carrying clay bricks on their backs. Others knelt on the steps, replacing worn with new. Silent and mangy earth-colored dogs slinked around alleys leading off the main steps. They looked both hostile and scared at the same time.

"Former monks," joked Ken.

We came to a flat place, like a landing, and I walked over to the low wall to look down. It was as if the world spread beneath my feet, silent and still. I picked up a small stone from the earthen floor and rolled it in my hand, feeling the warmth of the earth and sun. I closed my hand over its smooth surface and my eyes against the glare of a cloudless sky. Air sang in my ears, as it does when soaring in a glider, and embraced my face. I slipped the stone in my pocket, a special stone to keep by my bed.

The Potala Palace is actually two buildings joined together, the White Palace and the Red Palace. Our guide had no idea how many rooms were in the Red Palace—not that we needed more rooms to explore, there were more than enough to keep us busy, and there were no restrictions; we could go anywhere. We soon found that most of the rooms were empty, abandoned, lonely spaces void of the thousands of monks who had lived there before the Dalai Lama was forced into exile.

There were no maps, no floor plans, no signs, and rooms opened up in unexpected ways: to other rooms, to dark, winding passages leading to other rooms, to open rooftops connected to other buildings. In fact, the Potala Palace is so complex I felt I could get lost inside and never find a way out.

A bell rang, then another, and I followed the others and the sound to a room where monks sat in prayer. Lines of them faced each other but not in any pattern I could determine. Ed and I stood together behind the seated saffron- and red-robed men, their shaved heads bent over holy scrolls, prayer rugs touching. Incense smoldered, candles flickered, and the hypnotic tone of the monks became all there was as I forgot that I was a foreigner in a strange land. I breathed in the warm, scented air. A flash of light, the click of a camera. I looked up to see Ken, smiling at us. The magic was broken.

"Let's go, Ed," I whispered. I walked toward the door.

"You are naughty, Ken," I said.

"You'll forgive me after you see the shot," he smiled. He was right.

We climbed higher and entered empty rooms with doors and shutters open, their floors made of wide wooden boards, their walls and pillars painted with sacred images the color of earth and sky. Brass gongs gleamed like beacons in the sun, waiting to call monks to prayer. I squinted at the bright light, hearing again Ed's greeting as he came home from work, "Hi there, light of my life." I tried to remember when I last heard those words.

Ragged barefoot men carrying huge clay pots of water strapped to their foreheads and backs climbed along narrow trails and onto the steps, and a few monks passed us, prayer beads rolling between their fingers, but the thousands of monks who had inhabited this heavenly place were gone, leaving behind a sense of longing I could almost touch.

There were no entry fees, no collection boxes. I looked at the paint, fading, peeling off clay and wood, the loose stones scattering the steps. I felt the unrelenting light trying to pierce through my sunglasses, the dry wind on my face, and wondered how long this massive complex could stand without perpetual care.

Once back in our room, I started to pack for the early-morning flight.

"Ed, what do you think will happen to these people?"

"Beats me." He opened a bottle of beer.

"Can't something be done?"

"Nobody cares," he replied. "They don't want to piss off the Chinese."

I unwrapped the pieces of jewelry I'd bought from their dirty newspaper and picked one up, the one with pieces of deep red glass in its corners imitating rubies. I could see the tool marks of craftsmen who had hammered the metal into shape, feel the warmth of the copper backs worn smooth from wear. I felt the whirls of silver threads holding the gems. I picked up a chunk of turquoise with a hole in its center where a young woman's hair had been threaded. I turned the bead in my hand, its craggy surface smooth under my fingers.

"Should I have bought these?" I asked.

"Why not? If you didn't, somebody else would."

He was right, I supposed, and I rewrapped them and laid the packages in my hand carry.

I dreamt I was running on leaden legs toward broken buildings, open to the wind and rain. I knocked on a door and saw my mother walk toward it, only to turn back again without seeing me, without recognizing me, hearing me cry.

Ed opened the door to the apartment, and we took off our shoes and put on the slippers Ai-yi always left in place for us.

"I need a shower," Ed announced, carrying the bags into our bedroom. I looked around the apartment. Dorothy and Wanda swam happily in their porcelain bowl. Light entered the room in shafts through net curtains. The palms thrived. I looked at the small brass carriage clock shinning in the bookcase: 3:30 on a Saturday afternoon. It was the same time all over China. All time zones were overridden by Beijing time. What time was it in Lhasa? I wondered Did they have clocks? I hadn't seen any outside our hotel. I heard the shower running, a hollow, empty sound.

Sharing knowledge

Looking for treasure

Reflections

Sharing a moment

A holy place

Apprentice monks

Looking for frogs feet

How many steps?

CHAPTER 26

MANAGER CHANG

A man should attain high rank
In the prime of life.
Honor tis to be won on the battlefield;
So why should I stay at home?
Comes a call to the colors,
Which brooks no delay.

From: *"Later March Beyond the Frontier," Du Fu, 755

We'd been back four days, and all I did was sit around the apartment trying to remember all the things I'd seen in so short a time, wondering if I would ever go back to Tibet.

"What's up?" Ed asked the second night I cooked cheese omelet for dinner.

"Just tired."

"It's the climate change. Just take it easy, you'll be okay."

I don't know how long I would have stayed in that space if Rebecca hadn't called.

"When did you get back?" she asked.

"Come over for tea?" I offered.

"Did you have a good time?" Rebecca asked, moving the leaves to the side of her cup with its lid and sipping the tea Ai-yi had made for us.

"You'll think I'm nutty, but I don't really know. I can't distance myself," I told her. "It was so very different. Unforgettable."

"You've fallen under Tibet's spell," she told me. "It happens sometimes."

It was easy to talk to Rebecca, and I showed her the things we'd brought back.

"I just have to keep this little carpet," I told her, guilt pinking my cheeks. "I couldn't find another. So sorry." She patted my hand and smiled.

I unwrapped the beads and silver boxes. Lying on the glass dining table, they looked shabby, and their crude leather cords made them appear discarded.

"Know someone who might help you. Doesn't speak English, though," Rebecca said when I told her how much I'd like to see them restored. His name was Manager Chang, a silversmith working on the other side of town. Rebecca had met him at the embassy when he gave a talk on amber and how it had been used to decorate those long silk jackets worn by wealthy men since the Han dynasty.

After Rebecca left, I called Shan Shan and arranged for her to stop by the next day. I discarded the crumpled newspaper and rewrapped the jewelry in soft paper towels, smiling at the thought of Ai-yi's response to the extravagant use of her precious towels.

Manager Chang turned out to be a very handsome Chinese man probably in his late thirties, early forties. He was wearing a well-cut Western suit, jacket open to show a white shirt and dark blue tie. He operated out of two rooms, a showroom in the front where his work was displayed and a room at the back where six men sat at tables, soldering guns in hand.

I brought some of the chains from the flea markets with me, and, with Shan Shan acting as interpreter, we agreed which pieces could be restored and which replicated and how the beads would be used. Manager Chang made suggestions and pulled out a box of loose amber and turquoise to supplement mine. He let me choose. I noticed his hands, smooth skinned, unscarred, his face unlined, his eyes warm and direct.

"Turquoise and amber are sold by weight," Shan Shan translated.

Relieved of my burden, we shook hands when I left, and I knew I'd met a man I could trust. Shan Shan approved of him too, an educated man, she told me, and Tzu Chow drove us there, not a ragged man on a pedicab, which made her doubly happy.

Once back in the apartment, I took our last chuck roast out of the freezer and cooked a pot roast, adding potatoes and carrots peeled by Ai-yi.

"Smells great," announced Ed as he walked into the kitchen, removing his coat.

"To make up for the omelets," I told him.

It did smell good, rich and oniony, and I took it out of the oven ready for Ed to carve, my mouth watering with anticipation. He sharpened the seldom-used carving knife and sliced the meat, so tender it shred at the edges. I looked at the sharp blade in his hand, the chunks of meat on the platter, and thought of the beautiful Tibetan girl, so desperate for money that she saw no option but to maim herself, of how many people this meat could feed . . . of the years I was fed only bread and potatoes.

"Up to you, more for me," said Ed when I turned my meal into meat-flavored vegetable soup.

The next time Shan Shan came to the apartment she noticed the paintings that Ed had so painstakingly hung on the walls.

"You like paintings?" she asked. I assured her I did. "There is an art show at the Fine Arts School today," she said. "Shall we go?"

I called Ed and asked to borrow the car for a bit. Twenty minutes later, Tzu Chow arrived. Unless Ed was using it, I could now have the car whenever I wanted. A welcome change.

The school was located in a stone-faced building in an area I hadn't yet visited. Like lots of places in this amazing city, it looked unique, with its flat façade and boxy windows in the style of Frank Lloyd Wright. We went inside and into a huge auditorium with no windows and very poor lighting, but, even so, I saw a painting that took my breath away. It was a large oil painting depicting three young women, fishing nets in hand, red flowers behind their right ears. I wanted to know all about it.

Shan Shan explained that the women were a minority people from the south and that they were widows, without children. The flowers behind their ears signified that. And, according to their tradition, they weren't allowed to marry again.

I looked at the ornate clothes they wore, the long green grasses surrounding them, their bare feet, the fish in their silver net, and knew I had to own this work. I was to find out more about this painting before we left, but Shan Shan was considering how we could buy it.

"It's not a sale," she told me, "just a show." She looked around for someone in charge while I tried my best to look as inconspicuous as possible, though, as far as I could see, we were the only visitors.

It seemed like ages before Shan Shan came back. In the meantime, I'd tried to find interest in the other works displayed. Finally, I felt her touch my arm, and she whispered her findings.

"Your lucky day," she told me. "The master said you may buy it. And he told me to 'tell your foreign friend she has a good eye.'"

"Can we take it now?" I asked. To my relief, Shan Shan nodded "yes."

Tzu Chow walked into the building, his swager still in place, and carried my new treasure to the car. I had no idea how much I paid for it; I was still so delighted it was mine. But the money passed hands, FEC, and the master bade us goodbye.

On the ride back to the apartment, Shan Shan told me about her father. He was a "national treasure," she said. A famous classical painter. "When his work gets mounted, they fight over his written instructions." While I considered Shan Shan close, she hadn't shared much in the way of personal information. This was a new side to her, and I was duly impressed and encouraged that one day she might share more.

Back to the apartment we went, and I invited Shan Shan in for a cup of tea.

Ai-yi always fussed over Shan Shan and happily fixed the tea while I got out my selection of horded English biscuits. We sat around the coffee table to enjoy our treat.

"If you hear of any other shows, will you let me know?" I asked.

"Of course," she assured me.

It had been such a special day, so I decided to be brash and ask a personal question. Everyone loves to brag about their children; it was a safe subject and had worked with Ai-yi and me, so I asked Shan Shan. To my delight, she told me about her daughter. Her one child per family. Her name translated to White Snow, obviously a winter baby. And out came the pictures, which were stored in Shan Shan's enormous bag. (I'd been curious as to what she kept in there.) White Snow was eight, and a more precocious little girl would be hard to find. There were pictures of her in an American cheerleader's costume, including pom poms, various poses, pictures of her dancing, and several with mike in hand actually singing, explained her proud mother. Her bedroom walls were covered in posters of film stars. Whatever I had imagined, I wouldn't have come up with this.

"What a lucky little girl, Shan Shan."

"She is our only one," she replied. We sat there, contemplating that thought and what it meant.

"I get pregnant easily," she said. "I have abortions." Then she told me that she did this to support her country and its ideals.

After dinner that night, I told Ed about Shan Shan's method of birth control. He wasn't surprised at all. "If you toe the party line, you can have a good life here," he said.

"But what about the women? The baby girls who get aborted? Only boys are worth living here," I said.

"Them's the rules. Nothing can be done about it. Just out of luck, I guess."

Of course, he was right. There was no point trying to hide anything here. You were watched by your leaders at all times, from your neighborhood watch to watchers at work and school. And, among the poor, the cherished son was prized over anything else. He was a parent's security in their old age.

CHAPTER 27

ENTOMOPHAGY AND FRIED ANT COOKIES

Fairies dance in a haze of incense,
While honored guests in mink and sable
Wallow in the rapturous music of pipes and zither,
Nor forgetting to do justice to
Camel's knuckles and all.

From: *"Thoughts on the Way From Capital to Fengxian," Du Fu, 755

F riends were coming to town, Peggy and Tom from Taiwan. They were bringing a group of Taiwanese travel agents for a quick tour of Beijing. It was always good to have friends around. They formed a bridge for Ed and me to meet on.

"You're in for a treat, Joan," Ed told me. "We're invited to a health-food restaurant."

"Does that mean vegetarian?"

"Hell if I know. I know it's expensive, that's all."

Tzu Chow drove us to the Sheraton Hotel where Peggy and Tom were staying with their twenty guests. They were in the bar, a boisterous crowd of Taiwanese Chinese, whiskey glasses in hand, swirls of cigarette smoke above and around them.

"You letting Joanie use the car yet, Ed?" teased Peggy.

"Can't stop her," he replied as he shook Tom's hand.

"Do you want to go shopping, Peggy?" I asked.

"Yes, want to buy a carpet," she told me. We arranged a time for the next day to go to the Friendship Store near the apartment.

"They have a good selection in now," I told her. "I just bought one for the apartment." In fact, I'd seen the red-and-blue jewel-colored carpet when I shopped for Ed's hot peppers. I'd almost fallen over the two-foot-high stack when the bright carpets caught my attention in the dark room. Tzu Chow had picked it up for me, and it now brightened the tired beige fitted carpet in the living room.

"You paid *what* for it?" Ed had asked.

"It's less than a hundred dollars. So, what's the problem?" I was annoyed. Shopping was my domain, and I thought I was good at finding bargains.

"That's just it," he'd said, laughing. "You paid for it in *renminbi*. How'd you get by with that?" At the time, I didn't know only westerners working for Chinese companies and paid in *renminbi* were allowed to use local money, but Ed was impressed.

"Go with Joanie," he told Peggy. "She can get you a great price." He told Ken the same thing, and I ended up buying five of the beautiful carpets for less than the FEC price of two.

Peggy and Tom walked hand in hand to the jeep, close like lovers, like friends. He held the door as she climbed in. Tzu Chow drove us to the restaurant; the others followed in a bus.

"They wanted to go," Tom told us, leaning his arm on the back of his seat. "We don't guarantee anything."

The restaurant was glass fronted, gold lettering on the outside. We walked through the main dining room, which was empty, to a smaller private room and sat at the three round tables waiting for us. Not knowing what to expect, Peggy and I sat next to each other, husbands to either side. A barrier against the unknown. Mao Tai and whisky bottles were passed around by our noisy companions while waiters stood, hands behind backs, their faces blank.

When a stern-faced woman appeared wearing a doctor's white coat shiny with starch, I knew we were in for trouble. She proceeded to tell us that entomophagy, bug eating, had existed in China for thousands of years and that the food we were about to be served was designed to enable the chi, ying and yang, to flow effortlessly through our bodies. Only the choicest ingredients were used from the remotest parts of China.

We had a lecture on every dish that was presented, all relayed in effortless English. And I must say, the presentation was beautiful.

"That's what the doctor says about cod liver oil," I whispered to Ed.

"Don't be so hasty," he said unsympathetically.

It was a special menu, preordered by the Taiwanese. The stiff waiters left the room to appear again, soup tureens in hand. Oh God, there were little turtles floating on top! First thought: were they alive? One hand behind their backs, the waiters served up the soup.

"Do I have to?" I asked Peggy, looking at the little turtle floating in my bowl.

"A little," she laughed.

"Put hair on your chest," teased Ed. I sipped some soup and chewed a deep-fried scorpion (think tiny lobster) but pushed the bull's testicles and a deer's goodness-knows-what around my plate while Ed ate everything with feigned enthusiasm. Each dish proved to be more terrifying than the last. Fat shiny silkworms on a stick and fried cicadas ("Think of crispy bacon," Ed said) were some of the scariest. And bird's nest soup the saddest (I'd recently seen a documentary on how the little birds made their nests in enormous caves and how they were harvested. I'll spare you the details. They're probably extinct now anyway). There was food "for ladies," which meant just Peggy and me, and food for men meant to increase potency and help hair growth, all with the promise of a longer, more successful life.

Peggy and I chatted away like long-lost friends. She was so comfortable to be with, no airs and graces unlike most of the wives I'd met, just someone who would drop in for coffee and brighten a day.

"Tom was telling me that you travel a lot, Joan. Don't think I could do that." Her remark took me by surprise. While it was true, I spent the time with my children, and it never occurred to me that I was doing anything wrong. Others had said the same thing: "Don't think I'd leave my husband alone that often." While I didn't care what others said, I did care about Peggy. How tempted I was to tell her the reason. It would be such a relief to have someone to share my anxiety with, to get another perspective. But I couldn't betray Christopher's trust.

"Ed doesn't mind at all," I said with a smile. "In fact, we seem to get along better after each trip. Absence . . . you know what they say."

"That I do," Peggy agreed.

And I thought of the old saying: "many a true word is spoken in jest." On my last three trips, when I came back from Hawaii, Ed had met me at the airport. When I commented, he said it was for all the food and cigarettes I brought back with me.

"Oh, not me, then?"

"Maybe that too," he said.

It was a welcome change to see him waiting there, helped with the anxiety I felt leaving Christopher and the guilt I felt knowing how hard he worked to lead an independent life. How he had to fight all the time to keep the darkness away. Maybe Ed and I could talk about that one day.

The last dish was removed, and I sighed. Our guests were engaged in heated discussions about the merit of each dish. They were very pleased, and it made this strange experience worthwhile somehow.

"Here you go, Joanie," said Ed. "Dessert."

Plates of almond cookies dotted with black sesame seeds were placed on the tables. Gratefully, I picked one up to feed my empty stomach. It was dry, and the overcooked seeds stuck to my teeth, but I finished it.

"Like it?" asked Tom, smiling.

"Yes, a bit dry though."

"My wife," Ed laughed as I gulped down scalding tea to wash away the dried ants sprinkled on the cookies. Next time, I'd wear my glasses.

It was good to hear Ed laugh. It didn't matter that I was the butt of his joke. In fact, I went out of my way sometimes to make him laugh. His brown eyes softened behind his dark-rimmed glasses then; his face lightened; his jowls disappeared. I recognized him when he laughed—he was the man who had made me feel wanted, safe, protected, all with just a smile.

CHAPTER 28

INDIGO-BLUE BOXES

Contentment with poverty is Fortune's best gift:
Riches and Honor are the handmaids of Disaster.
Though gold and gems by the world are sought and prized,
To me they seem no more than weeds or chaff.

From: "Dream of the Red Chamber," Cao Xueqin, c. 1750

I'd been away a month, first to Hawaii for spring break, then to London to visit my mother for her birthday. It hadn't seemed long at the time, but, when I walked out of Beijing Airport, the trees were covered in blossoms and white clouds floated in a blue sky.

Ed met me, and we talked about the children. Zhu Chow greased the right palms and greeted me with his wide, cocky grin.

It felt good to be back.

Once in the apartment, I told Ed the latest. "Chris has a girlfriend."

"When did that happen?"

"Not sure, but it was by chance I met her. I was watering the banana trees as she drove up. She seemed very surprised to see me, as much as I was. Anyway, she told me her name was Amy, and she was just stopping by to see Chris. They were arranging a volunteer project for the booby birds. He must have heard us, as out he came, hair dripping from the shower, and introduced us."

"That's some news!"

"He did say they were just friends. Met while working on base with that nesting project."

We sat at the kitchen table and, for the first time in years, talked together about Christopher. Avoiding his illness, of course. Ed seemed really happy that Chris was in a relationship. I, on the other hand, voiced my concerns. "What if they get serious and break up?"

"Why would they do that?" he asked. "Look at us, we're still together."

Not wanting to spoil his enthusiasm, I joked, "Yes, miracles do happen."

He laughed. "Come here, you," he said and pulled me onto his lap.

I smile now thinking of it, but the concerns I had were real. Nobody wants their child hurt, no matter their age; we cringe at the thought of it. How could Chris handle a broken relationship without a negative impact? His doctor had told me that sudden change would be very difficult for him and could lead to a relapse. But this was my concern, and I shouldn't put it on Ed. I would just have to wait and see. Be prepared.

"I'd never leave my husband alone that long," said Rebecca. We were in her car on a mission to find where they manufactured the blue cloth-covered boxes used in China to hold everything.

"Ed encourages me to go," I answered her, a bit too quickly. "Besides, your children are older than mine. My mother's not well," I added. Even though I was used to this comment, it still disturbed me and, I must admit, made me defensive.

"Of course, honey. Don't mind me," she said, patting my hand. But I did mind her. Other friends in Hawaii had voiced the same opinion this last trip. "I trust Ed," I had told them. Our night of glorious passion hadn't been repeated; when we made love, it seemed like something we both had to do, and, for a reason that was beyond my understanding, I now hastened to dress, scared Ed might see my breasts, my skin, and want me.

We drove past pale orange clay fields freshly planted in straight lines, waiting to sprout. Hamlets sprinkled flat fields far away from the road. As navigator, I looked at the penciled lines on the scrap of paper drawn by Old Mr. Hu. There were no maps; the roads were nameless and hamlets anonymous to outsiders.

"Should be coming up soon on the right," I told Rebecca, and there it was, a grove of skinny trees hovering over cottages built out of the same orange clay. We drove over rutted ground and parked.

"This must be it, Joan," Rebecca said, opening the door and climbing out of her car.

The hard-packed clay was swept clean, brush marks swirling in lazy circles. Pink pigs routed for scraps of cabbage littering their pen. Red chickens looking important pecked hopefully at the hard earth. I looked at their knowing, beady eyes and wished I'd brought a camera. No dogs barked; no birds sang; no children laughed or cried. An old man coughing broke the eerie silence, and we walked toward him. His face was as wrinkled as a prune. Smile lines cut deep from his eyes to his hairline, and they deepened when he returned our smiles.

Rebecca showed him the blue box, and he nodded his head and pointed to an open door in the largest of the small buildings. We ambled inside. The floor was packed clay, the thick walls and ceiling whitewashed, accentuating the dark wood of the wide, rough-hewn beams. Planks resting on clay bricks filled the room, and paper pulp pressed flat under more planks and bricks lie on top, drying.

"It's just recycled paper!" I said to Rebecca, amazed at how the end product could support the weight of a man.

Silent women walked into the room, patted the paper, and left again, shyly taking peeks at the two foreign women with their lipstick, painted nails, and curly hair.

Rebecca tried to communicate, and, though they turned to one another, they responded with flustered looks and mumbles in a dialect I hadn't heard.

"Won't work," Rebecca sighed. She'd wanted boxes made for porcelain bought from our old friends. Old Mr. Hu had offered, but Rebecca didn't want him to see the pieces. "Never know," she'd told me.

As we turned to leave, a middle-aged woman stopped us at the door, a rose-patterned thermos and two mugs in hand. She pointed the cups toward us, inviting us to take one each, and poured the steamy golden liquid. We sat on a wooden bench under a large tree and sipped our tea. "Only poor people do this," I heard my grandmother say again, "take care of each other." We had tried to visit my cousins that day, and a neighbor of theirs invited us in. "They're out, luv Come on in and rest your poor old feet," and in we went for tea and precious cream biscuits.

CHAPTER 29

SPRING

Asleep in the spring, dawn comes to me unawares;
I hear the bird singing all around.
When night comes there's the sound of wind and rain;
Who knows how many blossoms fall to the ground.

From: **"Daybreak in Spring," Meng Haoran, 689–740

Trees turned green overnight, or so it seemed., and plum trees' pink blossoms covered the pavement in a soft, sweet-smelling carpet. It was the kind of weather that reenergized you after a bleak and brutal winter. The streets around our compound boasted ginko and the grand scholar trees, with their gnarled, ancient-looking trunks, and so I went out, no destination, just to walk in the shade of these beautiful trees. Some reached out to each other across the roads, providing a green tunnel to walk under. The air was soft, like a gentle blanket. Petals floated slowly.

Shan Shan arrived at the apartment, and I told her how I longed to become immersed in the local culture. Opera season was over, and I was looking for things to do. Right away, Shan Shan came up with a suggestion: an old tea house, one with a theater and comedy shows. Sounded wonderful to me, so we arranged to go that night. I did ask Ed, just in case, but his response was typical: "You go. I have stuff to do." I didn't mind. With Shan Shan in charge, I could just sit back and enjoy whatever presented itself. Tzu Chow drove us to the Beijing Hotel, where I hid while Shan Shan arranged a pedicab. It was her way of ensuring a fair price, she explained. My face would triple the expense.

Off we went, our destination Zhangyiyuan Tea House, the other side of Tiananmen Square. We stopped outside an inauspicious building hosting various shops. The teahouse entrance was the door right in the middle. Up the stairs we went, dark and wooden, and into a large room. Square paper lanterns hung from the ceiling, edged in red fringes, providing a soft yellow glow. Open woodwork screens created cozy spaces. We were seated at a small table near the front of the stage. Others were arranged at different levels, one step up at a time, around us.

Tea was served in delicate white porcelain cups. Bowls of sugared nuts and various dried fruits were placed before us, along with long bone chopsticks. A gong was struck, and the show began. It was a comedy show, with two musicians—one playing the erhu, the other doubling on the pipa and gong—and two elderly men dressed in Ching Dynasty costumes in somber tones of charmeuse. The barber act was first, the customer and the proprietor. We watched the hour-long show of classic slapstick humor. No interpretation was necessary; no matter the language, the skits were universal. Applause was light and the laughter loud, with some enthusiastic foot stamping.

We walked outside, waiting for a pedicab, and it was then that I realized we had been the only women there, including staff, and that nobody paid us any heed.

Shan Shan went through her usual bargaining routine, but this time I had nowhere to hide. So, she bullied the driver to make up for the inflated cost.

The moon was full, the air soft with a breeze strong enough to snap the huge flags along the immense expanse of Tiananmen Square to attention. The street was so empty I could hear the flags playing in the wind. We arrived at the Beijing Hotel too soon, and I said my goodbyes and got in a cab back to the apartment. Pedicabs weren't allowed, more's the pity.

I was becoming the "China travel expert" among my friends, and I really enjoyed sharing what little I knew of this amazing country. The favored destination, besides the Forbidden City, was the Great Wall. Ed and I had visited there several times, once with the children right before we moved here, but, no matter how many times, I always found it mind boggling.

That year we had a host of Company visitors, "visiting firemen," Ed called them, and I was elected to be their guide. Tzu Chow drove us; it was an easy trip from Beijing. Most seemed to go just to have their pictures taken to impress friends. Tzu Chow would park the car, and out we'd hop straight to the undulating section that provided a great backdrop. There were a few who were genuinely interested. One was Peggy—I knew her well, and she was truly fascinated. Her reaction made it so much more fun for me, and I could see it again, fresh through her eyes.

I shared Humphrey with Peggy. Humphrey was a camel tethered on the mountain side of the wall. Ed and I met him on our first visit with our children, and Lisa had named him. "Hump, get it, Mum?" That was ages ago now, when Christopher and Lisa came for a five-day crash course on Beijing. For a small fee, you could sit on his smelly motheaten back for a photo op, which Peggy did. I then showed her a path that led up the mountain from which you could see the immense span of the wall.

"Take my picture," she requested. And I did, only to find out after she went home that I'd cut her head off. "Nobody believes it's me," she moaned. Her only other disappointment was the toilets. Money had to be paid, handed over at the entrance, in exchange for which you received a ticket and two sheets of pink crepe toilet paper. The ticket you placed on a nail outside the door, the crepe paper . . . I think that's why most of the visits to the Great Wall were hurried ones. We westerners are so spoiled with our indoor plumbing and abundant toilet paper. We had no idea it could be turned back into wood with just a little moisture and a lot of pressure.

Humphrey and friends

CHAPTER 30

BLUE SOFT-SHELL CRABS

Inside your sharp pincers,
Packed meat is so smooth,
Purer than white jewels.
Under your thick surface,
Treasured substance
Piled together in abundance.
How awesome it is with eight legs,
You crawl faster than anyone else.
But in your long spears and iron armor,
You meet your fate sent by your karma

From: "Dream of the Red Chamber," Cao Xueqin, c. 1750

Apart from morning coffee and the occasional cocktail parties, the expat community didn't entertain at home. However, Ken called from Shanghai and told me he was shipping their famous blue soft-shell crabs; I would get them the next day. "How many?" I asked, and he said two crates.

Two crates of crabs. I had no idea how many crabs were in each crate, but I thought Olivia might. She had lived here ten years. Olivia told me how lucky we were, how delicious the crabs would be this time of year, and that two crates should feed between ten and fourteen people. But I didn't know fourteen people, so I started to panic.

I called Ed, asked him how many people he knew who would like soft-shell crabs. He assured me everyone would. "So, give me names," I demanded. Luckily for me, the two young Americans from Shanghai were in town, and they brought two friends, and I asked Ed to see if the office ai-yi could help. Turns out, she was delighted at the prospect of a little extra money, even more so the opportunity to see Loaban's penthouse.

Then I called Rebecca, invited her and John, then Monica to invite her and husband Dave, then Olivia, who was delighted at the invite and happy I asked her to bring her ai-yi to help with the cooking.

At ten o'clock the next morning, Tzu Chow delivered the crates of crabs. He hung around a bit, hoping for some crabs, until Ai-yi sent him off with a few choice words about being lazy. The crates were placed in the kitchen. It was a very large kitchen, divided by a center counter, and the crates were placed on the floor, farthest away from the work area.

Ai-yi pried open the top of the first crate, exposing damp straw—which moved!

Of course, they were alive. They had to be alive, I somehow knew that, but soon the kitchen floor was covered in blue crabs scurrying away, looking for places to hide. I rushed to the broom closet and tried my best to sweep them back toward their temporary home. With Ai-yi warning me to watch out for their claws, I did a lot of jumping. As I wielded the broom, Ai-yi held the large dustpan, and somehow we were able to recapture these very energetic creatures.

The crate lid went back on, and we two sat down and had a cup of cha. Then I realized they had to be cooked—boiled to death. My kitchen would once again become a place of execution. I needed Olivia.

Olivia arrived with her ay-yi, huge pot in hand. "We'll leave them to it," she said. "They know how to do this."

Sounded great to me, and Olivia and I set about placing dishes on the large round glass-topped table, along with napkins and chopsticks. "We don't need much," she told me. "Every bit of the crab is edible."

By the time our guests arrived, the apartment smelled like Fisherman's Wharf. Nobody seemed to mind. The soft-shell crabs were a rare treat here in Beijing, and our guests sat anywhere they found a place, plates piled high with crab. Ai-yi went around with a tray holding various sauces made specially and little dishes to put them in. That's all we served, soft-shell crabs, no salad, no bread, nothing but these succulent little creatures.

It was one of the noisiest dinner parties I'd ever been to. The food itself was handheld and messy, a great equalizer. We served wine of course, and Ed brought in extra beer. "Have to have beer with crab," he assured me. And I had pastries for dessert, but who wanted cake when they could have the rare and delicious?

Ed enjoyed playing host to such an appreciative crowd, and he did it well. "Think everyone's enjoying themselves," he told me with a self-satisfied smile.

The few crabs left over went home with the three ai-yis—their reward for standing over giant boiling pots and handling crabs fighting for their lives.

My reward for participating in their death was a very serious infection on my right thumb from a poke with a very sharp claw.

On his way out, John took me aside. "Your ai-yi," he told me, "is highly educated."

I didn't know what to say to this, but it made me think.

Before the Blue Shelled Crab Feast, Ai yi on my left

CHAPTER 31

SUPERIOR DRAGON'S WELL TEA

You ask for what reason I stay on the green mountain,
I smile, but do not answer, my heart is at leisure.
Peach blossom is carried far off by flowing water,
Apart, I have heaven and earth in the human world.

From: **"Questions on a Mountain," Li Bai, 701–762

Rebecca, like a lot of expat wives, went home during the summer months. I would be going too but later, when Lisa arrived home from school. So, I was delighted to get a call from Urs and Isabelle, friends from Zurich. Urs had worked with a very dear friend of mine, also an architect, and we had spent many happy times together in Hawaii. It seemed they had planned on a group trip to Wuyishan City in Fujian Province, which had fallen through. They still wanted to go; would I like to go with them? And could I help with the language? Maybe the arrangements?

The furthest south I had been was Shanghai. Fujian hadn't made it to my must-see list, but, like eating in a different restaurant, I found it much more interesting going where somebody else chose and that way be exposed to new experiences. So, of course I wanted to go! Ed helped make the plans, but he had no desire to go with us. "I hardly know them," he said. "You go, enjoy yourself."

After a quick sightseeing stop to the usual—the Forbidden City and the Great Wall—off we three set. This would be my first trip without every minute planned with meet-and-greet guides in place—and where I would be the one responsible for the trip's success. Scary thought, especially as my limited Mandarin wouldn't be much help outside of Beijing.

It took several flights to get there, and we were the only foreigners traveling on the small domestic planes, but we would have stood out anyway, as Urs and Isabelle are both over six feet tall and were unable to stand up straight in the tiny cabins.

Through the concierge at our very basic hotel, I was able to arrange car and driver, with a guide who spoke Mandarin, no English, for a sightseeing tour around the spectacular local scenery. We drove up and around and through mountains with views of crystal-clear rivers peeking between trees. The area was lush and green, which made it the capital for the most expensive oolong teas in the world, of which *Da Hong Pao* was the most famous. There were six "mother" trees clinging to the mountains that grew the famous flame-red tea. The next day, we were to climb up to see them.

The Wu Yi Mountain Villa nestled in the midmountain range. With its whitewashed walls and dark timber trim, it resembled a classical private compound of the Ming dynasty, beautiful, peaceful, quiet. Topiary trees lined walkways; not a blade of grass was out of place. This was our starting point.

Our guide left us at the foot of steps cut into the mountain. He assured me we couldn't get lost—just one way up and one way down. He would be back later with the car.

The sun was blazing high in the pale blue summer sky, and my face felt scorched from the heat.

"Wish I hadn't forgotten my hat," I moaned.

"You can use my hankie," Urs offered with a smile.

The steps ended, and we entered a small plateau. Out of nowhere, vendors appeared. Crowding around us, vying for attention, they showed us their trinkets: three wise monkeys carved out of rock, plastic sunglasses, postcards of the mountains that reached up and around us—and umbrellas.

The umbrellas were small, like the dainty parasols used to protect fair-skinned ladies from the sun lifetimes ago. Their frames and handles were made of bamboo and their canopies paper, adorned with flowers, or birds, or butterflies, and covered in a coat of shiny lacquer.

"Just the thing," I said, choosing one ablaze with the pink blossoms of a cherry tree. It was light in my hand, and, when I opened it, I found it barely wider than a big straw hat. When I held my it in my hand, the shade it cast deflected the rays of the searing sun. I was very pleased with my purchase—twenty cents' worth of beauty and comfort.

Urs and Isabelle, my two long-legged friends and I, began to climb the crumbly pathway along the side of the mountain. Donkeys passed us by, carrying those too lazy to make the climb in the sultry climate.

The path was steep. I grabbed dried bushes to steady myself and scrambled along until we arrived at another small plateau, the last lookout on the narrow earth-packed path that led to the mountain trail we were to climb that day.

The donkeys could go no farther and blocked our way to the mountaintop and our destination—the teahouse that served mountain-grown teas. Isabelle was a Cordon Bleu cook and had a culinary school in Zurich catering to business types looking for a hobby. She had obviously been captivated by stories of the tea's reputation for curing all ills, from colds to calluses to cowardice, and wanted to see the source of this magic nectar. Walking gingerly around and between the dust-covered donkeys and their passengers, we managed to reach the narrow trail that snaked its way farther upward. The higher we climbed, the cooler and dryer the air became. Birds chirped and trilled around us, and lacy trees replaced the scrub.

We had climbed for about thirty minutes when Urs held up his hand. In front of us, a gorge cut the path in two. A once-rushing river had carved its way through the mountain, taking rock and earth with it—except for nine skinny spindles of mountain standing up from the dry riverbed. Like sentinels, they spanned the gap that stood between us and the tea. I stared at these tall, unevenly spaced spindles with dread. Together they formed Horse Tooth Bridge.

"A nice surprise," said Urs. He took the first step, placing his foot in the center of the eighteen-inch rock. Of course, being Swiss, he and Isabelle had climbed mountains all their lives, so to them it was merely another group of rocks, amusing, interesting, but for me it was the high wire at Cirque Du Soleil.

I let my tall friends pick their way across the thirty-foot span—and then, when they were almost there, I opened my umbrella, took a deep breath, and, on an act of faith, stepped out across nothing and placed my right foot on the first odd-shaped flat rock.

Step by hesitant step, I made my way across, balancing on each rock, fighting the urge to look down. I was walking on steppingstones in the sky with nothing but air for thirty feet down to the dry, yellow-colored rocky riverbed.

Urs, being an architect, speculated about how the bridge was created, how much longer it would last, while I worried about how I would get back.

Our pathway veered gently to the left, and before us appeared a cottage built from the yellow-brown rock of the mountain. Around the cottage, a shady garden with rock tables and wooden logs provided a place to rest while drinking the famous teas—all of them empty, as if waiting for us.

We went inside the cottage and sniffed the tea leaves stored in the tin-lined wooden chests that ran the length of the building. Our hostess explained the different qualities of each of the teas, ranked by their position on the mountain, the amount of rain that spring, and when the tea was harvested. The procedure seemed as complicated as grading fine wines.

Isabelle chose our tea, *Qiqiang Lung Chin*, Superior Dragon's Well, the most expensive, it seemed. We went outside and sat under ancient trees on wooden logs at our rock table. Long-spouted kettles filled with boiling spring water were taken off woodburning stoves by our smiling, toothless host, who stood nearby waiting to demonstrate his skill with the kettle. Our hostess placed the chosen tea into tiny white translucent porcelain cups placed in front of us. From two feet away, the water flew across the empty space, making a rainbow-shaped arc between cup and kettle. The dried-up sage-colored leaves gratefully absorbed the water and unfurled before us into their original wide jade-green flower form.

As soon as we emptied our cups, more hot water spiraled its way into the delicate vessels and became tea. No matter how many times the tiny cups were filled, the tea's light, perfumed flavor remained unspoiled. And, each time our host poured the water, he stepped farther away from us—the greater the distance, the wider his smile. Even at twelve feet, he unerringly filled our cups without spilling a drop.

"These little cups would make good eye-bath cups," said Urs. He was right. They were maybe an inch in diameter, equal in depth.

We bought assorted teas and little cups, then it was time to leave this restful place.

"Did it work?" asked Isabelle, meaning the tea.

"We shall soon see," I said as we approached the bridge.

My friends laughed at the way I exaggerated my balancing act with the little umbrella.

"Seems like it does," I said.

Our next stop was the river, where we rode flat bamboo rafts steered by a gondolier like the gondolas of Venice. There was no sound except for the gentle sigh of water, as it slipped between the slats, gently washing our toes. This was Urs's idea; he wanted to see the caves carved in the steep mountain sides, multi levels, like apartment buildings, used for thousands of years as dwellings.

"How on Earth did they get in and out?" I asked. The mountain face was flat; there were no steps or handholds that I could see. And the river we were on reached to the foot of the mountain.

"Don't know," admitted Urs. "That's why they're so fascinating. Some of these are still occupied," he continued. "They have mountain villages throughout China, self-contained and remote. My next trip will be to visit Sichuan Province. There are places there that can only be reached by vine ladders."

"I won't be on that trip with you," said Isabelle. Neither will I, I thought.

Our days were spent touring off the regular tourist routes and our evenings in recuperating. Ten days flew by, and too soon it was time we parted company. Urs and Isabelle went to Shanghai for another five days before returning to Zurich and I to Beijing, where I couldn't wait to share our experiences with Ed.

Sharing trips with friends, visiting places they'd read about, places special to their interests, was a real bonus for me. Sharing their experiences broadened mine. And, while Ed didn't want to participate, he was always supportive of my going. "That way," he said, "I can be an armchair traveler." He really was a poor traveler, impatient and demanding. While we had travelled a lot together, it had always been to safe locations, where service and standards were predictable. "Too old for Lonely Planet tours," he'd say. But then he'd said that when he was thirty. It worked for us, though. While I enjoyed the exotic and unusual, Ed was content to stay at home.

On our bamboo raft with my trusty parasol

orse Tooth Bridge

Tea awaits

The Tea House

CHAPTER 32

THE SUNG DYNASTY PILLOW

> *The pillow's low, the quilt is warm, the body smooth and peaceful,*
> *Sun shines on the door of the room, the curtain not yet open.*
> *Still the youthful taste of spring remains in the air,*
> *Often it will come to you even in your sleep.*
>
> From: "Spring Sleep," Bai Juyi, 772–846.

"Glad you had a good time," Ed said on my return from Fujian. "Keeps you from buying all these pots. Don't know what the hell you're going to do with them." He had a point. My last lot of purchases had been clay pots, probably dug up by farmers after being lost in the earth for hundreds of years. Some were Han dynasty, making them between 200 BC to 220 AD. Apart from their graceful shapes, their age appealed to me. To have something made from clay survive all those years fascinated me, especially the larger pots. My favorite pot of all was eleven inches tall, made in the curled rope method, the soft gray-blue color of a Pacific dawn. Though my favorite find was a Sung Dynasty pillow, bought from a new friend of Rebecca's.

"Want to get a coffee?" Rebecca asked. That request was code for shopping—not only shopping, shopping from someone without the

Chinese government's seal of approval. We didn't see it as breaking any laws, more a way to add a little excitement to our otherwise very dull lives while supporting the local economy. "Everyone does it," Rebecca insisted. "The government shops are way overpriced." She was right, of course. And the official shops had little to offer in the way of porcelain, especially the earlier pieces I collected.

    Rebecca drove, following a sketchily hand-drawn map. Another aspect of our special trips was that we went through parts of the city not on the tourist maps; with no street markers we could understand, it was an adventure every time. Redevelopment was changing the city even during the short time I lived there, with massive gray concrete buildings reaching up to the equally gray sky, huge black or red numbers painted on their sides their only distinguishing marks. Our destination today was in the older section, with its dark, narrow alleys leading to what had been large family compounds occupied by the wealthy and now chopped up and changed into buildings within buildings. Our instructions were not to park too near our final stop, so Rebecca parked on the main street. There were no other cars in sight, and we walked through an ally, then through a building to a little shed in the back—no door, just a wooden table under a corrugated roof over corrugated walls. Our host was a young man in a suit with soft hands and a good haircut. I saw the prices go up. That day, I didn't purchase anything, Rebecca did; she had checked him out and knew he had the pair of ox-blood bowls she wanted.

    His merchandise was mixed, mostly Ching dynasty porcelain, a few pieces of furniture, and what I knew to be Sung dynasty bowls, delicate open shaped-bowls white glazed with incised clouds. "If they're the real thing," I said to Rebecca, "bet he wants a hefty price." I knew enough not to show interest, and, as we left, we promised to return another day. That day I bought the Sung dynasty porcelain pillow, engraved with a poem in ancient calligraphy. He even supplied the poet's name, Yen Meng Yao. You could tell its owner had treasured it, used it, by the fading of the incised characters in its very center.

    I didn't really want it. What I wanted was the tri-colored plate he showed us. He went behind the inevitable heavy curtain, came out, hands behind back, looked furtively around, then, like a magician, produced a small plate, what we would call a dessert plate. "Two thousand dollars," he said, hands shaking, and he proceeded to tell us he had a buyer coming by later. "But you have first choice." It was perfect. He said it was Ming, showed us the identifying marks on the back, and we believed him. Then he kicked something under his table and asked if I wanted it. "Sung Dy," he said. It looked like a white porcelain box. It was in fact a pillow. I didn't, but the thought of this thousand-year-old treasure sitting on a mud floor, being kicked, had me feeling guilty, so I bought it at a whopping two hundred dollars, my most expensive purchase ever.

Our young entrepreneur carried my treasure out to Rebecca's car wrapped in a grubby blanket. Once he left, we started to laugh, giggles at first, then escalating to near hysteria. With tears streaming down my face, I asked, "Who do we think we're kidding? Us, inconspicuous?"

"We can only hope," responded Rebecca. We laughed all the way home.

"What are you going to do with that?" asked Ed. I told him I would have to hide it from Ai-yi, that it was very old and I wasn't supposed to have it. That I wanted to take it home. "I'll get a box made for it from Mr. Hu's, take it back next trip." In the meantime, I hid it in a suitcase, which I locked.

"They're going to arrest you," Ed said as he lifted the now heavy suitcase back into the cupboard. "I won't bail you out." He smiled when he said it.

"I'm going to take it to the Academy of Arts," I said, "see if I can get the poem translated." The museum is in Honolulu and has one of the largest collections of Asian art in the US.

"Okay," Ed said.

"The man who sold it to me said it had belonged to either a high-ranking soldier or a high-ranking court official."

"Don't know how anyone can sleep on those things."

"I know. Even children did, though. Supposed to be cool in hot weather."

"Crazy lot," Ed said.

The pillow had an interesting escape from Beijing. The Hus' blue box was wrapped in brown paper, tied with string, and appeared in the overheard when I boarded the plane. Tzu Chow and more cigarettes. It had to change planes in Shanghai and miraculously appeared once again. At the time, I didn't know that, except for rare pieces, Sung dynasty porcelain was okay to export. It might have spoiled the fun if I had.

CHAPTER 33

SUMMER PALACE, HEBEI PROVINCE

A sorrowful stream flows over a broken path.
A million sounds from the Earth are the true flutes and reeds,
Autumn is sprinkled in colors positively sad.
Palace beauties have turned into yellow dust,
And what's more, scattered are their powders and paints.
Where once they awaited a glorious golden chariot,
Now, of those things, only the stone horse remains.

From: *"Riverside Lament," Du Fu, 757

Justine called: would I like to go with her and her cousin who was visiting from the US to Hebei and the Qing Dynasty Summer Palace? Ed was off to Chicago for a week of meetings; the timing was perfect. Justine made all the arrangements, so I packed a small case, gave Ai-Yi a holiday—except for fish feeding—and was ready.

Justine arrived with her cousin Amy, and Ai yi made tea. Ai-yi was much more reserved around Justine than with Shan Shan or Kathy, and I couldn't help but think she knew all about Justine's parents' fall from grace and was showing her disapproval. I was glad we didn't have long to wait for Tzu Chow, who was driving us to the train station.

The Beijing railway station resembled the likes of Grand Central and Waterloo—it was mammoth, and, although relatively new, it had taken on the look of a building that had been in place for decades. It was so crowded we had to steer our way across the wide pavement through a solid mass of bodies, all holding various bundles and rice sacks and battered cardboard suitcases. It looked as if everyone in the city was traveling somewhere. Once past the standing mass, there were still others we needed to skirt around, families sitting on the ground, backs against the buildings, bundles at their sides, waiting... Dressed in their multilayered rags, matted hair, faces burnt from the sun, they looked abandoned.

"From the country," Justine said to my question. "Probably came here looking for work. No one will hire them. They don't have papers." No papers no job, no job no house, no house no stove or oil or cabbage.

Justine led the way through the maze of people to our platform and our train, which was waiting. Wooden benches were our seats, with wooden floors and windows that were open, (don't know whether they closed). It was crowded, but we were lucky enough to find seats near each other. I sat on the inside next to a man who I found out during the course of our journey had a sinus problem that required him to blow the contents of his nose and cough up the contents of his throat about every twenty minutes. This he did with abandon—onto the wooden floor right in front of us! Luckily, he got off after his third bout, and Justine joined me. We had apples Ai-yi had packed and which Justine peeled with the tiny Swiss Army knife, a present from Urs. With the caged chickens and ducks and the obvious predisposition of the Chinese to sinus problems, I could manage only a few slices of apple.

We rode through pristine, lush green countryside and watched hills turn into mountains. In fact, the palace was called the Chengde Mountain Resort during the Qing dynasty and rests in an area of pastures and forests and lakes, some of which were man made to follow the natural landscape.

There weren't many of us left on the train by the time we reached our destination, and by then I had learned that Amy was born and raised in the United States, was in fact a professor of Chinese history, and this trip was for her to explore the places she had studied. Unlike Justine, with her long, lean body, Amy was my height and compact, a hiker, I thought, with a round face and easy smile.

Justine and Amy hoisted their backpacks, and I felt positively ancient with my suitcase. I looked and felt like a middle-aged tourist. There were other suitcase holders like me; they were German tourists in a group of six with one guide. But we parted ways as we went to our guest house and they most probably to a hotel.

Our guest house catered to Chinese nationals, and I was looking forward to the experience. What's the point of traveling to other worlds and spending half your time as if you were still at home? The structure was very basic, as were the rooms, rather like a hostel, though we had our own bathrooms. The only glitch was hot water—it was turned on for one hour between eight and nine in the morning and for another hour at six in the evening. There was always cold.

That evening, we went for a stroll around the palace gardens. It was much cooler than in Beijing, the air sweet and clean, free of pollution. Ancient trees, their trunks twisted and gnarled, still thrived, unspoiled, but everything else looked sad and neglected.

"How forlorn everything looks," I said. While my friends agreed, Amy told us there were no funds to maintain, let alone repair, this enormous compound.

Breakfast was the usual, tea and hard-boiled eggs, but, instead of chook, we were served hot buckwheat noodles in broth. We soon set off for the palace. There was little in the way of information, but Amy did her best to enlighten us and answer my many—I'm sure annoying—questions.

In many ways, it reminded me of the Forbidden City, probably because it was built with the same palace architecture, but here the thick posts reaching up to the ceiling were void of paint and looked weatherworn. Windows were open to the elements, the stone floors cracked and uneven, and weeds grew out of the brick walls.

We continued to explore the outlying buildings, and Amy explained that elements of Han, Mongolian, and Tibetan architecture had been incorporated in its construction. "Even the landscapes are copied from famous places. It's like a collection of the best places in China all in one." Some of their names—Green Lotus Island, the Tower of Mist and Rain—sounded straight form a fairy tale, and the Chinese pagoda covered in glazed tiles with a round gilded spire looked like the tower containing the princess who waited for her prince. In its heyday, it must have been magnificent, with the lakes and gardens and temples painted with birds and flowers edged in gold leaf. It was only two hundred or so years old, and it was falling down. I asked stupid questions: "Why is it not protected? Why is such a unique place like this left to rot?" There were no answers.

We meandered along paths laid out to entice one to go farther, to see what was waiting just around the bend, just beyond that tree. It was pure magic. Amy saw it through a scholar's eyes; she made copious notes and took an equal number of photographs. Maybe her efforts would result in this enchanted place receiving the attention it needed to put it to rights before the forests took over. With that encouraging thought, we went to dinner.

We arrived at a small local restaurant where Justine ordered for us, explaining that Northern food was a little different. And so it was; we had *guo bao rou*, fried shredded pork with bamboo shoots arranged like a pyramid, steamed buns with mutton filling, bean curd with onions and ginger and garlic, and my favorite, *Qizi*, sesame seed cake, crisp on the outside and soft inside, which we called gin dui in Hawaii. Once the food arrived, Justine handed Amy and me each a pair of chopsticks in little cases. I unpacked mine under the table so nobody would see and think that I was too stuck up to use those provided. Of course, we fooled no one. Ours were cloisonné, in bright reds and blues.

We spent two glorious days exploring this magical place, and we only touched on the highlights, then it was time to leave. We paid our bills separately—three difference prices, three different methods of payment: Justine *renminbi*, Amy AmEx in dollars, me FEC—at a slightly lower price than Amy but still 10 times that of Justine. Fair enough, I thought. That's how it should be.

We parted ways at the Beijing railway station after Justine arranged for my taxi. We shared hugs, something uncommon in China but totally appropriate for us. And I arrived to an empty apartment. I was alone, and it felt wonderful. After days of cold showers, I decided to treat myself to a hot bath. Rose salts in, Dettol in, then, just to remind me where I was, no hot water. I didn't care and shivered as I soaked, enjoying reminiscences of the past two days.

I found out later that, once a year, the hot water is turned off to do some sort of cleaning . . . Another mystery of glorious China.

CHAPTER 34

BEAUTY IS DEFINITELY IN THE EYE OF THE BEHOLDER

The River Chu cuts through the middle of heaven's gate,
The green water flowing east reaches here then swirls.
On either bank the blue hills face toward each other,
The flatness of a lonely sail comes from out of the sun.

From: "Viewing Heaven's Gate Mountain," Li Bai, 701–762
(translated: Burton Watson)

Peggy wrote and asked if Ed would arrange a trip for her and Tom on the riverboat in Guilin. The weather was getting warm, trees were sprouting summer leaves, and I felt the urge to get out of the city.

"Ed, let's go with them. We can be back in a day."

"We'll see," he replied, his polite way of declining.

But his friends at the travel bureau saw this as an opportunity to show favor, so he was trapped, no matter how hard he tried to decline.

"Tom can't get away," he told me the day before the trip, throwing his briefcase onto the desk. His fate now sealed, he poured a stiff drink and yanked off his tie. "Damn!"

Ed didn't frighten me, but his temper did, and my skin crawled. I heard a voice from long ago. "Stop crying," it screamed, and my foster mother crashed into the room, her face red and swollen, her hair sticking up. She held my shoulders in her sharp claw-fingers. She shook me and wouldn't stop.

The sun was shining, and Ed's anger from the night before was forgotten as we walked aboard the one-story pleasure boat. Ed chose a seat near the back for the four-hour journey down the Li River to the village of Yangdi.

Once out of the busy town of Guilin, we entered a world unchanged for centuries, a magical place of round stone hills, called karst hills, standing in rows leading from the rocky shoreline back as far as the eye could see. Odd shapes, with magical names: Elephant Trunk Hill, Old Man Mountain, Nine Horse Hill, Crescent Moon Hill, whose summit contains a cave shaped like a half moon, and, my favorite, Folding Brocade Hill. On both sides of the river, we were surrounded by these steep towers of stone covered in multicolored vegetation, the more distant softened by mist and rain.

Fishermen on flat-bottom skiffs glided by, using long poles to navigate, two men to a boat, a big round woven basket balanced between them, waiting for the catch to be emptied from the net. Others fished with trained cormorants, large, ugly birds until they dove into the water. With strings attached to necks, they catch the large silver fish in their beaks and return to their owners. Unable to swallow due to the string restraint, they drop the fish to the deck.

Children stood in the shallow water by the banks, skin golden from the sun, shiny black river rocks under their feet. They called and waved to us as they washed huge water buffalo in the clear water, long sticks at the ready.

There was no rushing on the river; it had its own pace, slow and easy, and Ed's camera clicked away. "Stand there," he told me, and I'd move in the direction he pointed and pose. Ed was always taking pictures of me, sometimes when I was just sitting still, unaware of his presence.

"Listen," said our guide, telling us we would hear the sounds of gongs and drums. The captain switched off the putting engine, and, as we turned a bend, a waterfall emerged, emptying deafeningly into the rippling river. The boat swayed away from the sounds and pressure of the water, and fine cool spray fell on my hot skin, making me gasp.

"That was refreshing," I announced.

"You'd better wear your hat," he said, handing it to me. I could feel my face tingling from the sun and held the straw hat on my head against the puffs of breeze that tried to pull it away.

The boat chugged its way to an unpainted wooden dock. We had arrived at the village of Yangdi, nestled at the foot of twin mountains shaped like upside down goats' feet, hence the name, *yang*: sheep or goat. There were only ten of us, all German and Russian tourists, Ed and I the only Americans. Our guide told us we had one hour before the return trip to Guilin.

Leaving behind the tranquility of the boat, I stepped onto the dock and was immediately gobbled up in the crowd of peasants and fishermen. The fishermen were vying for a photo opportunity with their cormorants, fine grass strung around their necks as they balanced gracefully on bamboo poles held in eager, bent arms. A hundred peasants pushed and shoved one another in their attempt to sell food and trinkets.

I looked around for Ed. I couldn't see him. When a man's along, peddlers talk to him, their conversations aimed at the woman. While visitors were few, they knew Western women have influence, especially when it comes to spending money, and that was their purpose, to get as much as they could in the short time we were docked.

I still got a little panicked when surrounded by aggressive salesmen, especially when they were talking as loud as they could in a language that I didn't understand. Mandarin didn't work here. Keep on walking, I urged myself. Don't stop or you're done for. So, I waded through the extended arms toward the narrow lane leading up from the dock. Once on dry land, the panic eased, and, by then, Ed had been able to reach me.

"Now what do we do?" I asked, aiming my camera back out at the green satin waters of the Li River.

Ed pointed to the houses on the other side of the lane. "Let's see the town," he suggested.

It wasn't much of a town, mainly small, low houses, whitewashed with flat roofs. A young man stood idly by an open doorway; he had that universal "nod and a wink" look of a salesman. He inclined his head, and Ed walked toward him. The young man held a bundle in his arms closely, as if it were a precious treasure, and, as Ed approached, he slowly removed the top cover to reveal a large vase.

"Here, Joan," Ed called. "Come look at this."

I stood beside him, staring at the vase. I felt a rush, like a miner striking gold, as I reached out to touch it. It was so beautiful. The oxblood background shone with a deep, rich glow. I'd never seen anything like it before, not in the open markets, not in the Friendship Store, not even at Rebecca's. Looking around to make sure nobody was watching, this seller of treasures beckoned us into the whitewashed stone room behind him. Aladdin's den.

I pushed the tatty curtain aside and stepped over the wooden threshold onto the earth-packed floor. It was dark and cool as a cave. There was one narrow window placed high in the wall and a dark passageway ahead, leading to the back of the house. I felt prickles of fear creeping up my neck. Knowing the glance over my shoulder to Ed meant an imminent exit, my host started jabbering in the local dialect and pushed the vase into my arms. I marveled at the bold strokes of blue and white and green that shaped the chrysanthemums painted around the bowl and up the narrow neck of the heavy vase: a pink-breasted phoenix in full flight, its blue beak open in greeting, branches of cherry and apple blossoms and two blue butterflies gobbling up the sedate background with their vibrant pinks and blues and greens, each one of them a symbol of long life and happiness. As I traced these bold patterns with my fingers, I saw an apple green mottling under the oxblood. I'd read about that technique somewhere—very rare, I think the article said. Turning it upside down, I looked for markings; there were none. This intrigued me even more. My heart beat faster. Acting as casually as possible, I turned it around in my hands, trying to estimate its age. The lacquer inside the vase was crackled, the base smooth and uneven around the edges, definitely an old piece. "Ching Dy," my new friend assured me, "Kang Xi," making it early eighteenth century. Time for negotiations—time for Ed.

Gazing absently out the open door, Ed turned when called and looked with a disinterested eye at the vase. "It's all right," he responded to my question. "Get it if you want." We had played this game before, naturally falling into our roles—mine as a half-interested buyer and his as a bored, impatient man, ready to leave in a heartbeat. Ed was my clout.

"*Tai gui!*" I replied to the entrepreneur's price. By Western standards it wasn't too expensive, but I knew to start at half the asking price. And so we bargained back and forth, using fingers, writing in the air, on our palms, each of us pausing reflectively after the other's offer. It was when I turned to leave that I got a price I was willing to pay. Ed handed the bowing, smiling vendor the *renminbi* notes, small, scruffy, torn pieces of colored paper, and the forever grateful man wrapped our treasure in old newspapers, which he then placed into a large thin plastic bag.

I felt exhilarated thinking about all the excitement my mysterious vase would generate back in Beijing. I couldn't wait to show it to friends and relay the story of our great luck and cunning negotiation techniques.

Ed carried the precious bundle under his arm as we walked back to the boat for our return trip. We were the last on board, and our tour guide asked, in excellent English, if we had enjoyed the village. I worried he might ask to see our purchase, so, with a hasty "Yes," I followed Ed to the back of the boat.

The river was quieter now. The last of the net fishermen's rafts rested on the rocky embankment, their nets draped over bamboo poles, and the children were gone from the riverbank. Black water buffalo still plodded and dunked their way to nowhere, and the occasional bird swept between lake and sky, but, other than that, we were surrounded by stillness.

The verdant green mountains gradually turned into the darker blue of the sky, like kingfisher plumes, a vibrant, soft blueness, and suddenly I was looking at a Chinese painting. Before this moment, I'd looked on those classical paintings with cynicism, adamant in my conviction that mountains could never be *that* shade of blue. But there they were, from cobalt blue to a hazy mauve, forever changing with the light and mists swirling around the stone mounds. And we floated in this magical place, the water as still as glass, its surface reflecting the mountains around it. The trance-like state abruptly changed when we approached wide bends in the river and their bubbling rapids. These were navigated carefully, with wide turns of the boat along the narrow banks, avoiding the dark, churning center.

Breathing in the cool, sweet air, I thought of how Ed found my magnificent vase and felt a rare contentment. Ed had nestled it carefully under the bench.

"Thanks," I said moving close so our bodies touched.

"What for?"

"This." I swept my arm in front of me. "And the heavenly vase."

"As long as you're happy," he replied. I moved closer and squeezed his arm.

After Ai-yi had left for the day, I called Rebecca to come for tea. "Something to show you," I said.

The vase was in the center of the glass dining table when Rebecca arrived, shinning in all its glory.

"Interesting," said Rebecca. "No, you're right, haven't seen anything like it before." I saw the corners of her mouth twitch.

"Are you laughing?"

"No. Yes." She grinned at me. "Joan, if you like it, that's fine, but, honey, I think it's just awful." She dabbed her eyes as she laughed—at my vase!

I appraised it again. What I had thought beautiful now looked garish, the patterns thrown on without thought, ill proportioned, like an artist's drafts when he breaks down his work. A student's practice piece. Why had I thought it beautiful? I had an "eye." The reigning porcelain expert of the expat community had told me so.

"You're right," I conceded. "It's too ugly to put flowers in."

"Poor Joan," she chortled. "Never mind, let's go shopping tomorrow."

"Thought you didn't want Ai-yi to see it," Ed said upon seeing the vase on the window ledge in the den.

"Yes, I did at first, but I think it's okay. Besides, I want to look at it," I told him. "It fascinates me."

"Glad you like it."

The vase wasn't a complete disappointment; it had provided an opportunity for Ed and me to share an enjoyable experience in a rusty old boat on an enchanted river. So, despite its garish appearance, I left it there to serve as a memento of a happy day spent hunting for treasure.

Photo op with cormorant

The Vase

Going fishing

After bathing buffalo

time for water buffalo to relax

CHAPTER 35

THE LONG HOT SUMMER

Looking back we cannot see the people of the past;
Ahead of us we cannot see those who are yet to come.
I muse on heaven and earth, immense and enduring,
And lonely, engulfed by sorrow, my tears fall.

From: **"Climbing Youzhou Tower," Chen Ziang, c. 760

After our coffee mornings of Straus waltzes, we continued our Sunday walks to Tiananmen Square that had started in the winter. Fruit-flavored ice bars replaced roasted sweet potatoes and chestnuts, and, while we had eagerly feasted on roasted treats, we dared not try frozen.

Parents paraded with their precious only child: boys dressed in tiny grown-up suits, girls with huge red ribbons in their short dark hair, held high on the shoulders of their fathers or in the arms of their mothers. They gathered under the shade of the massif trees as they sucked on treats their parents couldn't afford.

"Expensive pets," said Ed, pointing to the well-dressed children.

"Yes." I smiled. "We all want the best for our children."

"Tell me about it," he laughed.

"I'm so glad Lisa's coming this summer."

Every summer for the past two years, I had gone back to Hawaii. This year would be the exception. I had hoped Chris could join us, at least for part of the time, but he had other plans. And he had his girlfriend now, so, what with his work and school, he was very busy. We'd always treated the children the same, indulging them in equal favors, but the older they got, the more difficult it was to participate in their lives.

"Just wish we could all be together," I sighed. I'd suggested other dates, shorter trips, but this year nothing worked. Maybe next year, I thought. They can come together next year.

"Want German food tonight?" Ed asked. It sounded good to me. The Holiday Inn Lido had several excellent restaurants, and their German place had an informal setting and outdoor seating.

It was a warm evening. Ed drove on wide streets that we had almost to ourselves. High streetlights shone straight down at sporadic intervals, and underneath their bright light stood young men around green-topped billiard tables. We could hear the clink of balls, the quiet cheers or jeers of players and spectators. I couldn't remember having seen so many before.

"Where do they go in winter?" I asked.

"Beats me," Ed replied. "Inside, I expect."

We entered the hotel and walked into the West. The only Chinese were staff—and English the predominate language. The restaurant vibrated with happy noises of people out for a good time. The clients were mostly young foreign men on business living in the apartments attached to the hotel.

"I never thought I'd get tired of Chinese food," I told Ed as I enjoyed the cold, tangy potato salad. "This is so refreshing."

"Get tired of Chinese myself," he replied.

"Who prepares it?"

"Westerners. If you want to make a lot of money, be a chef overseas, *and* they have contracts."

It was a sore point with Ed that the expats working for his company had nothing more than a handshake with their assignment. Whatever guarantees were in place before your move no longer applied. "They offer you something after your tour," he had told me when we first discussed it, "and other guys have made out okay. I'm not worried." I decided not to worry about it either. In fact, Ed was in his fourth year in Beijing, with no move in the foreseeable future.

One lazy Sunday followed the next, and the young men and their billiard tables seemed to multiply. The more I saw them, the more boisterous they seemed to be, the more cigarette smoke snaked up to the lamp lights, the more like a stage set from *West Side Story* these scenes appeared. No other people walked the streets; no lights shone through windows. Only young men were in view, standing around green-topped tables in the spotlight of streetlamps.

"Fred asked if we'd like to join him tonight," Ed announced.

Fred was a hotelier and had spent his life working in exotic places. He'd been married three times and was now alone. "Once the glamor wears off, it's a difficult life for a woman," Fred had opined. "They don't have a real home, and the kids have to go away to school." He told me this the last time we dined together, and I thought how lonely life can be even when surrounded by people.

It was a particularly hot evening, hot and still. We drove our usual route, but something was different, strange. I couldn't tell what at first, like when you suddenly see a new building in a familiar spot and can't remember what was there before.

I realized what was missing. "Ed, the billiard tables are gone."

"You're right," he answered, leaning toward the windshield. Only last week it was a regular sight at the corner of each block to see a billiard table set up under a makeshift light, young men, suit jackets off in the warm weather, standing around and waiting for their turn to play.

"What's going on?"

"Don't know. Probably a government crackdown. Can't have too much fun here, you know." I did know, and I felt unsettled by it. These people have so little. What's the point? I wondered.

Fred met us at the entrance and guided us to the open seating area in the beer garden. He was immaculately dressed as usual, in a summer-weight silk suit. When I'd first met him, I thought he was overweight but soon realized he was a barrel chested, muscular man.

"Where is everyone?" Ed asked, looking around.

Except for us, the beer garden was empty. The only sound I could hear were crickets frantically calling to one another with their scratchy legs.

"It was like this yesterday, too," Fred said, holding a chair out for me. A waiter followed us, beer jug in one hand, mugs in the other. We could see the road from the garden; no traffic went by, not even a bicycle. The extraordinary quiet made me uneasy; icy prickles rushed up my spine. "If you reach 'three one thousand,' you're all right," the boy told me as we huddled in the dark room and waited for the bombs to drop.

"Are you all right, Joan?" Fred asked.

"What? Yes, sorry, fine." I took the proffered menu from his hand, shaking off the dark thoughts.

Over dinner, Fred regaled us with fascinating stories of his life. It was so easy to listen to him; his voice was quite soft, and every tale ended in humor, even the sad ones.

"You know," he said as we all stood up to leave, "this reminds me of the time the Japanese invaded Shanghai. The quiet before the storm kind of thing."

"I feel it too," I told Ed on our way back to the apartment. "Like something bad is going to happen."

"It certainly is quiet," he observed, and we drove home in the uneasy silence.

The next day, I decided to take an early walk under the amazing trees along the streets wrapping Ritan Park. The trees stood tall and straight; their branches greeted one another across the road. I tried to find out their name, and the closest was "scholar's trees." Silver leaves, or seedpods, spiraled down like a spring snowfall, white against a blue sky. I looked for the old men who sunned their precious birds in ornate cages. I saw no one. Not one old man sat under a tree; not one birdcage swung in branches. Disappointed, I turned toward the main road, and out of nowhere came a flatbed truck. Banners hung from the wood-slat sides. Young men in short-sleeved white shirts crammed together yelled slogans, their usual restrained, serious manner replaced with wild enthusiasm, as if they were heading a celebratory parade. Amazed, I stood and watched them drive by, the old truck rattling its way toward Tiananmen Square. Three more followed, their occupants equally jubilant. It was a joyful sight, and I felt light, happy.

From what little I understood, they were students from Beijing University, mostly men. It wouldn't be tactful to question Ai-yi, or Shan Shan, but I wanted to know what was happening.

"Maybe this is why they don't have time for billiards," I joked.

"Ask your teacher," Ed said when I told him. Ernie was my language coach, though he used our time together to practice his English. Justine had recommended him to me months ago, and this chubby, affable young man, eager to know the West, challenged my political knowledge with his questions. Every Saturday, after Ai-yi left, he arrived, and we drank coffee and solved the problems of the world. I gave him *Time* and *Newsweek* magazines off inbound flights, camouflaged in Chinese newspapers from prying eyes.

Ernie didn't come that week, nor the next. Young men on foot joined the trucks, and megaphones helped carry the students' words to busy people who seemed not to notice their presence. The parades became commonplace, and the young were contagiously happy with their flight of fancy, singing their songs and waving their flags, and soon they were greeted with tolerant smiles and friendly waves.

"I hope Lisa gets to see this," I told Ed one evening. Lisa would be arriving in a few weeks to spend her summer vacation with us.

"Don't worry. They're not going to stop any time soon." We spent every evening speculating on the events, confused and amazed at why the rigid government tolerated this open defiance.

"They had a bus today. They'd tied silk flags to it."

"Only one?" he asked with a grin.

The next day, they had more, all confiscated. Nobody intervened. They got bolder, and the happy convoy paraded around the streets of the city on trucks, busses, foot.

Young workers now joined the students. Still, nobody intervened. The more they paraded, the stronger in numbers they became, and I envisioned truck drivers joining in for the sheer fun of it. It was as if the circus had come to town for the first time ever.

Saturday afternoons, Ed and I walked to Tiananmen Square, and there they would be, day and night, sitting under makeshift shelters on the huge granite slabs paving the vast expanse of the square. We didn't stand around or take pictures; we just ambled and tried to look casually disinterested, then popped into the Beijing Hotel for a soda.

As the days passed, I noticed the banners tied to the trucks and busses had become tattered, some of the bus windows broken. The prior jubilation of the crowds seemed flatter, angrier.

"How can they end it now, Ed?" From small beginnings had come this huge situation, and not even the police did anything to stop it. "This isn't Trafalgar Square or the White House."

"Let's hope it doesn't get nasty." His words sent chills up my spine and over my scalp.

The White Lady

Joyful rebellion

And the busses joined the trucks

And here they camped

And they walked to join the parade

And still they came

CHAPTER 36

TIANANMEN SQUARE

> The country torn apart,
> What thought the mountains and rivers are as before?
> And the greenery—too profuse for a city in spring.
> Grieving over the times, the flowers are bedewed with tears.
> Loath to part, the birds are stricken to the heart.
> War has been blazing for three months;
> A letter from home is worth ten thousand pieces of gold.
>
> From: *"Spring View," Du Fu, 757

Lisa arrived June 2, 1989, exhausted from her journey halfway round the world. After a light snack, she stumbled to bed and waited for me to tuck her in.

"Get some rest, kid," Ed said.

"Rest, sweetheart. We'll go out tomorrow." I smoothed the tiny blond curls from around her face and kissed her forehead. She wrapped her arms around her threadbare stuffed teddy bear and, with a "'Night, Mom, 'night, Dad," closed her eyes.

Lisa was up early in the morning, and a delighted Ai-yi fussed over her, face beaming. She unpacked Lisa's case, pressed her clothes, and hovered around eager to do more, practicing her name, "Lee-sah."

"Like your camera, kid?" Ed asked. He'd bought her a Nikon for Christmas. She asked for one for her photography class. It was, she told us, why she really, *really*, needed the light meter, telescopic lens and other camera gadgets too complicated for me to understand.

"It's great, Dad," she beamed, taking it out of the box. She was so organized and took such good care of her things, even as a four-year-old. I knew she'd always store that camera in its box.

"Ready for a walk?" Ed asked. "Your mother wants you to see the parade."

It was one of those hot, muggy days hazy with pollution as we set off for Tiananmen Square. Along the street, young people gathered in silent groups. It was like that all the way to the square. They were parading the day before, but now the streets were still, void of the decorated trucks and busses. There were other people too, silent men walking, riding or pushing bicycles, all dressed in dark pants and white short-sleeved shirts, heads turned toward the silent groups.

"Wonder what's going on," I pondered. I felt the air, now thick with tension, the carnival spirit gone.

"Don't know. Want to go back?"

"Let's walk a while longer," I suggested, watching Lisa practicing with her light meter, taking the odd photo as inconspicuously as possible. We kept on walking toward the square, ignored in the soggy heat.

The crowd got thicker, the humid heat more intense, the smell of sweat more pungent, piles of trash littered the street, and Lisa wilted.

"You all right, sweetheart?" I asked.

"Just hot," she said, her face flushed. "It's so crowded." We had passed the Beijing Hotel, and the crowd was becoming a solid, unmovable mass. Tiananmen Square stood to our left. The world's largest plaza resembled a campsite, unkempt and untidy. Broken-down busses and trucks stood abandoned and looked sad with their torn, worn flags. Garbage was piled high, like remnants of a vast New Year's Eve party. It was the first time I'd seen trash anywhere in China. And there, in front of us, stood a whiter than white statue, her hands holding a torch, reaching up to the sky. She must have been over thirty feet high.

"Ed, this wasn't here last week, was it?" I didn't hear his answer; young men had walked up to us, quietly and whispered in passing,

"Tell your countrymen about us." It was a plea, a desperate last-minute entreaty.

And there was the pole on which perched the student on hunger strike. He was so high, so isolated. His supporters stood below him, waiting. And hundreds or thousands more young people sat on the ground or stood, looking forlorn, lost. To see so many people standing around, a tangible but muted anticipation hanging over them, was disquieting, especially after the weeks of lighthearted play. The hairs on my neck prickled. Sweat ran in straight lines down my back.

I looked at Lisa. My daughter's face looked worried, confused. "We shouldn't be here, Ed," I whispered.

"Think you're right," he agreed. "Hey, Lisa, want a soda?"

We walked in silence back toward the Beijing Hotel, wrapped up in our own thoughts and feelings. Ed led the way; his size gave us easier passage. I was glad he was there with us.

Taxis and cars filled the parking lot in front of the main doors, their drivers and passengers nowhere to be seen. We walked into the poorly lit lobby, over worn red carpet, and past tacky counters selling cheap souvenirs to the coffee bar. The expat community and a few Chinese sat sweating in the shabby, oppressive space. The atmosphere was tense and expectant, as if everyone was waiting for the unthinkable to happen. As if the air-raid warning had sounded and there was nowhere to hide.

There was no air conditioning that day, no waiters to take our order. Ed walked to the bar and came back with flat cokes. We hurriedly drank the warm sodas from their sticky glasses in silence.

"Ready?" Ed asked.

Outside, the crowd seemed thicker, and in front of us a group of young men were viciously punching and rocking an empty parked car. There was nothing for it but to walk right past them. I looked at them, then my daughter. How could I have misjudged this situation and brought her into harm's way? Just like the students, we had all been carried away with the enthusiasm of sudden, unprecedented freedom, like teenagers whose parents have left them alone for a weekend.

"Keep walking," Ed instructed, picking up the pace. The young men didn't seem to notice us, but I held my breath until we passed them. We hurried home to the relative security and absolute silence of the apartment complex.

Ai-yi had left for the day, and Dorothy and Wanda just floated lazily in their palace home. I tapped some food into the water and watched them nibble.

"Not hungry, thanks," answered Lisa to questions about food. None of us were hungry, so I put out crackers and cheese and nuts to snack on.

"Try not to worry, sweetheart. It's going to be all right," I assured her. Useless words. We were all worried. Ed turned on the television. Optimistic agricultural reports were energetically discussed but nothing of the happenings in the capital. We really hadn't expected news—there had been none at all since it started—but it was something to do while we waited. I was good at waiting. Pictures flashed in my mind of dark, crowded closets under the stairs, damp, dark holes in the ground smelling of earth and graves where I had waited. Thoughts I had suppressed my entire adult life tried to claim me again and take me back where I didn't wish to go.

I joined Ed and Lisa on the long, narrow balcony off the living room. It was now in its own shadow. The concrete balustrades were all that I could see if I sat on a patio chair, so I stood, arms resting on the flat top of the wall, staring at the trees lining the way to the square. Not a truck went by; not a bicycle moved along the Ring Road below us. One of the city's major arteries sat silent and still. Lisa and Ed were talking photography and looking through her new telescopic lens.

"Coconut wireless," Ed responded when I asked how the entire population of this city knew to stay off the streets. "They've done it for generations." I was just about to ask him what he thought they knew when I heard the sound of engines. Brand-new bulldozers plodded their way past our apartment building toward the square. Army trucks followed and parked across the road; their uniformed occupants stood on the grass verge alongside them.

"What's going on, Ed?"

"Wish I knew." We stayed there a while longer in the smoggy stillness. Nothing else moved. It began to get darker, and my legs ached.

"Let's go inside," I suggested, opening the glass door. The others followed, and we sat in the kitchen snacking on our luxury reserves:

buttered popcorn, onion-flavored potato chips, macadamia nuts, and apple pie I'd made the day before. A real junk-food feast.

I saw Lisa to bed and left her door ajar. My tall, athletic daughter looked like a little girl again, isolated in her room where Count Dracula was hiding in her closet or under her bed. Ed stayed up much later, waking me from a restless sleep. That night his snore comforted me for a change, and I dozed.

Popping sounds broke the night's silence. It's not New Year, I thought, then fear turned my body to ice. Lisa stood at our bedroom door.

"Guns don't sound like that in movies," she remarked. It was true. These sounds were like those from toy guns, innocent pops. We heard the grinding of heavy vehicles on the road outside our bedroom window. Ed pulled back a corner of curtain to peek through. Army trucks and tanks slowly crept past.

We sat together in the dark. Lisa rested her head in my lap, and I stroked her hair, just as I had every Sunday when she was little, while we watched the Walt Disney program.

"Don't worry, Lisa, it's going to be all right," I told her. "I'm sure they're just trying to get the students to go home, that's all."

"Your mother's right, sweetheart," Ed insisted, though, from his expression, he didn't believe it. I didn't believe it either. The hairs on the back of my neck told me otherwise.

I wondered about Ernie, my student-teacher friend. Why did I let him have those magazines? What if he was found with them? I thought I was being kind, that I was helping him understand the West, improve his language skills.

Ed sat in the chair across the coffee table from Lisa and me and lit cigarettes, one right after the other. Each of us sat quietly, our own private thoughts too unformed to voice. It was a long night.

June 4, 1989. As soon as daylight came, we took our places on the balcony. The road below us was lined as far as we could see, over the flyovers, every inch covered in parked trucks. Black smoke rose in straight columns into the air from Tiananmen Square, joining the heavy pollution, trying its best to hide the tragic scenes below. Helicopters flew back and forth in the cloudless gray sky, huge metal buckets swinging underneath—and I wondered why.

Small groups of young men lined the road, standing silently, waiting. We waited too. We stood on our balcony with an unobstructed view of the Ring Road right below us. I made coffee and opened a package of sweet rolls, and we watched tanks plod by past the army lorries lined up on the main highway as far as the eye could see. We looked down on canvas-covered flatbed trucks packed with men dressed in dark pants and white short-sleeved shirts, the only distinction between them and the crowd watching their yellow hard hats and wooden poles. They jumped out of the trucks and chased the crowds, who scattered before the vicious blows. Their attackers followed. Uniformed soldiers came and joined in the melee. I hadn't expected to see violence—until then I had wanted to believe no one would be hurt. But the roads and bridges were covered in white-shirted men, hundreds and hundreds of them swarming like so many ants disturbed from their colonies. And a thought ran through my mind like an electric current. I looked at Ed. We stared at each other, eyes wide open, as if at that moment we knew the unspeakable. We knew what was burning in the square, what was in the huge buckets swinging on chains from the slowly moving helicopters. I couldn't breathe. I couldn't think. Nobody spoke.

All morning we stood there, watching. I wanted to yell at the unsuspecting people below, like I had at pantomimes a lifetime ago, "Watch out! Run! He's behind you!" And, each time a deserted army vehicle burst into flames, we silently cheered the invisible hero.

Lisa bent down low, hiding behind the balcony railings, and took black-and-white photographs with her new Nikon camera and telephoto lens, took rolls and rolls of film: the tanks, the trucks, the people. She managed to capture the panic on the streets below us, while we remained spectators as if watching a play from our balcony seats at the theater or the coliseums of ancient Rome. We weren't the only ones; our neighbors stood on balconies below, eating breakfast, then lunch, drinking wine. Hours went by as we waited for something else to happen. Then Lisa stood up too quickly and bumped her head hard on the balcony ledge. Tears welled in her eyes, but I knew it wasn't just the pain. Why were we doing this to her, watching this devastation? "Let's go in, sweetheart."

"What shall we do, Ed?" I asked as I rummaged for easy food to cook.

"Just wait, I guess. The embassy said this isn't directed at foreigners. We'll be okay."

Ed made his scheduled calls to home office, finding out what was happening here. We had no news except what we could see from our balcony. The big item, of course, was whether to close down. He decided not to, though other expats did. We picked at food we didn't want, made light conversation hoping to ease some of Lisa's fears, and got ready for bed, street clothes and emergency bags at the ready. We left our bedroom doors wide open.

"They used the Beijing Hotel as a hospital last night," Ed informed me in bed. "Nobody knows how many were killed. They must have cleaned it up fast."

"Is it over?"

"Nobody's sure, but they think so." He told me the news reported from overseas, of the Beijing soldiers who had refused to take action against the protestors, of the soldiers shipped in by train from the provinces who had. "That's why it's dragged on so long," he explained.

I tried but was too frightened to close my eyes that night, haunted by the sight of smoke rising from the square. I knew what it was like to burn alive, to see my flesh melting from my body, to try and run from fires that consumed me. It was my nightmare from the past, the one I could never escape.

Grating sounds penetrated the silence, coming from the ceiling above our bed. "That's the sound," I said. "The noise I told you about. What do you think it is?"

"Beats me. It's definitely not plumbing."

Guns popped sporadically during the night as soldiers shot rifles aimlessly in the air. We saw the holes in the brick walls of our building the following day.

"I'll be okay," Ed said after he told us he was going to the office. "Nothing's happening out there now." He was right. Most of the army trucks and tanks had moved during the night, except for the tank on the bridge, and nothing moved on the road outside. The sabotaged trucks and tanks were the only evidence of the devastation. Not one person could be seen.

Ai-yi didn't come. I hadn't expected her—there was no public transportation—just hoped she was all right. None of Ed's staff arrived, except for the two young Americans from Shanghai.

It became unbearable sitting in our tower apartment, isolated from the world. The phone line had to be kept open, though Ed was the only one who called. He was having a hard time managing the phones at the office, so Lisa and I offered to help, relieved to have something to do.

Ed came to pick us up. As Ed locked the apartment door, the elevator came down, and five or six Chinese men in engineer-type overalls got out and continued their journey down the stairs. We were on the top floor, and, besides long, low brick structures—"for air conditioning," we had been told—we were unaware that there was anything above us or that the elevator went higher. Ed and I exchanged glances. We didn't say anything, didn't want to alarm Lisa. I wondered why the men had walked instead of using the elevator. We soon found out it was locked, so stairs it was for us too.

The apartment landings were covered in mattresses where our neighbors had slept and now camped. They said the bullets were too close for them. But it's not a war, I told myself repeatedly; it's a civil disturbance. Nothing to do with us—it'll end soon.

Lisa and I busied ourselves in Ed's office. It felt good to be useful, to do something to help the panicking people who called. But I knew we should leave soon; rumors were circulating that things would get worse; it would be the foreign community next, though I didn't want to believe that.

Most of the calls, of course, where from Chinese residents, and all we could do was pass the phones over to Ed's two young American employees who spoke fluent Mandarin.

I heard Lisa say, "I'm a volunteer," before she called for Ed. I asked her what that was about. She said it was one of the national news programs looking for information. "I didn't want to tell him I'm a relative," she said. His parting comment to her was "I didn't know the company was so hard up they used volunteers." I saw her face, so serious, so worried, and the comment from the reporter was so ridiculous that I started to laugh. We two gave into the need to release the tension accumulated during the last days and ended up wet faced from near hysteria, pleasantly exhausted.

Kathy came to the office during the day. She lived close by and wanted to know if she could help. It was good to see her, though she was obviously frightened.

"I lent Ernie my bike last night," she told me. "He wanted to get home fast. He lives on the other side of the square." Ernie had called to tell her he heard chanting coming from behind the gates of the Forbidden City. He couldn't make out the words, but the sound terrified him so much that he left her bike alongside the road. "He's in hiding," she said.

I became compelled to watch the streets on either side of our building. I began to like the excitement. I felt alert, energized. I wanted to see what would happen next—though I kept this to myself. What kind of a person was I to find this exciting? I felt ashamed, guilty, horrified, so I rationalized my feelings with the absolute knowledge that the worst was over, and, every time I felt goose bumps of excitement slither up my spine, I thought of Ai-yi, of Ernie.

Creeping out onto the balcony early that evening to join Lisa, I looked down and saw what appeared to be a young man. I nudged Lisa. "Look," I said as he came crawling out from his hiding place under a sabotaged army lorry. We watched as he took a running jump at the brick wall surrounding our apartment building and rolled silently onto the ground inside the compound. My heart skipped a beat—how I wished he were Ernie. We watched as he scrambled up and ran away, bent low, into the shadows. We held hands and silently cheered him on.

Watching was so much better than hiding in the dark, waiting.

I became a spectator of life and death once more. I had no feelings of fear—except for a deep sadness, I had no feelings at all. I was an outsider this time and observed the little things: the absence of the elderly men and women dressed in their dull gray Mao suits who practiced tai chi on the street opposite, the tank on the bridge where a young man lay dead, the terrible silence. I thought of that young man and wondered why his body had been left on the road for such a long time. Why the tank hadn't been moved. And then I knew that, even though this wasn't a war, for all these people, the soldiers, the protestors, the spectators, the results would be the same.

Our son called—frightened. He wanted us home. It was harder for him not knowing. Lisa wanted to stay; it was a unique experience, and her photo portfolio was growing. It seemed prudent to leave, though, so we packed one suitcase each. Ed too; he would move into the Holiday Inn Lido with the employees who were able to get to work. It was outside the city center, safer for them there.

I looked around the apartment one last time. Silk cushions waited to be patted, tables and chairs gleamed from the oil Ai-yi rubbed into the wood, and palms flourished in their porcelain pots. I let them go with a sigh; they were just things. Then I saw Dorothy and Wanda swimming around in their blue-and-white bowl and looked at Lisa. We couldn't leave them. So, into a Tupperware container they went.

The elevators still weren't working, so we trudged down the stairs, Ed carrying two of the heavy suitcases, his briefcase stuck under his arm, and Lisa one, while I carried the fish and a hand carry. We climbed over mattresses and said our goodbyes, not certain we would ever return.

Like in a bad dream, the jeep wouldn't start. The key ground, but the engine refused to turn over. We looked for the guards and saw none. Apart from us, the area was empty.

"Damn!" Ed cursed. "Needs a push. Joan, you sit behind the wheel." He and Lisa got out to push. It didn't budge. Then, out of nowhere, two round, toothless ai-yi toddled to our aid. Smiles on their worn faces, they pushed until the jeep started, then waved us goodbye.

We passed abandoned trucks on the lonely road and saw no one until we entered the airport. Hundreds of people yelled and pushed in a swaying mob. Joe stood on a chair, yelling announcements in Mandarin and English, trying to calm the panicking crowds. Ed checked us in, and words of goodbye came tumbling out: "Take care." "See you soon." "Don't worry." "Call me." "I love you." All those things we say in parting. Lisa and I understood Ed had to leave us, and we sat in the relative calm by the departure gate, waiting.

There was a tall elderly woman, a westerner, walking around in circles amongst the panicking crowd, her hands raised in confusion, tears streaming down her lined face. Not wanting to get separated, Lisa and I walked toward her. Taking her hand, I walked her to an open space with a wall behind us, asked her name, tried to calm her. But she couldn't respond to us. Lisa went over to Joe, asked him to make an announcement about a lost elderly lady, and soon we were joined by her son. He was so relieved to find her and explained that she had dementia; she had wondered off in all the confusion. They were on their way back to Michigan, where she would stay with her daughter. He had business in Beijing and would return as soon as he could.

Our flight was packed, late, and our stewardess openly annoyed at the inconvenience this mob caused her. More passengers joined us in Shanghai, and, when we arrived in Tokyo, news crews pushed microphones and cameras in our faces, asking questions impossible to answer, moving on to the next bedraggled passenger. The flight to Honolulu was oversold, so we went to Los Angeles, and news crews waited for us there as well. It was a relief to climb on board our plane to Honolulu. We were anonymous, relaxing among the happy chatter of tourists and returning locals, apart from them, in a no man's land.

When we were given our agricultural forms, though, I had a moment of panic. Live animals, including fish, were prohibited unless they had papers. While tempted to sneak them in via my hand carry, I have enormous respect for our island home and all of the unique life there. So, with a heavy heart, I sought out the ag man sand waited for his verdict. "What do we have here?" he asked. "Goldfish," he answered, appraising them. And, to our relief, he said, "They're okay."

A very happy Christopher met us at the airport with leis and picked up Chinese food from our favorite restaurant, Kin Wah, which made us all laugh. It was a relief to be back.

Lisa developed her pictures. Some she gave to the local paper to use, but she wouldn't give them her story. Dorothy and Wanda swam contentedly in the aquarium Chris had bought. And I watched the news coverage on television, impressed with the quality and accuracy of the programming, which was mixed with commercials for hamburgers, cars, magic bathroom cleaners. Only then did I tremble with the horror of it all. Memories of black night skies ablaze with fire, planes screaming right outside my bedroom window, of hiding under the bed wishing I could disappear, of fear that burned in my mind and turned my body cold. Nightmares that came and wouldn't go away.

During those five days in Beijing and throughout the turmoil afterwards, I felt connected to every other human being on this Earth. I knew without a doubt we are all walking the same path, confirming what I knew as a child: life and freedom are fragile—not one second can be taken for granted. What we perceive as reality can change suddenly and irrevocably in a heartbeat, never again to be the same.

We are all, friend and foe alike, at the mercy of the powers that be.

That night

waiting for the night

Watching the aftermath from our balcony

Still they come

Where did the come from

And the soldiers came with white shirts, hard hats and big sticks

the following day

The next morning

CHAPTER 37

BETWEEN TIMES

In these peaceful times there is much to enjoy
For those with little talent,
Relishing lonely clouds at leisure
And monkish ways at peace.

From: **"Going up to the Pleasure Gardens," Du Mu, 803–852

Lisa went to the beach and to the stables to ride but avoided all but her closest friends. We both found it hard to get back into a pattern of normalcy. Everywhere we went friends asked about our experiences, too eagerly. The same questions: "What was it like? What did you see? Were you scared?" We were exhausted by it all.

My daughter's grand holiday now spoiled, I planned another trip, somewhere quiet and peaceful—England. I wanted Chris to come with us, but he had worked lined up and couldn't spare the time. Lisa promised to bring back his favorite candy, Smarties.

We went to London to see my mother, then off to Devon for pony trekking. Riding through lush fields and woods on easygoing horses salved our spirits. Living in an old-world country hotel eased our nerves.

"Help, he won't stop," I yelled to Lisa and our guide, Alf. My little horse, now through with his drink, was pawing the stream, drenching me with water.

"Oh, aye," Alf laughed, "should 'ave warned ye about that. Tommy likes a bit of splash, 'e does. Nothing for it but to wait. 'e be through in a bit," Alf assured me, whereupon he sat back in his saddle, looked down the hill at, me and rolled a cigarette.

"Wish I had my camera, Mom," Lisa teased.

"You can come back now if you like," Ed said during our weekly telephone call. I'd begun to wonder if we would ever be able to return. It was the end of July, and Lisa agreed she would like to finish her visit to China.

This time I had no illusions about Ed and me. Somehow, all the anxiety of the past three years, the fears, the hopes had been washed away by the tremendous upheaval of Tiananmen Square, and our trip to England had smoothed the edges. It was as if a blank slate had been placed in front of me with no pressure to fill it in. I would just take it one day at a time. See where everything would take me.

Ed greeted us with hugs. "Good to see you," he said, taking my hand carry. It was good to see him.

"How are you?" I peered around. "It looks grim here."

"Yeah. It's tough."

This airport always had the effect of dampening any mood, but it now seemed as if the porters, the immigration officials, the custom agents had withdrawn into the dull grayness of its walls in an attempt not to stand out, not to be seen. No stamping papers too loudly, no banging suitcases, and absolutely no eye contact.

Tzu Chow drove us, his face serious. I missed his cocky grin. Ai-yi waited for us at the apartment door, face worried as she nervously pushed up sleeves that refused to stay. She smiled her shy smile and chatted away, telling Lisa how pretty she was, how glad that she was visiting China. How good it was to have us back. I had a feeling that she was embarrassed at the happenings, as if she was to blame in some way. I wanted to hug her but knew it would make her uncomfortable.

Ai-yi took Lisa's suitcase, the small one, and beckoned Lisa to follow into the bedroom she'd left last month in such a hurry; she helped put her things back in the cupboards and drawers.

In spite of the warm welcome, the apartment had an empty, lonely feel, and I was reminded of another homecoming after a war. How much I had longed for the day when I would finally come home, see my family once more. Concrete air-raid shelters lined the street. Debris covered the place where a house once stood. I followed my mother up the stairs into our flat. The lath skeleton of its walls lay bare in parts, the wallpaper torn. I looked at my brother, my sister, my mother. I didn't know them, and they didn't know me, and I felt more alone than ever before.

Rebecca came over to meet Lisa; we hadn't had time before. We three sat sipping tea and talking about everything except what really occupied our minds. This we did in Rebecca's car.

"We had to leave the day after you," she explained. "The army came to escort us out. It was frightening. One of the guards at the gate spat at my face. He'd always smiled at me before." Her voice was sad.

We drove to Hobo Town searching for our old friends. I wanted Lisa to meet them. A few were there, but it was a while before they all returned. I watched as they fussed over Lisa, and, though she had no idea what they were saying, their toothless smiles and gentle hand movements communicated how pleased they were to see a young person for a change. There wasn't much to buy, but I saw their anxious glances and bargained for a pot. "But I only want one," I told my old friend. In reality, I didn't want any—they were stoneware in dull colors—but I felt obligated somehow to pretend that everything was as it had been before. The stubborn old man wouldn't break the lot down, so I bought all five. He smiled his toothless smile, totally understanding the game we were playing. Other vendors set up shop on pavements, their wares placed on dirty scraps of fabric or wooden boards. We didn't stay long; it was just too depressing.

"Surprise," I called to Ed when he came home from work. "I got the elevator operator to smile today."

"How about that." He laughed and pulled me onto his lap. I wrapped my arms around his neck and kissed the top of his head.

"Got lipstick on you."

"My badge of honor."

That Saturday, Lisa, Ed, and I continued our interrupted walk to Tiananmen Square and the Forbidden City for a tour. Scars marked the paving, gouged from tanks or bulldozers. The Forbidden City appeared to be opened just for us and a handful of others, all Chinese. We walked through courtyards and into buildings, their magnificence frozen in time, their walls silent to all they had witnessed.

Sunday, Ed drove to the Great Wall, and we climbed steps and walked the undulating path. We drove to another section topping spectacular hills named Badaling. This spot we had to ourselves. It was so quiet and peaceful, the song of air the only sound. The small villages below us looked like toys.

Ai-yi bought persimmons, the soft ones, and showed us how to eat them, along with large sour apples she helped slice for pie. The three of us stood around the kitchen table, Lisa and Ai-yi peeling and slicing while I made pastry. Ed arrived home just in time for hot apple pie, and I served the four of us as we squeezed around the kitchen table, Ai-yi shyly protesting. I knew Ai-yi didn't like the pie by the expression on her face, and, when Ed placed cheese on his, she turned green. Struggling to finish, she said, "*Ming tien, jiaozi.*"

True to her word, the following day Ai-yi made a fine meat filling and dough, which she rolled with a thin dowel and cut into circles. She showed us how to stuff, seal, and crimp the edges of the dumplings and pop them into the boiling pot, laughing at our clumsy efforts.

Ed joined us for lunch that day in our floury kitchen, and we feasted on Ai-yi's dumplings dipped in rice vinegar.

"*Hou che*," I told her while she beamed and piled more on our plates. Ed patted his belly and smiled at her. Praise indeed from Laoban.

Shan Shan arrived. She had heard we were back—the coconut wireless in action. There was so much to show Lisa, special things, and, with Shan Shan in tow, we could visit one that evening. Tzu Chow drove the three of us to the old teahouse down the street from Tiananmen Square. It hadn't changed from the last time Shan Shan and I were there. The old men still told the same corny jokes, singers sang arias from Chinese opera, tea was poured from long-spouted pots, and sugared nuts and tiny rice crackers tempted the appetite. While the room wasn't as full as before, it was still heartening to see that some things still remained, untainted by the events a few steps away. Shan Shan sat back, disapproving of our presence in such common surroundings. She approved even less once outside, and I told her Lisa and I would get a pedicab to the Beijing Hotel, but she hailed one for us, settled the price in *renminbi*, then left us for home.

In we climbed. I wanted Lisa to feel the exhilaration of riding through the city at dusk, past huge flags flapping, snapping in the warm breeze, under lamps along tree-lined streets, all to the sound of bicycle wheels humming. Our driver was a chubby one, and he puffed away in the summer heat, pedaling slowly, and stopped at a hotel—but not the Beijing Hotel.

"*Wo shi Beijing ren*," I told him. He insisted we were at the Beijing Hotel. I wanted him to know I lived here. I was a Beijing person, not a tourist. Smiling, he climbed back on his seat and continued our journey. Every so often, he turned around and said, "*Ni*," to which I responded in like, "*Ni*." And we laughed our way there. He tried to get more money; when that failed, he insisted the fair agreed to was in FEC, not *renminbi*. But I wouldn't budge, and we walked away as his fellow drivers laughed at his protests.

Eager for news about Ernie, I arranged to meet Justine at the Jingyou Hotel for coffee. Tzu Chow drove Lisa and me there. Without the Viennese waltzes, it seemed a sad, grubby place—though their bakery was open, with its lovely selection of pastries and the comforting smell of freshly baked bread.

Justine must have been in her mid to late thirties, Lisa nineteen, but the two students ended up chatting about things common to all, no matter the country or subject. This was the most relaxed I'd ever seen Justine, as, if for a moment, she could forget all the stress and unhappiness in her life. I felt awful bringing up Ernie, but I just had to know.

"I haven't heard from him since that night," she informed me. Tears welled in my eyes as I imagined the worst.

Justine was well, though very distressed over the events. To her, it was history repeating itself, and she was worried that she wouldn't be able to get her student visa to America. I wondered how long it would be before the mood of the city returned to how it had been just a few months ago.

"Years," Ed projected when I asked. "That's what the brains at home office project. Things are certainly slow here now."

Olivia called and invited Lisa and me to tea. We hadn't seen each other in ages due mostly to her very demanding job. Like a lot of expats, she had been called back to London to wait out the political unrest. She had returned just a few weeks ago. "Not all bad," she said when I asked how things were. "They've moved me to that new apartment hotel." I knew the one; it wasn't too far away. "Great, I've wanted to see what it's like," I said.

Ed was still at work, so I called to let him know where we would be. "We'll get taxis," I said, and off we went.

While my friends in China were few, I wanted Lisa to meet every one of them—Olivia especially. She had a very interesting life, and I filled Lisa in with as much as I knew, which wasn't much at all, as we soon found out. Olivia was born in Shanghai, moved to Hong Kong, then to London when she was still a girl, and now full circle back to China, though I didn't know the details. The expat community was like that—we didn't go into our pasts; life was mostly about the here and now. But I had noticed that Olivia was more English in a lot of ways than me, so I knew there was a story there.

We were greeted by her ai-yi, who was just leaving for the day, and we walked into the bright apartment, fresh paint shining on the walls.

Olivia greeted me with a hug. "Welcome, Joan," she said. "And, Lisa, how lovely to meet you. Come and sit down." Olivia put her arm around Lisa and led us to a table loaded with imported treats, mostly from Marks and Spencer's, with a fruit cake from Fortnum and Masons for good measure, the table set with Royal Doulton china. No tea bags present here, and Olivia poured with the aid of a porcelain tea strainer that I admired and which she insisted I keep. "Chinese style," she said. "That's why I hid the Ming vases before you came."

We sat around the table sampling all on offer: McVities digestives, with and without chocolate, scones with clotted cream and raspberry jam, chocolate Swiss roles, and lemon cream biscuits. "How do you get all this fabulous food?" I asked.

"Well, this being classified as a hardship posting, I get two months holiday a year—and six round-trips, first class, so off I go back home and shop."

"Very nice!"

And the evening flew by as Olivia told us about her early days in Shanghai.

Her family were bankers, her mother the powerhouse. "Mother would hold opium parties," she recounted, "for her most-valued clients. All men of course." Evidently, opium parties were much more complex than your average cocktail party. Each guest had a servant, supplied by the hostess, experienced in the use of all the drug paraphernalia, including collecting the tar residue, which would be returned to the shop, where it would be bought back and resold to less affluent customers.

"I used to sneak out of bed to watch. We had a large house, and Mother's guests spread out over two rooms. There were four beds, you know, the Chinese day beds. In each guests would sit or lounge. I remember the satin pillows piled everywhere, the silk screens, and how dark and quiet it always was. The pipes were long and beautifully carved, and cups of tea were constantly offered to each guest. They did chat but very softly, and Mother walked around making sure everyone was enjoying themselves.

"I was very young, of course, and had a nanny who hovered around me night and day, but I got clever at hiding from her. I knew she wouldn't tell or Mother would punish her. I remember our garden with its fishpond and the little bridge that stretched over it and the foreigners who would visit, mostly English businessmen. My mother made a point of my meeting them to practice my English—'and your manners,' she would say."

Lisa and I listened, fascinated, as Olivia continued her story.

"My mother saw the end in sight with the Japanese right at the door, so she made plans to leave for Hong Kong." The safety they hoped for was short lived before the Japanese invaded Hong Kong too. "My father had died by then. It was just Mother and me, and she decided to move to London."

Our tea now cold, Olivia reached for the electric kettle and refilled the pot.

"Let's sit over there," she said, pointing to the settee. We three sat on a chintz-covered sofa covered in big fluffy cushions, fresh cups of tea at the ready.

Lisa leaned back, hugging a cushion, wide eyed, drinking it all in, wanting more, and Olivia obliged. By the time they had bribed their way to the United Kingdom, their enormous wealth had dwindled. "Money was put aside for my education, and she held on to most of her jewelry," Olivia recalled. "My mother was very women's lib. And a lot was used in various clinics to treat her opium addiction. But she made it, and she adjusted to a life without maids and cooks and chauffeurs . . . and drugs."

It was as if we'd spent the evening listening to one of those radio Storytime programs. By the time her story was over it was 1:00 a.m., and, while I sensed there was more, and I had questions buzzing around in my head, it was time to leave. Olivia had to work the next day.

Wrapping up the leftover treats, Olivia handed them to Lisa. "Chinese style," she said, smiling.

We hugged goodbye, and I knew that Olivia had shared a great deal of her very private life with us. I felt honored and told her so. We became lifelong friends. Years later, I did find out more, including the history of her huge eleven-carat yellow diamond ring.

In the taxi on the way back to the apartment, Lisa closed her eyes, sighed, said, "Wow," and collapsed back in the seat.

Guilin's famous mountains

Tommy and friends

On the boat to Guilin

My favorite transport

CHAPTER 38

SUZHOU: SILK SCREENS AND CLASSICAL GARDENS

Planting flowers serves to invite butterflies,
Piling up rocks serves to invite clouds,
Planting pine trees serves to invite the wind...
Planting banana trees serves to invite the rain,
Planting willow trees serves to invite cicadas.

From: "Planting Flowers," Zhang Chao, 1650–1707

"You girls want to join me in Shanghai?" Ed asked. He was due that week. Silly question, of course we wanted to go, if only for the food.

Happy, busy sounds pervaded the bright airport. The heavy oppression of Beijing hadn't reached Shanghai.

Ken met us with his usual enthusiasm, and off we set, Chang Zhang at the wheel, to Ken's new office. He was now ensconced in the Hilton, and, even though I really liked the seedy atmosphere of his old office, with its shuttered windows and high ceilings and lazy fans, I had to admit this was a vast improvement. For one thing, the air conditioning worked!

After everyone in the office fussed about Lisa, Ken told us he'd arranged a day trip to Suzhou for Lisa and me. His office assistant would be our guide. Her name was Ling. She was in her early thirties, pretty and bright with very good English. Chang Zhang would pick us up around seven the next morning and bring us back around seven that evening.

By the time we set off, it was closer to eight than seven. Chang Zhang obviously had a difficult time with punctuality. Ken had given him a watch that year, but it didn't seem to make much of a difference. His smiling face and eagerness to make up for any inconvenience smoothed over the irritation I felt at having to get up early only to wait.

Suzhou is west of Shanghai, about a two-hour car ride away. As we drove through country as lush and green as Hawaii, I was struck again by how different Shanghai was from the stark dryness of Beijing. The only thing in common, I thought, was the pollution.

Once parked, Ling led Lisa and me along a narrow road that opened up to equally narrow canals on either side. Houses lined the banks, some with gardens and brick walls in front of them, others where the house walls met the water as it glided gently past. They were made in the traditional folk-house architecture and looked as if they'd been there for hundreds of years. Made of wood and earth, painted white, with thatch or tile gabled roofs, each was unique, no one exactly like the other. They were absolutely delightful. We crossed a small bridge with low stone balustrades and continued down this enchanting street, past more canals lined with houses and the occasional restaurant. We were on a tour of the old part of town, the area famous for its silk fabrics and carpets.

Ling stopped in front of an open door of what looked like a house and beckoned for us to follow. The door was wider than usual and, except for a small window, let in the only light. Two gray-haired men were inside, both wearing shorts and wifebeater t-shirts. One stood against a wall under the window, working a spinning wheel, while the other sat at a horizonal loom, creating an intricate silk carpet. So far, he had finished about ten inches, and in that space were four different patterns. Deep in concentration, they didn't seem to notice our presence, and the only sounds were the soft hiss of the spinning wheel and the click, click, click of the loom. I'd seen wool carpets made by hand; they were on vertical looms, and a pattern had been transferred onto the warp yarns in the colors of the finished carpet. I saw no such markings for this carpet and marveled at the skill required to produce it.

We stood there, fascinated, until Ling signaled for us to leave. Our next stop was a shop selling all things silk, from yardage to double-sided embroidery. Bolts of silk lined the walls of this small shop from floor to ceiling—solid patterns, floral prints both delicate and bold, different weights, from charmeuse to chiffon. There were just too many choices, so we settled on the double-sided table screens, one with a ginger cat chasing a grasshopper, the other a yellow bird sitting on the branch of a cheery tree in blossom.

The air was heavy, and Lisa and I started to wilt in the humid heat. Time for lunch, Ling announced. She knew we weren't that adventurous, not like Ken and Ed, so played it safe, and we found ourselves in a small. immaculate restaurant, with glass-covered tables and blue-and-white dishes. Here, we enjoyed a delicious meal of Suzhou-style dim sum. My favorite had to be the fried crab cakes made with potatoes and carrots, though shrimp fried with green tea leaves was a treat, while Lisa enjoyed moon cakes, spring rolls, and fried steam buns—"Just like manapua," she declared.

Suzhou is also famous for its classical gardens. There are over a hundred of these, each with its own unique features and name: Lingering Garden, Master of the Nets Garden, Mountain Villa with Embracing Beauty, to name a few. Ling was taking us to Humble Administrator's Garden, the largest, and one that was in the process of being restored.

On the short drive there, Ling did her best to explain the history of Chinese gardens. Designed and built mostly by scholars, each would contain four primary elements: water, rocks, plants, and structures. Except for the higgledy-piggledy rock gardens of England, I'd never thought of rocks as a garden feature.

And there it was, dating back to the eleventh century, a quiet haven inviting us in. Have you ever watched an acrobats' performance, thinking there's no way they can improve on that? Well, that's what these exquisite gardens presented to us. Huge rocks pockmarked by time and seasons stood regally, demanding attention and wonder at their survival. Trees, with their gnarled, arthritic branches, leaned and reached, teasing the eye to follow. Ponds, serene green pools, reflected all that is around them. And the pavilions and pagodas were placed just right to stand under and contemplate.

We strolled from one such scene to another, and I felt as if I were walking through a classical Chinese painting, one that had no ending. The scenery seemed to wrap itself around us, unlike the garden of Beijing's Summer Palace, which was spread out around an enormous man-made lake, where finding shade meant long walks through the bare grounds—though the white marble boat was a fascinating thing to behold as it stood at the edge of the lake in all its regal glory. I suppose the boat represented a structure in keeping with the four elements; it certainly couldn't float. There were plenty of visitors to that garden, mostly families out for a day. But here, in this ancient place, it was cool and quiet, and nobody spoke, as if we were all under its spell. We didn't see anyone else during our stay, and I wondered if entry was limited.

Too soon it was time to leave this magical world where the air was sweet and clean, time to head back to the polluted, crowded reality of Shanghai. We talked about the gardens on our ride back, and Lisa and I shared thoughts on the structured gardens of Hampton Court Palace, the classical gardens of the West, where man chopped trees into shapes, grass was mowed short and in stripes, and ornate fountains shot water into ornate pools, about how those gardens caught the eye and demanded attention, while the classical gardens we had just visited invited their guests to become one with nature.

That evening, Lisa and I enjoyed Shanghai's famous noodles in the Hilton café. It was one of many small shops placed behind the copper-covered elevators. A narrow, ornamental river sliced through the white marble floor dividing the lobby into the lounge and business area. A low ornamental bridge connected the two sides. We were both tired after our excursion, so we decided to relax in the elegant hotel lobby before going to our rooms. With its lush carpets, softly shaded lamps, and comfy chairs, it was just right, and we sat sipping sodas and listening to the pianist as he played Gershwin. Except for a western businessman, we were the only guests, and, as I looked around, I caught his eye. He raised his glass to us, and I returned the gesture.

"Mother!" scolded Lisa, to which I responded, "It's perfectly acceptable for a man to acknowledge two beautiful women." We both laughed. I leaned back in the comfy chair, looked at my daughter and sighed. Life doesn't get any better than this.

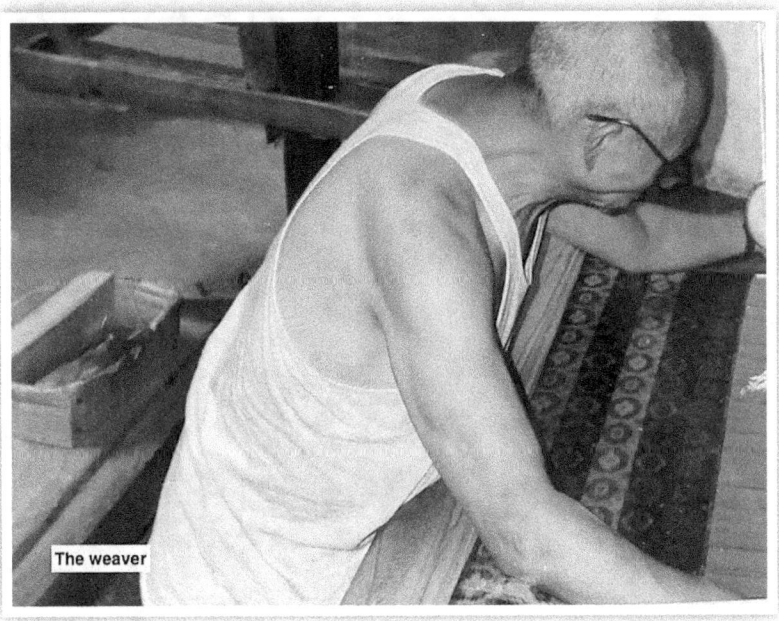

The weaver

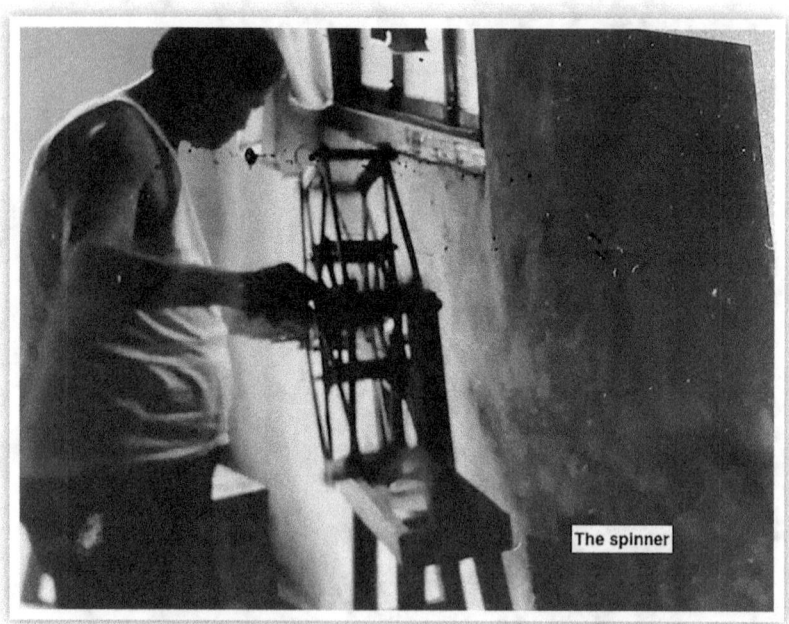

The spinner

Charming Suzhou

Hard working pair

A master holds court

In a garden

CHAPTER 39

TERRACOTTA WARRIORS, YURTS, AND YAK BUTTER TEA

I find the country in hubbub—mustering in, sure enough.
I ask the officer in charge,
"Why no grown-ups? Place too small, perhaps?"
"Commandant's orders came last night;
The draft age is lowered to eighteen."

From: *"The Officer at Xin'an," Du Fu, 759

"Where do you girls want to go?" Ed had those tempting tourist flyers with him and placed them on the dining table. "My friends at CITS are almost out of work."

We decided on Xian, Guilin, Mongolia, and Tibet. Ed would go with us to Xian and Mongolia, places he had yet to see.

Once out of Beijing, we became curiosities. Three people from outer space, colorful people with strange hair and bright clothes. I had found on other journeys that returning stares with smiles made me feel brave, so I smiled and received a predicable response of open mouths or the beginnings of a smile, like a practice smile. In any case, I felt easier acknowledging our strangeness. "We're just like you," I tried to communicate with my teeth. Lisa received the most attention, especially from young men. With her lustrous, long blond curls, she was accustomed to turning heads, but I could see she was uncomfortable here. She was expected to do something and didn't know what.

We were all expected to do something during our time in Xi'an. Our shabby hotel boasted a dance floor in which Western music blared from speakers and young people jumped around, awkwardly imitating what they thought were the latest Western dance steps under one of those rotating balls of chipped mirrors. They tried to get us to join them, show them the moves, but Ed doesn't dance, and Lisa and I weren't about to be on display, so we left the happy crowd earlier than I would have liked.

The next morning, we set off to see the wall surrounding the city of Xi'an. Our guides advised us on which part to visit for the best view and the neglected parts to avoid. So we ventured off, up crude steps and onto the wide wall, where we were rewarded with an amazing view of both the bustling city and the encircling areas. We didn't stay long. There were vendors everywhere, pushy and bold. Not at all our usual experience.

It was the same out on the street. "Stay close to us here, Ed," I requested as we walked down a narrow brick-walled alley crowded with young men who pushed cheap trinkets and puppets made from dried ox skin used in shadow-puppet theaters in our faces.

Xi'an's most famous attraction, the terracotta warriors, we had to ourselves, as well as the inevitable guide. We walked the earthen floor and wooden planks placed between columns of figures and looked down into pits where life-size soldiers marched forever in the crude building enclosing them. Ed was in awe of the Terracotta Army, and, while I admit to amazement at their individual faces and the sheer size of the army, I wasn't as enthusiastic, and neither was Lisa.

"So, there are thousands of them," she said. "It's still a grave."

We were impressed with the magnificent bronze carriage with its fine detail and size, pulled by elegant horses, but Ed still voted the warriors as his favorite. Maybe if there were just one or two . . .

After a short rest stop in Beijing, we set off again, this time for Mongolia. We were in the hands of the local tourist office, and they wanted to spoil us. Not the cities for us, Ulaanbaatar, Urumqi, but the plateaus and steppes.

Lisa loves to ride horses, and, as Mongolia has its own breed of small, sturdy horses, not to mention their fierce riding history, our first stop was to a farm, where each of us, Ed included, got to sit in a wooden saddle on top a skinny, bad-tempered horse. Ed's feet almost touched the ground, but the little horse kept walking, and Ed actually smiled, his standard "horses are big and stupid" forgotten.

Mongolia covers a huge area, and we spent many hours in cars getting from one place to another, but the scenery more than made up for it, from the magnificent deep blue Tianshan Lake and its backdrop of snow-covered mountains to the steppes with their rock prayer shrines, prayer flags blowing in the wind, and a clear bright sky that went on forever.

"Tonight, you're in for a treat," Ed announced, a sneaky smile on face. No matter how much Lisa begged, he would say no more. We'd been driving on the grasslands all day, the overwhelming isolation broken only by the occasional horse looking like it was about to step off the Earth and into the sky. We found out later that they were all hobbled, not the lone majestic animal claiming its rightful place in the wilderness but a skinny old nag having a bit of a rest. There wasn't a tree in sight, then, out of nowhere, appeared a house, more a cottage, made from the same earth that surrounded it, smoke rising from its chimney.

"Tea break," our guide said, and out of the cottage came a tall thin golden woman wearing traditional handwoven clothes. She held out her hands, welcoming us into her home, where we were treated to yak butter tea. The house was one room, with one small window and low ledges around all four walls, broken only by the door. Our guide told us the ledges were heated from the fire burning in the open hearth and used as beds. That impressed me. How comforting that must be to come in from this open, windy world and curl up on a warm bed in this cozy cottage. I would have liked that growing up in wet, windy London.

Our hostess was probably a prop used to impress us foreigners, but I still enjoyed meeting her and feeling welcome in her immaculate home. The yak tea? Quite another matter.

"No, that wasn't it," Ed replied when Lisa asked if that was the treat. "That is still to come."

It had started to get dark—and I discovered for the first time what dark really meant. There were no lights except those from the car. I couldn't wait for night to see the sky.

The car stopped/ Our guide retrieved our bags and led us to an innocuous one-story concrete building and handed us over to a sharp-faced, dark-skinned man with cropped, graying hair who smiled his welcome and led us outside again to a yurt. This was my first yurt, and, while I knew it would be round, I had no idea it would be made of what looked like rolls of thick felt wrapped in canvas and tied like a birthday present, ready to be packed up and moved to another place.

"Surprise!" Ed declared. The yurt had thick mattresses plonked on the earthen floor, with cushions and pillows and blankets piled on top. There was a narrow path leading in and out and an opening to the sky in the center. Lisa and I looked at each other, knowing that we both expected all kinds of creepy crawlies to attack us in the dark.

"What?" Ed asked. "It has plumbing." And it did—a small sink alongside the felt-covered wall. I sighed. Lisa gave him what in Hawaii we call "stink eye."

Our host signaled to us that food would be served in the main building, and Lisa and I followed him out. Later, I checked to see if they had any inside rooms for rent. But, of course, they didn't.

The huge dining room boasted round tables dressed in white starched cloths and about a million dead flies lying on the windowsills and floor. Huge, dead flies. Ed, unaware of our displeasure, sat at one of the tables and helped himself to the beer that was waiting.

Lisa and I exchanged glances. "I have a plan," I whispered as we joined Ed. "Don't worry."

There were no menus, and our meal arrived on three plates. Each plate held the best part of a boiled leg of lamb. I like lamb, as does Lisa, but we like it roasted, with roasted potatoes, golden and crunchie, and sweet peas and mint sauce.

"Ed, do you think they have anything else?"

"Nope," he said, pointing to the only other guest, whom I hadn't noticed until now. He was dressed in a very expensive suit, white shirt, dark blue tie, as if he were in London—or Tokyo, as, on second look, he was Japanese. He too had a plate of boiled lamb in front of him. A high-flying businessman by the looks of him. I wanted to ask him if he was staying somewhere other than a yurt, but my courage failed me.

"How do we eat this?" Lisa wondered. Good question. There were no utensils bar a long narrow knife at each place setting.

"Like this." Ed proudly demonstrated how to carve off a hunk of gray meat and pierce it with the two prongs on the end of the knife, then shove it in your mouth, which he did with relish. "Put hair on your chest," he said. Lisa rolled her eyes.

The meat was so dry I don't think my mother could have made lamb stew out of it, even if she cooked it all day. Poor old sheep probably died of hunger before it was boiled.

Once back in the yurt, I proceeded to empty Ed's suitcase of his clean t-shirts and underpants, which Lisa and I used to dress up our pillows. We also used his long socks, into which we shoved not only feet but the bottoms of our jeans.

"Not bad, sweetie," I observed, and Lisa and I snuggled down on the very soft mattress, facing the round hole in the yurt's top. "And at least we can see the stars." As soon as the words were out, on came the spotlights. Real spotlights, bleaching the sky.

"Do you think it's to keep the bad guys away?" Lisa asked. Ed and I had no idea at the time and said the most reassuring things we could come up with—but, soon enough, we found out.

Exhausted after a busy day, we soon fell asleep, and a second later, or so it seemed, Lisa woke me up. "What's that sound, Mom?"

Oh no! Sheep or goats. Lots of them, filling the night with bleats. Lisa and I peeked out the flap door, and there they were, skinny, grubby sheep coaxed along by a man with a long stick toward another large outbuilding. On their way to be slaughtered. That was the end of sleep for us girls. Ed snored through it all.

Breakfast consisted of boiled eggs, no plate, and a bowl of chock. Thankfully, no mutton.

So much for Mongolia, I thought. Maybe that's why tourists go to the cities, where I'm sure they have plumbing and beds, and restaurants that serve more than boiled eggs and mutton.

Home Sweet Home

On the road to nowhere

CHAPTER 40

RETURN TO TIBET

Its whitened walls and crimson pillars
Shimmer with light and color;
Its portraits of spirits and ghostly beings
Fill it with green and red.
I mount the steps and bending low
I offer food and ale,
Wanting with these humble things
To show my heartfelt feelings.

From: **"The Rocks on the Mountains," Han Yu, 768–825

"Here are your papers," Ed said, with his usual cautionary "don't lose them." These were the documents Lisa and I needed for visiting Tibet. Ed had also managed to obtain a very special letter "granting us safety" from the head of the internal travel bureau. Why that was necessary I didn't know, but we were officially real VIPs.

For some unexplained reason, it was necessary for us to go via Chengdu, where we stayed overnight going and coming, wasting precious days. It wasn't until we were in Chengdu Airport waiting for the connecting flight that I began to feel uneasy. For Lisa's sake, I pretended to know more than I did, but Mandarin wasn't spoken at our transit stop, and the flight board was set by hand and in Chinese. There were lots of open spots on the board where departure times should have been displayed. Maybe they were short on numbers or didn't care—or, worse, didn't know. We soon found out it was the latter, and it was one mad rush when a departure was announced, as if the passengers were late getting to the gates, not the other way around. As I waited, straining my ears to hear something that sounded like Lhasa, I noticed a man sitting across from us wearing a shabby Western suit, elbows resting on his knees, looking down at the dirty floor. He was the only one besides us that didn't have a bag of peanuts or dumplings and a flask of tea at the ready. His skin had that glorious golden glow of high altitudes. He looked up, perhaps feeling my stare. He was Tibetan, and I hoped was waiting for the same flight as us.

He stood up as I heard what sounded like "Lhasa." I urged Lisa to pick up her hand carry, and we followed the man in the shabby suit out onto the tarmac to our tiny plane. Other passengers steered around us, heading for their own planes that were plonked in what appeared to be no order at all, the only identifier the number displayed on its tail. There was no time lost in boarding or takeoff; everyone scrambled for a seat, any seat, strapped in, and off we went.

A car waited for us at the other end with a driver and guide. No sign in hand, this was a discreet meeting, and our guide knew who we were immediately. Of course, it didn't hurt that we were the only tourists. Our young Chinese guide was lean and serious, no smile to spare. She told us her name was Miss Fan. Her English was perfect. There was a sadness about her; maybe this wasn't a choice location for a guide, not enough tourists, especially now, after Tiananmen Square. Knowing how the government discouraged contact with the Tibetan people, it must be a lonely place for a young woman too, I thought.

We drove through the glorious landscape for two hours, and I asked to stop on the way so we could see the rivers that cut ice blue through the golden-red land and see the mountains above brought into the glossy water. My last trip was in winter, but the only change I could see was an extra softness in the colors of the land, the sharp glare of the sky not so harsh.

Prayer flags started to become more frequent, colorful pieces of cloth waving their way up the mountain to the sky, and there, suddenly, like a mirage, stood the magnificent white walls of the Potala Palace staggering up the Marpori Mountain. Thirteen stories of buildings. More than one thousand rooms. Stupas, covered in gold and gleaming in the sun, reaching even higher.

We arrived at the Holiday Inn where we had stayed last time. It looked even more neglected, and I thought maybe we were the only guests. At the time, it was the only Western hotel available. Miss Fan bade us goodnight, reminded us to stay safely in the hotel, and told us she would be back at nine the next morning.

Today, Miss Fan informed us, we would visit the Potala Palace. She and our driver would be waiting for us where we were dropped off at the end of our visit. Guides on our previous trip had done the same, left us to our own devices. It was always a relief not to have to listen to their constant talking, informative though it may be. I found it distracting and would rather just ask questions than be fed facts I would soon forget. I did want to know when it was completed—1648 Miss Fan told me.

The natural light seemed brighter than bright as it reflected off the whitewashed buildings, so, sunglasses on, we climbed the steep wide stairs carved out of the mountain. Each step stirred up puffs of golden dust. Earth-colored dogs sat in doorways or slinked along, tail between legs, nose to the ground, sniffing out scraps. They gave us quick, edgy glances. I wondered if they were rabid.

Lisa walked alongside me, new Nikon camera around her neck, multi lenses in her photographer's vest, along with extra rolls of film in black and white and color and pens for marking finished roles, looking every bit the college student impersonating a *National Geographic* photographer. We pretended not to see the machine guns aimed at the monasteries or the Chinese soldiers dressed in civilian clothes trying to blend in with the Tibetan people . . . or know they were there to control the monks.

There were no other tourists, no other "big noses," and there were fewer monks than last time and many more hungry dogs. Ragged cloth prayers streamed up the mountainside like abandoned laundry. They reached up to where the red-gold earth touched the cloudless Botticelli blue sky. Coral and turquoise and amber, the treasurers of Tibetan women, braided in their black shinny hair and worn like crowns.

We continued past walls made from the same red-gold earth and climbed until we reached what appeared to be a rooftop, a wide expanse of rock paving surrounded by a low wall. I felt I could touch the sky, like the stupas, covered in gold. And there he stood, our first monk. He walked toward us, his blood-red robes flowing with his graceful steps. He spoke no English, we no Tibetan, but, through signals, he made it clear he wanted to borrow Lisa's camera. He placed his palms together in a wai when she offered it and took it carefully in both hands. We followed him over to the low wall. He held the camera up to his eye and adjusted the telescopic lens. Up and around he gazed, as if in wonder of what he saw. I looked closely at him and wondered if the walls of the palace had been his only experience. He was perhaps twenty-five, handsome, with golden skin and a closely shaved head. The muscles on his arms were long and defined. He reminded me of my tai chi master and the inner strength that radiated around him. With a beaming smile, he handed Lisa back her camera, bowed, and began walking past us.

"May we take your picture?" I asked, using hand signals.

"Mom!" Lisa scolded with her eyes. But her new friend didn't mind. He stopped and signaled that we could take a picture together and asked a passing monk to do the honors. His gift to us.

That done, he continued on his way. I took another picture of him walking down the uneven steps as we followed a few strides behind and saw him enter an open doorway. Miss Fan had given us a set of rules to follow: no taking pictures of soldiers in uniform, machine guns, or engaging in any way with local inhabitants. But nothing was said about entering open doors. We entered the dark room.

The floors were smooth, unpolished wood planks, dark with age. Wooden posts reached up to the high ceiling, each one a work of art, painted in faded shades of red and orange with demons and flowers. High, narrow windows let in shafts of light, and silk flags grouped in circles moved gently from the breeze. A large drum painted red stood in the center. The room smelled like a pine forest on a dry spring day. Four monks sat in the middle of the room, young apprentices behind them. All sat cross-legged on a worn dusty carpet, busy filling small boxes with tiny Buddhas, earth, and dried leaves. Those were to be given to the devout and worn close to the body to ward off evil. Incense burned and smoked around us, creating a soft haze. It seemed so peaceful.

"I smell pot," Lisa said. What a thought! And how did she know? Maybe she was right, but I preferred to think of the rarified atmosphere as spiritual rather than chemical.

We stayed there, unnoticed, watching this silent activity that had probably gone unchanged for hundreds of years, until I remembered that our guide would be waiting.

"Sorry, Lisa, but time to go."

She sighed, and a monk spoke, "You are welcome to come back," he said—not just said but in perfect Oxford-educated English! I looked at the monk who had spoken; he was perhaps thirty, hands busy gently sorting the contents for his next prayer box. I was flabbergasted. He was amused, and, hands in a wai, he told us, "*Tashi delek.*" How I wanted to talk to him, hear his story, but it would be like chatting frivolously in a cathedral during high mass, so I just returned his greeting, marveling at the secrets contained within these walls.

Then, just as we left the room, a very old monk walked up to us, a smile exploding from his wrinkled face. "*Tashi delek,*" he said, raising his hands in a wai. "*Tashi delek,*" we repeated. The old monk just stood there in front of us, leaning on his knobby walking stick, his smile never faltering in spite of the fact he had no teeth. With his enormous smile and sticking-out ears, he looked rather like a mischievous elf. Then, through a series of signals, he told Lisa she could take his picture in exchange for one of her ballpoint pens. He directed us over to a low stone wall where we sat while another monk took our photo. It was a fabulous exchange, and Lisa and I knew we had received the better part of the bargain.

On the way to meet Miss Fan, Lisa shared a thought: "I bet the monk who borrowed my camera was looking for soldiers and machine guns." My thoughts exactly.

Off we went to visit the Jokhang Temple, where scarecrow men and hollow-faced women completed their journey of a lifetime. taking them months to reach this sacred place by foot, or prostration, a trip that, for us, involved just days in the comfort of planes and private cars. The women's black and silver hair, smoothed with yak butter, hung behind them in thin unraveling braids. Their bony hands rotated huge prayer wheels that surrounded the outer walls of the temple, and they hummed sacred mantras as they shuffled along, shadows of one another.

It was as if time had stood still since I was last here, like Brigadoon, where life continued in an otherworldly sphere, separate from the outside world. Precious food, potatoes and radishes, barley and yak butter were placed on ledges in the courtyard, offerings from the faithful. Stone pots, crammed with incense sticks, sent straight spirals of vapor into the sky, and their fragrance filled the air. Crimson-robed monks, linked together by a continuous cord, sat cross-legged in prayer, chanting mantras, ringing tiny bells just as before.

"*Tashi delek,*" a woman greeted me, then whispered words I couldn't understand. I examined her face, etched in lines of worry and bronzed as the earth around us. She continued talking in her soft, gentle voice. I looked at Miss Fan. "What is she saying?"

"She wants to be reincarnated like you," she told me.

Miss Fan wouldn't join us inside Jokhang Temple, so we stood in the square, where Miss Fan shared legends around the origin of this very special place: a temple built by an emperor to wed his beloved, a temple built to house a sacred statue, about the dragon it is built on, the Earth Dragon, which keeps the buildings up, but the one constant is its age. It was built in 652, making it the oldest architecture in Lhasa.

Fourteen hundred years of worship. I felt uncomfortable, somehow not worthy of being in this sacred place, but it was too late to turn back. I took a last nervous look at our guide before leading Lisa toward the dark waiting rooms of the temple.

Dozens of hands ushered us gently in front of other pilgrims purchasing silk scarves. All stood aside and made room for us. Smiles lit up their faces. Their kindness couldn't be snubbed, so Lisa and I bowed our heads in acknowledgement and bought three white gossamer silk scarves and gave them to the waiting monk. Making marks in red ink, he chanted prayers over the scarves and put them into the waiting fire, their smoke and prayers destined for Heaven.

As if in a dream, we followed pilgrims along a narrow stone path, an act of faith, as the candlelight almost disappeared in the heavy smoke from the incense holders lining the walls, leaving us wrapped in a yellow fog, while the passageway under our feet undulated like an underground cave. Images of Buddha floated on the walls, the intensity of the jewels that decorated them softened in the smoldering light.

And I forgot I was the foreigner with the red hair. I became another pilgrim walking a sacred path of accumulated love.

We visited the last room. Narrower than the others, its rough stone walls were draped in thangka, Tibetan Buddhist paintings mounted on silk brocade. Reluctantly, I walked outside into a piercingly bright light to meet our guide.

I watched my fellow pilgrims walk past, soft smiles on faces. "*Tashe delek*," they said, "*Tashe delek*," I repeated. Still unable to grasp their kindness, I again asked Miss Fan.

"They hope to be reincarnated as someone like you and your daughter," she told me, "Westerners, free from poverty and suffering."

I wanted to tell them how wrong they were, how poor and unnourished my spiritual self had become, how I longed for their faith, but, without their language, I could only watch them, humbled by their presence.

Miss Fan was an expert on Tibetan Buddhism and went to great lengths to explain the sacred tankas and their meanings. I felt guilty with her wasting her knowledge on someone like me and secretly hoped there wouldn't be a test. We went into a shop that sold amazing paintings, but there were so many, and, what with the various designs and their religious meanings and the significance of the colors, the pressure was so great to choose one that I left with none. Lisa, too, seemed overwhelmed by choice.

I looked for the stalls that tempted me last time, but they were nowhere to be seen. Neither were the pilgrims with their sacred sheep. In fact, there was an emptiness all around us, as if we were late to the party and it was now over. And we had less freedom than our last visit, no more strolling down alleys, walking in the market, our visit confined to the approved sites, I expected. Or perhaps "VIP" had another meaning we were unaware of.

After our amazing day, we were glad to be back in our hotel, shabby though it was. Miss Fan left us with gentle but firm reminders to stay inside and not stray. We had other plans.

Kathy had given me the name and address of an art studio that was quite near the hotel, so, after a quick meal, we set off to find it. With Lisa's blond hair and my red, we hardly fit in, so we opted for the casual night-stroll look as cover. We found the shop easily enough, but the two-story wooden building was boarded up. Disappointed, we were turning to leave when a tall young man appeared from the shadows and whispered greetings to us in English. I showed him Kathy's note. He nodded and indicated to follow him around the back to a small door. Taking a key from his pocket, he took us inside and up a crude wooden staircase. There were no lights. The room we entered was filed with paintings, all with Buddhist themes and forbidden for sale. The lighting was poor, only what seeped through the dirty windows, but that didn't dimmish the beauty of the artist's work. So many choices, but we chose two, one featuring three monks standing tightly together, heads lowered, prayer beads in hand, faces as craggy as the rocks behind them, and another in oils depicting the worn, worried face of an old monk, arranged as if he were fading away, with a young apprentice below him with his steady gaze, his calm, unlined face looking hesitantly out. Our young friend rolled them up and disguised them as much as possible with brown paper. We paid the price, which was embarrassingly low, and went back to our hotel. I counted on Miss Fan not questioning our package; it would be impolite, as we were foreign guests, VIP status. The irony was the artist is Han Chinese.

The next day, we started our journey back to Beijing. Our paintings, rolled in brown paper and wrapped in string, held in one hand, a small hand carry in the other, with Lisa dragging the wheelie case, we made our way to the lobby and Miss Fan.

Three nights and two days is all we had, though they left impressions enough to last a lifetime. Except for the monks and the devout women, I never managed to meet a Tibetan—they had become ghosts in their own land—but the contact I had experienced created a bond and a deep respect for their culture and traditions.

We rode in silence most of the way, eyes taking in the magnificence around us. When we arrived at the airport, with its noise and chaos, it was as if our trip to those magical mountains was a dream.

It was frowned on to tip anyone in China—the government strictly opposed it—but we did it anyway. A gift with cash was more palatable, gave a better impression than money alone. To my surprise, our Chinese driver, who hadn't spoken a word, gave me a small stone in the shape of a mountain, and Miss Fan explained it was part of the holy mountain we had just left. I knew it was special to him, and it still sits on my bedside table.

Tzu Chow met us at the airport, and, by that time, Lisa was in panic mode about her return to school. Timing was tight, and she still needed supplies. And the reality of our real world overrode the wonderful state of peace Tibet had created for us.

Two days later, Lisa and I were on our way to a quick stop over in Honolulu via Tokyo, then New York. Once at the airport, the pressure eased up just a bit.

"Have to use the loo, Lisa," I said, and she sighed as she followed me to the women's toilets. I looked under the door, no feet, so I pushed it open, and there, her back to me, was a young woman in a white blouse and black skirt standing on the toilet seat, high heels on her feet. She turned around and gave us a little smile. And out we rushed.

"Oh my god," Lisa exclaimed, her hand over her mouth.

"She must think Western women are very athletic," I said, cringing with memoires of squatting over holes in the ground and the occasional narrow trench. I still don't know if that was the funniest or saddest thing I'd seen in a long time. It did, however, perk us up a bit for the journey ahead.

It was a nightmare trip, and the long five-hour layover in Tokyo turned longer when we learned our flight was cancelled due to a mechanical problem. Lisa was frantic, complaining about everything, as if I had something to do with the broken plane. And I was getting really annoyed. After all those wonderful trips, especially Tibet, a trip of a lifetime, my daughter was being a brat, I thought, fuming.

After several frustrating calls, I finally located a room in a five-star hotel, the bridal suite. "Only room available, madam," said the reservationist. "But you told me you had a standard." There was no response. By now it was midnight, and our flight was scheduled to depart at eight the next morning. We caught the airport bus and arrived at the magnificent hotel. Its huge marble lobby stretched forever toward the reception desk, where four bellhops stood staring at us, not making a move to help with our bags. I became the ultimate ugly tourist by dropping the luggage on the floor and continuing the long walk. I approached the receptionist by stating I wasn't about to pay for the bridal suite. Maybe because we looked like refugees taking shelter out of the storm, or maybe they didn't want a scene, but we were charged for a regular double room, and the bellhops carried our luggage up to our suite.

Lisa looked at the electronic gadgets for opening curtains and turning off lights, the bowl filled with packages of her favorite Arare crackers. She turned on the telly and made herself comfortable on the settee. Annoyed beyond being nice, I went into the sumptuous bathroom with its gold-plated hardware and used up all the bubble bath provided.

"Mom, these duvets are satin—and filled with down," said my now wide-awake daughter as she played with the gizmo for working the drapes. She was right; they were gorgeous. But all I could think about was how they were cleaned.

Still looking the worse for wear, we climbed on the very full shuttle to the airport. On our way in, we had been stopped by security, and everyone had to climb out of the bus, identify their luggage, and open it for inspection. Security was tight, and, I while I supported that wholeheartedly, I didn't want to have to get out of the bus, so I whispered to Lisa to help carry our luggage inside. I felt very smug when the other passengers got off while we sat there and weren't even asked to open our cases.

Dirty looks were directed our way as the passengers, all male and Japanese, all dressed in dark suits with pure white shirts and narrow black ties, looking grim and tired at five in the morning, climbed back on board. My smugness was replaced by embarrassment as first one then the other of our wheelie cases rolled down toward the driver and I had to rush down the bumpy aisle of the speeding bus and retrieve them before they hit him.

Lisa started to giggle. It was funny, this tousled, middle-aged redhead chasing cases, these dignified men staring on with horror, and I joined in. We laughed away all the frustration and stress of the journey.

Pilgrims Outside the Jokhan Temple

Can almost touch the sky.

Standing on the dragon.

Sharing

Double image

What does he see?

our curious monk friend

I can see forever

Jokhan Temple Square

Carrying potatoes up to the Potala Palace

Going home

Shrine on the way to Potala Palace

Craftsman at work

CHAPTER 41

TROUBLED TIMES

When parted by death we overcome our grief;
When parted in life our sadness is always with us.

From: *"Troubled Times," Du Fu, c. 750

I delayed my return to Beijing. Usually, I couldn't wait to get back, eager to go hunting for treasures, to become part of a city that thrummed with energy, but, after Tiananmen Square, that wonderful energy had felt flat. In spite of that, the pull of China was not to be ignored, so off I set again.

Ed was at the airport, and we sat in the jeep together, Tzu Chow at the wheel. We chatted about the children, how independent they seemed now, and I took the opportunity of Ed's relaxed mood to get hold of his hand. It was a test, an experiment. I wanted to see how long it would take for him to extradite himself. It didn't take long; he used his thumb to gradually slide his fingers free.

Ai-yi seemed so relieved to have us together again and proceeded to spoil me with cups of cha and the persimmons I loved. Did I want to get more fish? she asked. While I liked having the additional heart beats in the apartment, I decided not to replace Dorothy and Wanda, who were now happily ensconced in a filtered tank in Hawaii. What if we had to leave quickly again? But I did want more plants. Plus, I really enjoyed chatting with Mr. Wi, the gracious manager of the plant nursery. It was a relief to find that, like the gentleman himself, it hadn't changed a bit, still a steamy jungle of green, like a hot house at Kew Gardens—something from another, gentler time.

Sunday came, and we went out for our special treat: coffee, cake, and a concert. The tearoom, usually full, was barely inhabited. Empty tables peeked out through straggly potted palms. There were no musicians. "How forlorn it looks, Ed."

"Yep, guess we were having too much fun before."

I asked the waiter when the concerts would start again. He didn't know.

"At least they still have pastries," Ed offered. But it wasn't the same, and I wondered if it would ever be like it was.

"No idea," Ed said when I asked. And, on that sad note, we sat at the little round table, lost in our own thoughts.

While the plant nursery hadn't changed, I no longer saw the round shapes of tai chi practitioners performing their routine across the road from the apartment. I missed their graceful movements, their quiet harmony in stark contrast to the heavy, noisy traffic that sped past them. Gatherings were discouraged now, and I wondered if they would ever come back. Such thoughts depressed me.

But it was such a gorgeous autumn day, and I took myself off to Ritan Park. Maybe the old men with their prized songbirds in their elaborate cages would be there. With the noisy Ring Road behind me, I walked along the tree-lined streets toward the park. Seedpods from the scholar trees twirled down; like tiny shuttlecocks, they spun slowly around me, settling on the pavement, looking like silver coins. The air was soft. The sun filtered through the trees, making lacy shadows. But the old men weren't there. And the quiet became heavy, empty.

Ai-yi was folding laundry when I got back, and I grabbed the end of the sheet she was holding so we could fold it together. Her usual shy smile had been replaced lately with a little nod of her head, an acknowledgement—that was it. She seemed thinner too, her face drawn.

Something had to be upsetting her, but I knew she would never complain to me. I decided to share Lisa's latest news—it wasn't much, which I suppose was a good thing, but it was an opening—and then asked Ai-yi about her daughter. She sighed and held the folded sheet to her skinny chest. Her daughter wasn't happy, she told me. She lived with her mother-in-law. They shared a single room, all four of them, with one bed. A very small room, she added. Their baby girl cried a lot, and her daughter had a difficult time quieting her, which made her husband angry enough to hit her. "Angry, he's always angry," she told me. One child policy, and they had a girl. "Daughter cannot work, has to take care of baby and mother-in-law." Divorce is almost impossible in China, she answered in response to my question.

The Knot Lady lived in one room, and the tailor did too. The hutongs were a warren of single-room homes, so I knew this wasn't uncommon. But somehow the picture my head conjured up was a nightmare, and I saw them in one dark, windowless room, cooking on a two-ring burner if they were lucky, bringing water in from some outside source, sitting on a bucket instead of a toilet . . . sleeping on the floor. How could any marriage survive that?

"Ai-yi, *ne xi huan cha ma*?" I asked as I took the sheet from her. We walked into the kitchen, where the electric kettle sat waiting.

This is what we did in the England of my childhood when overwhelmed with life's curveballs. It was the only thing I could think of. Ai-yi poured the tea while I arranged my hoarded McVities digestive biscuits, a gift from Olivia, on a plate at the tiny kitchen table.

"*Wo hen baoqia*, Ai-yi," I said, feeling the inadequacy of my words.

"*Bie zhao ji*," don't worry, Ai-yi told me. I reached out and touched her hand and saw a tear roll down her tired face. "*Wo de fuqin*," she said, and she told me that her father had fallen two months ago, broken his hip, and had been lying in bed unable to move ever since. He was too old for the hospital; nobody would waste a bed on an old man. He was a quiet man, she continued, an artist, a painter of flowers. Ai-yi pulled a crumpled hankie from her apron pocket and wiped the tears from her face.

This was the first time Ai-yi had opened up to me. She had always been so cheerful, so energetic, and I'd been fooled into thinking that her life was happy, uncomplicated, with her two-ring burner, her one cup, one bowl and one pair of chopsticks each. With my limited Mandarin, it was impossible to convey my feelings, to comfort her. I felt useless, knowing the suffering going on around me while I sat in comfort and grumbled. We sat in silence until the tea turned cold.

Ai-yi didn't take a biscuit.

We were able to do something, though. I told Ed about Ai-yi's father, and, through the mysteries of *guanxi*, he managed to get her papers and train tickets to visit him. A small thing, but something.

Shan Shan stopped by and wanted to know what my plans were. Good question, very direct, something I hadn't given much thought to. Partly because I had no idea what to expect after the upheaval of Tiananmen Square. Over tea, we talked about Manager Wong and the ethnic jewelry—that seemed safe—and the Hu brothers' shard boxes, but all the while neither of us talked about the trouble a foreigner might cause a local entrepreneur like the Knot Lady; we handled it by not mentioning her name at all.

While in Hawaii, I had met a fascinating woman who owned a shop in one of the five-star hotels in Waikiki. She had asked for Beijing opera costumes to decorate her new store on Maui. She was also interested in pearl chokers, the small freshwater pearls so prevalent in China. I shared this news with Shan Shan.

First to the costume shop, in the old part of town, with its narrow, twisting streets busy with porters carrying incredible weights on their backs, anything from pallets of fabric to pots and woks and porcelain bowls precariously stacked, the loads heavy enough to have the porters bent almost double.

We walked up the broken steps to the poster-covered door and, to the sound of the bell hanging over the top, walked into the overstocked showroom. I'd already bought opera masks for Ed's office, so I tried to ignore the urge to buy more. Costumes were draped randomly on walls, alongside spears and swords and hats. I felt an immediate attack on the senses, making it difficult to concentrate on the job at hand. Color, that's what I would do, concentrate on the color of the costume, and I decided on pink. Bright pink satin covered in blue and white and gold embroidery depicting clouds and waves and pheasants. Shan Shan asked the salesclerk to open one of the packages containing the silk robes, but there were two in that color, one for aerial work and the other for everything else. Overwhelmed by decisions, I bought both. Then the hat—the beautifully embroidered hat, eight inches high with two five-foot long pheasant feathers draping down either side, used to emphasize various gestures and moves. I just had to buy the hat. Purchases in hand, it was time to leave, and, at that moment a porter, came in with a load of fabrics strapped to his back, and we had to fold ourselves over the display cases, bundles in hand, to allow him passage while I worried about breaking the feathers.

Breaking the feathers was the least of my problems. Due to the size and delicate nature of the construction, I would have to hand carry the hat with the feathers rounded gently over to make it smaller all the way to Honolulu. Once there, the customs agent had me wait while he called over the ag man, who wanted to know what kind of feathers I had. Kind? "Pheasant feathers," I said. "But what kind?" he asked. "I'm sure it was dead when they pulled them," I assured him. "Let me see." And he examined the feathers, declaring them not golden pheasant feathers, which evidently were on the endangered species list. I was free to go

Not wanting to use up our shopping list in one day, we settled on a cup of tea at the flat and a plan for the pearls. The Hu brothers were in the know, so we decided to start there the next day.

We walked to the CITIC building to get a taxi—much more fun than nosey Tzu Chow—and arrived at the shop early, the first customers of the day, which always guaranteed us a discount from the superstitious shopkeepers. Of course, old Mr. Hu had contacts, he told us, a cousin of some sort, himself related by marriage to the largest harvester in Shanxiahu. How many did we want? Best quality guaranteed. It was then I realized these pearls would be sold in bulk—no holes for stringing, nothing except the pearls themselves. And probably buckets of them. Now I was in an embarrassing situation. Having set old Mr. Hu up for a profitable transaction, not only for himself but for a relative, I would have to extricate myself from this sale and make another purchase. One that would keep me in good standing with the Hu brothers and especially their uncle. Luckily for me, there were many temptations in his shop: old-fashioned hair ornaments dangling with pearls and semiprecious stones and, of course, his shard boxes in their hammered silver casings. I bought an embarrassing number of boxes, probably 60 percent of his stock, and all the lovely hair ornaments in his case. I also ordered the indigo-blue boxes for each shard. We would pick the order up the next day. As we left the shop, I could almost hear old Mr. Hu rubbing his arthritic hands together.

Of course, Ed wanted to know what all the "damned" boxes were doing in the apartment. I ignored the question—it was easier that way—and told him dinner was ready. German sausages and sour kraut, a favorite of his.

CHAPTER 42

A NARROW ESCAPE

Lines of geese have already all gone back home;
Where are you heading, a lonely silhouette?
In the evening rain you call to the others, but they're lost;
When you land alone on the cold embankment, it's late.

From: "The Solitary Goose," Cui Tu, c. 854

Tourists were few and far between. Rumor was that it would take years to get back to where it had been that spring. Consequently, our travel-industry friends saw this as a great opportunity to visit China. It started with Ken's son and his three college friends who wanted to stop here on their way to Shanghai. He told me they had been "roughing it," his words, for the past three weeks going to all the off-the-tourist-path places they could fit in. I knew they'd be starving, especially for Western comfort foods. Christopher always was after his long hikes, and spaghetti and meatballs always revived him.

"How long?" I asked.

"Three days," he answered.

That meant shopping. Holiday Inn Lido would be the best place to get what I wanted—if they had it. And, if they didn't, nobody would. Ed and I went shopping, "You've enough food there to feed an army," Ed remarked.

"I'm excepting them to be starving." He nodded his head in agreement.

I was looking forward to visitors, and Ai-yi and I set about making beds for our guests. We had double beds in each spare room, and I decided that I would also make up two settees to give them the option of sharing beds or using the settees.

Tzu Chow delivered our guests to the apartment, and Ai-yi opened the door to four young men with sunburned faces, disheveled and grubby, backpacks hanging off their bent shoulders. They had been hiking the Great Wall at Huanghuacheng, a tiny village about fifty miles from Beijing, and they looked ready to drop.

Ai-yi gestured for them to remove their shoes and gave them slippers. I offered showers, and their faces lit up. They had no clean clothes, so Ed handed out t-shirts and shorts, and the transformation began while Ai-yi bundled their clothes for washing.

"Hope you like pasta," Ed said. We sat at the large round table, where all shyness dispersed, and these four young men devoured everything in front of them. They confessed to being tired of Chinese food and always felt hungry; I told them that they were still eating Chinese food—at least the pasta part. Revived, they shared their fabulous trip with us, the highlight being the reservoir they swam in that day, which covered part of the Great Wall.

"The way it climbs up and down the mountains is unreal. It just keeps going. And we got to swim over it." The best part, they all agreed, was there were no other tourist in sight.

They had a list of places they wanted to see in Beijing, and I enjoyed showing them the sights, not all of them old. They wanted to see the Colonel, the larger-than-life symbol for Kentucky Fried Chicken, which was on Qianmen Street where the Qianmen Gate once guarded the southern entry into the city. When it opened in 1987, I wasn't sure it would survive; the cost of a meal was more than the average weekly wage, but there he was, big mustache, bigger smile, still greeting guest. We didn't stop, and I left them on their own to explore the Forbidden City, which was just across the wide street, and explained how to get a taxi back to the apartment.

Guests, like fish, go off after three days, so says a Chinese proverb, and day three soon arrived. All were packed up ready for Tzu Chow, except for Fred, the medical student. Fred had a raving headache, he told me. His face was gray, and sweat beaded on his forehead. I took his temperature—104. There was no way he could travel. So, while the others reluctantly left for Shanghai to stay with Ken, Fred would have to follow later.

Ai-yi made him chock, but he couldn't swallow anything; he couldn't even sit up without help. There was no such thing as your local doctor that could be called in or visit, so we were faced with the prospect of a trip to the hospital to get Fred checked out. The thought terrified him—me too, but I couldn't let on. There was no choice. We would go to Peking Union Medical College Hospital, recommended for foreigners. I called Shan Shan and asked her to meet us there. I prayed hard there would be English-speaking staff.

Tzu Chow drove us, and Fred and I walked into the huge waiting room with seats arranged in lines across an asphalt-tiled floor that must have been the original from 1907. Blinking, hissing florescent lights in a high ceiling tried to illuminate the space and showed the chipped and faded industrial green walls. Doors with glass windows and shabby curtains hid examining rooms. Corridors led off the waiting area, and gurneys lined the walls.

We sat with the other patients, monochrome people with vacant faces who looked like they had been there all night. Poor Fred crossed his arms around his chest and leaned forward. I'm sure he just wanted to lie on the floor. I placed my hand on his back, hoping to reassure him.

Not unexpectedly, we were the only foreigners. I prayed we wouldn't be called before Shan Shan arrived. Then again, as noncitizens we would be required to pay, which gave us priority of sorts, and it wasn't long before I heard my Chinese name called by an immaculately dressed nurse: *"Xie Qiao Shan."* It took her three tries before I recognized it; I could barely pronounce it myself. She babbled away in Mandarin, telling us to follow her as she marched importantly toward one of the curtained doors.

"Oh God!" I thought. It was what I feared most. Shan Shan wasn't here! *And* they did not speak English! Panic filled every fiber of my being. I felt so responsible for Fred's welfare and so out of control at the same time. Should we leave now, make an excuse, sneak out, go to the embassy? But one look at Fred's gray, sweaty face told me no, not a good idea. Taking a deep breath to still my racing heart, I grabbed Fred's arm, and we staggered together into the examination room. It was dark in there. The window had either been painted over or was filthy, letting in only a grudging light, and the overhead florescent tubes sputtered. Blue-rimmed white enamel bowls sat on metal tables, and a wooden desk waited for the doctor. A chart of the human anatomy decorated one wall, and a table with what looked like some kind of sterilizer and trays of instruments waited at another . . . threateningly.

Suddenly and silently, the doctor appeared. A very young woman, who, without a word to either of us, picked up Fred's limp hand and took his pulse. (I had been told that doctors who practice Chinese medicine can diagnose an illness by doing just that.)

With a small torch in hand and a tongue depressor, she signaled for Fred to open his mouth. "*Biantaoti yan,*" she declared, "*shoushu.*" Operation? Over my dead body! My heart raced.

In my pitiful, nonshopping Mandarin, I told her his head ached, not his throat. "*Tou tong,*" I told her, tapping my head for good measure, and no one's going to operate, "*Maiyou shoushu,*" I said as the nurse attempted to get Fred into a wheelchair. (It was the best use I had so far for *maiyou*. 'We don't have.') Flipping urgently through my English/Chinese dictionary, I hunted for the magic phrase that would have her listen.

I couldn't find it, so I repeated, louder this time, "*Maiyou shoushu, maiyou bianaoiti yan!*" I thought of the waiting gurneys. There was no way they were going to take Fred out of my sight.

The look on my face was enough to get poor Fred panicking too. I had almost convinced him he had a sinus infection from the reservoir. That seemed the most likely diagnosis to me—and a prescription of antibiotics should do the trick. Using all my language skills, I tried again, telling the doctor I wanted either another opinion or antibiotics or we were leaving. "Leaving" was evidently not an option; once admitted, treatment had to follow. And Shan Shan wasn't here! Worse yet, I couldn't see an escape route. An argument ensued. The doctor took exception to being challenged in such rotten Mandarin—and by a foreigner yet. The ruckus attracted the attention of a passing senior doctor, and into the room she came.

In her sixties, tall and thin, her hair disheveled and her white coat open, she filled the room with her presence. She didn't ask what was going on. She didn't say a word. She just got to it.

Poor Fred was examined again, this time used as a prop for a lecture on correct diagnostic procedures from a senior doctor to a junior. She finally declared that he did indeed have a sinus infection, a very bad one, and wrote a prescription, which she plonked on the desk.

At this point, Shan Shan appeared, and I melted with relief.

It wasn't that easy to leave, though. The senior doctor thought it good PR to read the riot act to the now very quiet intern—in front of us while Fred turned greener by the second. Bold as ever, Shan Shan leaned between the doctors, picked the prescription up from the desk, and said our thanks and farewells. From there, Shan Shan led us through the complicated checkout procedures, then to Tzu Chow and home. Leaning back in the jeep, eyes closed, Fred spoke his first words since leaving the apartment that morning: "I thought I was never getting out of there in one piece."

We three on the Great Wall

CHAPTER 43

THEY ARE BACK

What place under Heaven most hurts the heart?
Lao Lao Ting, for seeing visitors off.
The spring wind knows how bitter it is to part,
The willow twig will never again be green.

From: **"Autumn Air," Li Bai, c. 750

Ed called to meet him for lunch at the CITIC building. He wouldn't tell me why, but I knew something was up. We rarely saw each other midday. The restaurant was crowded as usual, office workers from the building mostly, and Ed was already seated.

"Start packing," he said. The noisy restaurant was silenced as my mind tried to understand what he was saying.

"Pack?" I finally managed to ask.

"Word from above, we're leaving in two weeks—going to Seoul."

"Seoul?"

"Yep, not enough business here now, and they have problems in Korea."

I didn't care what problems the company had. I didn't want to go to Seoul. I was perfectly happy living here. And I was five years old again, leaving the comfort of old Mrs. Croft's cottage for strangers who didn't want me.

Appetite gone, I sat there, not knowing what to say, how to feel. This amazing country, where it was a problem to find a carrot, had become part of me. I thought I would live here forever—or at least until Ed retired. It could happen; Ed said other managers had.

"I'll have Kathy tell Ai-yi."

"No. I want to tell her." With that, I left the restaurant for home.

No sooner had I put the key in the lock than the door flew open, and Ai-yi stood there, arms outstretched, tears streaming down her tired face, and I reached out to hug her. I felt her bony shoulders, her thin arms, shaking. We cried together, right there in the hall. And I was angry that someone had told her before I had a chance. How dare they!

"Coconut wireless," Ed said when I asked who told Ai-yi. I'd seen it work before; I shouldn't have been surprised.

I couldn't sleep. I sat in the living room in the dark, the same thoughts running around in my head: I'm not ready to leave; I have yet to accomplish what I set out to do. My business was nothing but a pipe dream, a hobby. And my marriage? I was no closer than I was four years ago. In fact, while I had managed to gather some new insight, it was nowhere near enough to provide the key to unlocking the riddle of what made Ed tick. Maybe I never would figure that out. Just maybe the man I fell in love with all those years ago was a mirage, and the moody, difficult man had been there all along. With that sobering thought, I went back to bed.

And it started, the mad rush to pack up all the treasures I had so much joy buying, to decide what could be left behind. Ai-yi and I spent silent days sorting cupboards and closets, her usual smile replaced with that same sad, worried look she had when Lisa and I returned after Tiananmen. Unspoken words of regret, of sadness, hung between us... a heavy weight in my heart.

Every time I thought of how much she had done for us, how kind she had been, how protective... how devastating the events of Tiananmen Square and the aftermath must be for her, I wanted to put into words what I felt. But they wouldn't form. It was too painful for me to think too deeply about the last four years: how much my life had changed, how much I had learned. It would mean I would have to really look at my marriage, think about a future, one with or without Ed. Everything was happening so fast, and I didn't have an answer. No, this wasn't something I wanted to explore, not now. So, Ai-yi and I kept our worries inside. We didn't try to share them. We just quietly sorted and packed up all the things that make a home and kept our grief to ourselves.

Every cupboard I opened, every surface I looked at, I could hear Ai-yi's voice in my head exclaiming, "*Hen duo, hen duo dongxi.*" How right she was; there were just too many things. The porcelain pots, the antique silks, all of Ed's "hundred-dollar suits," beautiful fabrics but lacking style and shape. Tact was required here. Ed was very attached to his suits—or more the message behind them: "Look, I paid only a hundred bucks for this." The Emperor's New Clothes. He missed the point that he had paid for eight of them but finally agreed we could give them away. I approached Ai-yi carefully, not wanting to embarrass her, and offered her the suits for "someone you might know who could use them." Without a word, Ai-yi packed them all carefully and quickly away and left the apartment early that day. I'd heard from Rebecca that in parts of the country there might be only one pair of men's pants per family, so going out of the house was rotated.

Kathy arranged for the movers, but before that the customs agents had to sign off on all items bought while in the country. I asked Shan Shan to come over and act as interpreter. We were having a cup of tea, and in they came, two tall, severe-looking men in tan uniforms, clipboards in hand. Ai-yi fussed over them, clearly concerned, and gave them cups of tea, which they drank greedily. Everything had been laid out for inspection, and inspect they did. One surprising find was a small monochrome vase in a very pale lavender color. "Ming," the older of the two agents noted.

"Really?" I questioned. "Then it'll have to stay here." I handed it to Shan Shan as a gift. The agent looked surprised. I think he was looking for an argument. And so it went until they came to the two beautiful altar tables I'd bought from my young friend.

"Receipt," the agent commanded, hand outstretched. I didn't have a receipt. It was always a cash transaction whenever we bought things from our entrepreneur friends. It would have shown lack of trust to have asked for an invoice. In fact, the only shops that gave invoices were those owned by the government.

Now what to do? I couldn't divulge my sources; goodness knows what their punishment would be. I'd never thought of that until now. It had seemed like a game, an adventure going into shacks and finding treasures.

I bluffed. "I'll have to look for them."

"No receipt, no take." Well, that was clear enough. And, with that, they left.

"If you were German, you'd have no trouble," said Shan Shan. I knew that was true; they could buy and ship anything. I'd often wondered why they had this privileged status. That's one of the reasons I felt smug when they were forced to speak English in Hobo Town, it being the foreign language of choice.

"I'll call Manager Chang," Shan Shan said, and it was through this lovely man that we were able to get the red wax chop on the tables. Manager Chang, I discovered, had worked for the Department of Antiquities. He was considered an expert on antique textiles and clothing. His contact was an older man who spoke excellent English. Taking one look at my favorite table, he declared, "This belongs to the world." I felt tears well up, tears of gratitude to this man I'd never met before, tears of sadness at being able to change the fate of only a piece of furniture. But it was a victory of sorts. *Guanxi.*

We held a party in the apartment for all Ed's employees. *Jiaozi,* made by the company ai-yis, with Ai-yi in charge. And, of course, French pastries from Jianguo's bakery. I'd tried to buy paper plates to save some work, but they were exorbitant price wise and very hard to come by, so we opted instead for a complete china dinner service for thirty-six, costing around $8. *Hen duo dongzi.*

The days passed quickly and quietly while I tried to pretend it was all a big mistake. We weren't really leaving. . . . Except we were.

The American ambassador and his lovely wife gave us a farewell cocktail party. Ed had put together a list of guests, including Chinese business associates. They weren't included in the invitations. Things had changed. No matter how hard I tried to believe otherwise, the evidence was all around me. Rebecca and John were there, and that was enough for me.

We arrived at the residence, and our hostess met us at the door. "Hope you don't mind," she said. "I have two house guests, and they'll be crashing your party." The houseguests turned out to be Happy Rockefeller and Barbara Walters.

Two days later, I met these "party crashers" again at old Mr. Hu's shop. Rebecca and I were there checking out his latest, and there they were, buying his famous shard boxes. We chatted, and I was impressed with how down to earth these amazing women were, how comfortable they made those around them feel. Purchases in hand, they left. As the door closed behind them, I asked old Mr. Hu if he knew who they were. "*Bu shi de,*" he said. "Mrs. Rockefeller," said I, and I waited.

The explosion I'd anticipated left me smiling. Old Mr. Hu repeated her name, first reverently, with awe, then gradually louder. By the time he had repeated it four times, all the hammering in the back workshop had stopped to be replaced by the same mantra: "Rock-e-fell-er!"

July 4, our shipment was waiting to be loaded, no wooden crates, just cardboard wrappings, and it rained. Out of a clear blue sky, the rain poured down, a short shower but heavy enough to wet the cardboard. There was damage to my two precious tables, and, when they were unpacked, I wept.

Two years had turned into four, but the day had come. It was time to leave. I looked around the apartment—how bare it looked, how unloved. All the paintings and porcelain so joyfully collected now gone, it had reverted to its dowdy look of a third-rate hotel. And I thought of my crafty old friends in Hobo Town and remembered the very last time Rebecca and I had been there before the uprising, my favorite rascal holding a delicate white teacup up high above his head, its cherry blossom handle chipped, pointing to it with the other hand, bouncing up and down, vying for my attention. I knew it was Ming, and I wanted it, but I was completely out of cash. As we hurried by, I told him "*Mingtian,*" and saw the disappointment on his face. But there was no tomorrow.

I had been so busy making a life in China it never occurred to me that it could be taken away, just like that, in the blink of an eye. And Seoul certainly held no appeal for me. But Chris was doing so well, with his girlfriend and with his business, and Lisa would graduate this year, though she wasn't sure of her career path yet—she claimed she might take a year off to decide on graduate school—and Ed and I bumped along now, not yet at peace, but I no longer felt the intense urgency to understand him, which had been my motivation when I first arrived. Maybe Korea would prove to hold adventures of its own. I should give it a try.... Maybe life would be easier, not as demanding as here. After I found a place for us to live, settle in, I would think about the future, but not yet.

Then again, if Lisa decided to spend a gap year in Hawaii, I would have to be there too. I couldn't leave her to handle any unforeseen emergencies with Chris. It wouldn't be fair to either of them. And there was the consulting job offered me when I went back last month . . .

My thoughts in a whirl, I went over to the living room balcony and looked out toward Tiananmen Square and the Forbidden City. The smog was too heavy to see clearly, but I could make out where they should be . . . and there, on the pavement across the busy Ring Road, were round gray shapes practicing tai chi moves. They moved like a flock of swallows, as if something unseen held them together as one. Graceful, measured movements, unchanged for centuries. I watched as if my life depended on it. I wanted to burn this image into my mind and have it be the last thing I saw before leaving.

They were back!

And they walked to join the parade

Our new best friend.

We three on the Great Wall

* and ** ENDNOTE: CHINESE POETRY

Chinese poets have been esteemed throughout thousands of years of history. The Tang Dynasty (618-907) was the most prolific and many poems have survived to this day.

    My curiosity with Chinese poetry began with the purchase of that Sung dynasty pillow with its porcelain surface carefully etched in a poem. It was while searching for a translation that I realized how much history is encompassed in these ancient works. Like Chaucer's Canterbury Tales, they provide a glimpse into the past, showing us the lives of the people, the social changes and hardships of the times, while embracing how life can be at one with nature. They are, it seems, a direct reaction to the world of that particular poet at that particular time.

    In writing this book I found many of the poems written so long ago could be applied today. I hope you will find them of interest.

From: *Selected Poems of Du Fu, Sichuan People's Publishing House

From: **Three Hundred Tang Poems, Everyman's Library Pocket Poets

APPENDIX

UNESCO World Heritage Sites referred to in this book, with year awarded:

China:

Classical Gardens of Suzhou (1997, 2000)
Historic Centre of Macao (2005)
Imperial Palaces of the Ming and Ching Dynasties in Beijing and Shenyang (1987, 2004)
Imperial Tombs of the Ming and Qing Dynasties, Beijing (2000, 2003, 2004)
Mausoleum of the First Qin Emperor (1987)
Mountain Resort and its Outlying Temples, Chengde (1994)
Summer Palace, an Imperial Garden in Beijing (1998)
Temple of Heaven, an Imperial Sacrificial Altar in Beijing (1998)
The Great Wall (1987)
South China Karst (2007, 2014)

Tibet:

Potala Palace (1994)
Jokhang Temple (2000)
Norbulingka Palace (2001)

ACKNOWLEDGEMENTS

This book began at Lillian Cunningham's Writing Retreats in a series of short stories. Through Lillian's "prompts and starters" I discovered a deeper way of reliving memories. Thank you, Lillian for the stimulating environment you always create.

To my dearest friend Shan Correa who continues to give her support and encouragement, I am forever grateful. And to the other members of our Tuesday Writing Group Mary Lombard Mulder, Mary Bell and Marie Fujii for their constructive criticisms and encouraging words, especially the criticisms.

To brilliant Penny Pence-Smith for asking, "Why did you *really* go to China?" Back to the laptop I went. Thank you, Penny for your revealing question. Hope all the rewrites have now answered it.

To Eunice Musgrave, my remarkable friend and author, for giving me the courage to dig deeper, to write from my heart and share my story in the hopes it will help somebody else.

To my early readers for their constructive input, Sue Tanioka, Janet Boomla, Frank Skilbeck, Ku'ulei and Ken Thompson. Thank you for your time, your enthusiasm and your kind words.

Thank you, Team Bublish for your dedication, patience, insightful editing and great cover design. Special thanks to my Project Manager Shilah LaCoe for always being there, for supporting my efforts and keeping me on track.

AUTHOR BIO

Joan Kelleher Gencarelli was born in London, England, and has lived in Kailua, Hawaii since the early 1960s, where she raised her two children along with various dogs, cats, ducks, and fish. In 1986, she left Hawaii to accompany her husband to Beijing. Over the next ten years they would move to Korea then Thailand. Joan's first career was as a technical writer. In 2002, she began writing fiction for fun, starting with short stories inspired by her childhood and her years in Asia. Her short story "Evacuation—There and Back," based on her memories of WWII became part of the BBC WWII People's War archives. First awarded the Golden Plover Award, in 2006 she received the Lorin Tarr Gill Honorable Mention for non-fiction. In 2021 she published *"When the Bough Breaks, Memories of Operation Pied Piper"*. Joan is an avid traveler and still has a few places left on her "wish list." She is drawn to the exotic, with an emphasis on **culture,** history and, yes, shopping!

www.ingramcontent.com/pod-product-compliance
Lightning Source LLC
Chambersburg PA
CBHW072043110526
44590CB00018B/3024